EXAM✓CRAM

MCTS
70-431

Implementing and Maintaining Microsoft® SQL Server 2005

Thomas Moore

MCTS 70-431 Exam Cram: Implementing and Maintaining Microsoft SQL Server 2005

International Standard Book Number: 0-7897-3588-1

Printed in the United States of America

First Printing: August 2006

09 08 07 06   4 3 2 1

Trademarks

All terms mentioned in this book that are known to be trademarks or service marks have been appropriately capitalized. Que Publishing cannot attest to the accuracy of this information. Use of a term in this book should not be regarded as affecting the validity of any trademark or service mark.

Microsoft is a registered trademark of Microsoft Corporation.

Warning and Disclaimer

Every effort has been made to make this book as complete and as accurate as possible, but no warranty or fitness is implied. The information provided is on an "as is" basis. The author and the publisher shall have neither liability nor responsibility to any person or entity with respect to any loss or damages arising from the information contained in this book or from the use of the CD or programs accompanying it.

Bulk Sales

Que Publishing offers excellent discounts on this book when ordered in quantity for bulk purchases or special sales. For more information, please contact

U.S. Corporate and Government Sales
1-800-382-3419
corpsales@pearsontechgroup.com

For sales outside the United States, please contact

International Sales
international@pearsoned.com

Library of Congress Cataloging-in-Publication Data

Moore, Thomas, 1961-

MCTS 70-431 Exam cram : Implementing and Maintaining Microsoft SQL Server 2005 / Thomas Moore.

    p. cm.

  ISBN 0-7897-3588-1 (pbk.)

  1. Electronic data processing personnel—Certification. 2. Microsoft software—Examinations—Study guides. 3. Database design—Examinations—Study guides. 4. SQL server. I. Title.

  QA76.3.M6487 2006

  005.75'85—dc22

                    2006019445

Publisher
Paul Boger

Acquisitions Editor
Betsy Brown

Development Editor
Deadline Driven
Publishing

Managing Editor
Patrick Kanouse

Project Editor
Tonya Simpson

Copy Editor
Kitty Jarrett

Indexer
Ken Johnson

Proofreader
Elizabeth Scott

Technical Editor
Randy Cornish

**Publishing
Coordinator**
Cindy Teeters

**Multimedia
Developer**
Dan Scherf

Page Layout
TnT Design, Inc.

Contents at a Glance

	Introduction	1
	Self Assessment	7
CHAPTER 1	Installing and Configuring SQL Server 2005	13
CHAPTER 2	Creating Database Objects	31
CHAPTER 3	Implementing Database Objects	69
CHAPTER 4	Supporting the XML Framework	99
CHAPTER 5	Data Consumption and Throughput	117
CHAPTER 6	Database Maintenance	133
CHAPTER 7	Monitoring SQL Server Performance	159
CHAPTER 8	Troubleshooting and Optimizing SQL Server	181
CHAPTER 9	Implementing High Availability	203
CHAPTER 10	Practice Exam 1	223
CHAPTER 11	Answers to Practice Exam 1	237
CHAPTER 12	Practice Exam 2	259
CHAPTER 13	Answers to Practice Exam 2	273
APPENDIX A	Suggested Readings and Resources	293
APPENDIX B	Accessing Your Free MeasureUp Practice Test	299
APPENDIX C	MeasureUp's Product Features	301
	Glossary	305
	Index	319

Table of Contents

Introduction 1

Self Assessment 7

Chapter 1:
Installing and Configuring SQL Server 2005 13
  Installing and Configuring SQL Server 2005 14
    Installation Requirements 14
    The Installation Process 18
    Installation Preparations 19
    Postinstallation Procedures 22
  Exam Prep Questions 28
    Answers to Exam Prep Questions 30

Chapter 2:
Creating Database Objects 31
  Creating and Defining Databases 32
    Using T-SQL to Create and Alter a Database 33
    The Makeup of a Database 33
    Standard Views, Indexed Views, and Partitioned Views 35
    Miscellaneous SQL Server Objects 40
  Defining SQL Server Tables 41
    Using Types and Schemas 42
    Using Columns with Automated or Calculated Values 46
    Maintaining Order by Using Indexes 47
    Primary/Foreign Keys and Relationships 50
    Using Cascading Actions 52
    Using DML and DDL Triggers 53
    Partitioning Tables 54
    Creating Partitioned Tables 56
  SQL Server Programmability Objects 60
    Stored Procedures 60
    Creating CHECK Constraints 61
    Creating Your Own Functions 62
    English Query Capabilities with Full-Text Catalogs 63
    Objects with Security Context 64
  Exam Prep Questions 65
  Answers to Exam Prep Questions 67

Chapter 3:
Implementing Database Objects **69**

   Data Querying and Reporting 70
      Listing the Contents of a Table 71
      Making a Report More Presentable 72
      Querying a Sampling of the Data Stored 75
      Relating Data from Multiple Tables 76
      Applying Conditional Data Filtering 78
   Data Querying Using Full-Text Indexes 80
      Creating and Populating a Catalog 80
   Using System Tables and Views 81
      Getting Information from System Tables 82
      Information Retrieval from System Stored Procedures 85
      Using Dynamic Management Views and Other System Views 86
      Inserting Data 87
      Using UDT and the CLR to Control Data Input 87
      Using the CLR Within Stored Procedures 88
      Inserting Individual Records 88
      Using a Query to Insert Complete Recordsets 89
      Disabling Functionality During Data Insertion 90
   Changing What Is Already Stored 91
      Updating a Single Record 92
      Doing Updates That Affect Multiple Records 92
      Performing Transaction Processing 92
      Upgrading Data from Previous Releases of SQL Server 93
   Removing Unwanted Data 93
      Directly Removing Records from a Table 94
      Indirectly Removing Data from a Table 94
      Escalating Privileges to Allow Deletion 95
      Controlling Privileges by Using GRANT, DENY, and REVOKE 95
   Exam Prep Questions 96
   Answers to Exam Prep Questions 98

Chapter 4:
Supporting the XML Framework **99**

   Managing XML Data 100
      Newly Supported XML Features 101
      XML: The Basics 102
      The xml Data Type and Methods 106
      XML Method Interactions 107

Other SQL Server XML Support 111
  Indexing XML Data 111
  Creating Primary and Secondary Indexes 112
  Native XML Web Service Support 112
Exam Prep Questions 114
Answers to Exam Prep Questions 115

Chapter 5:
Data Consumption and Throughput **117**
Importing and Exporting Data 118
  Using the Bulk Copy Program (BCP) 119
  Using OPENROWSET for Importing Data 122
  Using SQL Server Integration Services (SSIS) 122
Implementing Service Broker 124
  Designing a Service 125
Exam Prep Questions 129
Answers to Exam Prep Questions 131

Chapter 6:
Database Maintenance **133**
SQL Server 2005 Database Maintenance 134
  What's New in SQL Server Maintenance? 134
Performing Database Backups 136
  Recovery Models and Backups 136
  Recovery Models Using T-SQL 138
  Backup Types and Scenarios 139
  Setting the Options of a Backup 141
  Options of the T-SQL BACKUP Statement 142
Restoring Data from a Backup 146
  Using the T-SQL RESTORE Statement 149
Using Database Snapshots 150
  Creating and Deleting Database Snapshots 152
Automating Maintenance with Job Scheduling 153
  Viewing Job Details and History 154
Exam Prep Questions 156
Answers to Exam Prep Questions 158

Chapter 7:
Monitoring SQL Server Performance **159**
SQL Server Management Studio 160
Monitoring and Recording Performance 161
  Using Activity Monitor for the Here and Now 162

Management Studio: Log File Viewer 164
Server-Maintained Information 166
Using Windows System Monitor 169
Using SQL Server Profiler 172
Defining a Profiler Trace 174
Using Profiler Traces to Diagnose Locking 175
Trace Playback and Diagnosis 176
Using Profiler to Gather a Workload 177
Exam Prep Questions 178
Answers to Exam Prep Questions 180

Chapter 8:
Troubleshooting and Optimizing SQL Server **181**

Data Analysis and Problem Diagnosis 182
Tuning the Operating System and Hardware 182
Creating and Maintaining Statistics 183
Locks, Blocks, and Deadlocks 184
Tuning the Database Structure 188
Indexing Strategies 188
Data Partitioning Across Servers 192
Using the DTA 193
Server Configuration Maintenance 195
Using the Database Console Command (DBCC) 195
Setting Alerts to Automate Problem Identification 198
Exam Prep Questions 199
Answers to Exam Prep Questions 201

Chapter 9:
Implementing High Availability **203**

High-Availability Solutions 204
Implementing Log Shipping 205
Using Database Mirroring 207
Using Failover Clustering 209
Using Replication 210
Replication Strategies 211
Types of Replication 214
Elements of Replication 216
Microsoft Analysis Services 218
Exam Prep Questions 220
Answers to Exam Prep Questions 222

Chapter 10:
Practice Exam 1 . . . . **223**

  Exam Questions 224

Chapter 11:
Answers to Practice Exam 1 . . . . **237**

Chapter 12:
Practice Exam 2 . . . . **259**

  Exam Questions 260

Chapter 13:
Answers to Practice Exam 2 . . . . **273**

Appendix A:
Suggested Readings and Resources **293**

  Chapter 1: Installing and Configuring SQL Server 2005 293
    Books 293
    On the Web 294
    SQL Server Books Online Help Facility 294
  Chapter 2: Creating Database Objects 294
    Books 294
    On the Web 294
    SQL Server Books Online Help Facility 294
  Chapter 3: Implementing Database Objects 295
    Books 295
    On the Web 295
    SQL Server Books Online Help Facility 295
  Chapter 4: Supporting the XML Framework 295
    Books 295
    On the Web 295
    SQL Server Books Online Help Facility 296
  Chapter 5: Data Consumption and Throughput 296
    Books 296
    On the Web 296
    SQL Server Books Online Help Facility 296
  Chapter 6: Database Maintenance 297
    Books 297
    On the Web 297
    SQL Server Books Online Help Facility 297

Chapter 7: Monitoring SQL Server Performance 297
    On the Web 297
    SQL Server Books Online Help Facility 297
Chapter 8: Troubleshooting and Optimizing SQL Server 298
    On the Web 298
    SQL Server Books Online Help Facility 298
Chapter 9: Implementing High Availability 298
    On the Web 298
    SQL Server Books Online Help Facility 298

Appendix B:
Accessing Your Free MeasureUp Practice Test **299**

Appendix C:
MeasureUp's Product Features **301**

    Multiple Testing Modes 301
        Study Mode 301
        Certification Mode 301
        Custom Mode 302
        Missed Question Mode 302
        Non-Duplicate Mode 302
    Question Types 302
    Random Questions and Order of Answers 303
    Detailed Explanations of Correct and Incorrect Answers 303
    Attention to Exam Objectives 303
    Technical Support 303

Glossary **305**

index **319**

About the Author

Thomas R. Moore, MCITP, MCTS, MCSE, MCSA, MCSD, MCDBA, MCP, MCT, CSE, CTT+, has been in the computer industry for more than 25 years. Thomas has a wide variety of expertise in all hardware environments and with most Microsoft Server products. "My first and lasting love, besides my wife and family, of course, however, is database programming," he says. Thomas is comfortable in any programming language environment. He achieved his MCSD and MCDBA certifications from their inception; completed the Microsoft CSE certification as a certified software engineer with Dexterity and Microsoft Business Solutions products; and, most recently, completed the new Microsoft Certifications for MCITP and MCTS on SQL Server 2005. Over the past 20 years, he has been working for a variety of Microsoft partners, and he is currently an intermediate developer/technical consultant with Diamond Municipal Solutions in Paris, Ontario, where he has been for the past four years. Among his myriad IT certifications, Thomas also holds certifications in English and business/technical writing. Thomas enjoys staying up-to-date, although like most of us, he finds it a challenge to keep up with the pace of the industry.

Dedication

This book is dedicated to my eldest son, Daniel Thomas Moore.
In you I see a reflection of myself.
Always strive to be the best that you can be.

Acknowledgments

There are always so many people to thank on any significant project like this one that it is difficult to cover everyone involved without the fear of missing an important cog. Rest assured that all the hundreds of individuals directly or indirectly involved in the project all deserve a portion of the recognition for its completion.

First, I must thank my loving wife, Joy. You are a cherished part of my life, and I treasure your continued support and assistance in everything I do. I also thank my children, Daniel, Max, and Chelsea. As always, my family are the most deeply affected when I decide to take on yet another of my projects. The many hours that I spent typing away in the office were voluntarily given up by the people closest to me.

Next, I would like to thank the editors: Randy Cornish, with whom I have had the pleasure of working on other projects, came through as expected. Randy, you have an eye for detail, and you are, as always, the perfect technician. Kitty Jarrett proved to be an exceptional editor. This is the first project working with Kitty, and I hope I have many more. Kitty has a friendly approach, correcting my sometimes imperfect grammar. She improved on the content with a flair that is truly appreciated.

Finally, to the rest of the Que team. From the top down, the organization is professional, polished, and respected. I would like to thank Jeff Riley, the executive editor, for having faith in the project in the first place. Thanks also go to the rest of the editing team. The team survived a lot of diversity during the project and still came up with a top-notch finished product. Steve Rowe, Todd Green, and Betsy Brown were all a true pleasure to work with through the duration of the project, and Tonya Simpson, the project editor, really pulled things together and ensured that all the bases were covered.

It was a lot of fun, ladies and gentlemen. Let's all do it again sometime.

We Want to Hear from You!

As the reader of this book, *you* are our most important critic and commentator. We value your opinion and want to know what we're doing right, what we could do better, what areas you'd like to see us publish in, and any other words of wisdom you're willing to pass our way.

As Publisher for Que Publishing, I welcome your comments. You can email or write me directly to let me know what you did or didn't like about this book— as well as what we can do to make our books better.

Please note that I cannot help you with technical problems related to the topic of this book. We do have a User Services group, however, where I will forward specific technical questions related to the book.

When you write, please be sure to include this book's title and author as well as your name, email address, and phone number. I will carefully review your comments and share them with the author and editors who worked on the book.

Email: scorehigher@pearsoned.com

Mail: Paul Boger
             Publisher
             Que Publishing
             800 East 96th Street
             Indianapolis, IN 46240 USA

Reader Services

Visit our website and register this book at www.examcram.com/register for convenient access to any updates, downloads, or errata that might be available for this book.

Introduction

Into the world of database management we plunge! The selection you have made of this *Exam Cram* series book will help you along your way to passing the Microsoft SQL Server—Implementation and Maintenance exam (70-431). This book contains information that will help ensure your success as you pursue this Microsoft exam and the Technology Specialist or IT Professional certification.

This introduction explains the new generation of Microsoft certifications that center on SQL Server and how the *Exam Cram* series can help you prepare for the 70-431 exam. This introduction discusses the basics of the Microsoft Certified Technology Specialist (MCTS) and Microsoft Certified IT Professional (MCITP) certifications, including a discussion of test-taking strategies. Chapters 1 through 9 are designed to teach you everything you need to know to take and pass the exam. The two practice exams at the end of the book (Chapters 10, "Practice Exam 1," and 12, "Practice Exam 2") should give you a reasonably accurate assessment of what is on the 70-431 exam. In addition, this book provides the answers to the tests and their explanations (Chapters 11, "Answers to Practice Exam 1," and 13, "Answers to Practice Exam 2") to help you assess your knowledge. Along with the explanations, you will find some particularly useful links to more information on the topic. For each answer, there is a reference to the chapter of the book that covers the topic as well as a link to more information on the Microsoft MSDN site and a link to SQL Server Books Online.

If you read this book and understand the material in it, you'll stand a very good chance of passing the test. If you make use of the additional links to the other materials and points of reference, particularly those on the Microsoft website, and if you actually use the product, you should be in excellent shape to do well on the exam.

Exam Cram books help you understand and appreciate the subjects and materials you need to pass Microsoft certification exams. They are aimed strictly at test preparation and review. They do not teach you everything you need to know about a topic; instead, they present and dissect the questions and problems that you're likely to encounter on a test. *Exam Cram* books work to bring together as much information as possible about Microsoft certification exams.

The MCTS (Technology Specialist) certification requires a strong all-round knowledge of the features of SQL Server 2005, and in particular, the newer features. To move on to the next level of certification, you need to drill down into each feature significantly. The MCITP (IT Professional) Database Developer, Database Administrator, and Business Intelligence Developer certifications require considerable in-depth information about the particulars of each of the SQL Server 2005 features.

Every Microsoft SQL Server–related certification starts with the 70-431 exam that this book prepares you for. To continue along any of the tracks for IT Pro certification, you must pass two other SQL Server–specific exams. 70-441: Designing Database Solutions by Using Microsoft SQL Server 2005 and 70-442: Designing and Optimizing Data Access by Using Microsoft SQL Server 2005 are the database developer–based continuation points, and 70-443: Designing a Database Server Infrastructure by Using Microsoft SQL Server 2005 and 70-444: Optimizing and Maintaining a Database Administration Solution by Using Microsoft SQL Server 2005 are the two administrator-based alternatives. Exams 70-445: Designing Business Intelligence Solutions by Using Microsoft SQL Server 2005 Analysis Services and 70-446: Designing a Business Intelligence Infrastructure by Using Microsoft SQL Server 2005 are the business intelligence endpoints.

About the 70-431 Exam and Content Areas

The 70-431 exam, Microsoft SQL Server 2005—Implementation and Maintenance, includes a variety of content. For specifics on the exam, you can check the exam guide on the Microsoft website, at www.microsoft.com/learning/exams/70-431.asp. The exam includes the following broad topic areas:

▶ **Installing and Configuring SQL Server 2005**—You are expected to be able to validate hardware and software, perform an installation, and perform the initial configuration of the server and its associated elements.

▶ **Implementing High Availability and Disaster Recovery**—You should be familiar with how to provide uninterrupted service to applications and how to plan for and recover from failures in a controlled manner.

▶ **Supporting Data Consumers**—Getting data into and out of the system in a variety of formats to support an array of client end functionality is an important skill.

▶ **Maintaining Databases**—You must be familiar with general maintenance activities, including backup and restoration of data, automation of maintenance procedures, and other related topics.

▶ **Monitoring and Troubleshooting SQL Server Performance**—You need to know how to utilize the tools provided to monitor, troubleshoot, and repair the server based on standard scenarios.

▶ **Creating and Implementing Database Objects**—The server controls dozens of different object types, and you must be familiar with the creation, alteration, and removal of each one.

Each of these task areas represents elements of a system's design from the outset of a project. You need to know how to take a system from a rough design through to the specifics of the implementation and then follow up with fine-tuning of the application to improve performance and guarantee security.

How to Prepare for the Exam

The 70-431 exam is somewhat difficult to prepare for because it is broad in scope. This is not an exam that you can adequately prepare for by simply rote-memorizing terms and definitions. It requires you to analyze a scenario and answer problems related to it by combining various knowledge points from various topic areas. Successfully completing this exam requires thought and analysis to properly choose the best solution from several viable solutions.

The best way to prepare for this exam is by doing the work. You must work with the databases and all the related objects to be comfortable with the material the exam addresses. I also recommend that you leave no stone unturned. You should spend a considerable amount of time using SQL Server Books Online, a help facility that has a phenomenal amount of information. Another helpful resource is www.microsoft.com. In particular, you should visit the MSDN library site. These resources contain the answer to every question on the exam.

What This Book Does

This book is designed to be read as a pointer to the areas of knowledge you will be tested on. You might want to read the book one time to get insight into how comprehensive your knowledge of this topic is. You should again read the book shortly before you take the actual test. You can use this book to get a sense of the underlying context of any topic in the chapters for fuller understanding, or you can skim it for Exam Alerts, bulleted points, summaries, and topic headings.

This book draws on material from Microsoft's own listing of knowledge requirements, from other preparation guides, and from the exams themselves. It also draws on a battery of technical websites, as well as on firsthand experience with application development and the exam. The aim is to walk you through the knowledge you need. By reading this book, you will gain from the experience of real-world professional development.

What This Book Does Not Do

This book does *not* teach you everything you need to know about database development. The scope of the book is exam preparation. It is intended to ramp you up and give you confidence when heading into exam 70-431.

This book is also not intended as an introduction to database design and implementation. This book reviews what you need to know before you take exam 70-431, and its fundamental purpose is dedicated to reviewing the information needed on this particular Microsoft certification exam.

This book uses a variety of teaching and memorization techniques to analyze the exam-related topics and to provide you with everything you need to know to pass the test.

About This Book

You should read this book from front to back. Nothing in this book is a guess about an unknown exam. I have had to explain certain underlying information on such a regular basis that I have included those explanations here.

After you have read this book, you can brush up on a certain areas by using the index or the table of contents to go straight to the topics and questions you want to reexamine. This book uses headings and subheadings to outline information about each given topic. After you are certified, you will find this book useful as a tightly focused reference and an essential foundation of information systems and controls auditing.

Each *Exam Cram* chapter follows a regular structure and has graphical cues about especially important or useful material. The structure of a typical chapter is as follows:

- ▶ **Opening hotlists**—Each chapter begins with a list of the terms you need to understand and concepts you need to master before you can be fully conversant in the chapter's subject matter.

- ▶ **Topical coverage**—After the opening hotlists, each chapter mentions the topics related to the chapter's subject. A few introductory paragraphs set the stage for the rest of the chapter.

- ▶ **Exam Alerts**—Throughout the text, Exam Alerts highlight material most likely to appear on the exam. They look like this:

EXAM ALERT

This is what an Exam Alert looks like. An Exam Alert stresses concepts, terms, or best practices that will most likely appear in one or more certification exam questions. For that reason, any information presented in an Exam Alert is worthy of unusual attention on your part.

All the content in this book—even material not flagged as an Exam Alert—is associated in some way with test-related material. Everything that appears in the chapter content is critical knowledge.

▶ **Notes**—This book is an overall examination of database design and implementation. As such, it delves into many aspects of business systems. Where a body of knowledge is deeper than the scope of the book, notes indicate areas of concern. Here is what a note looks like:

NOTE

Cramming for an exam will get you through a test, but it will not make you a competent database implementation professional. Although you can memorize just the facts you need to become certified, your daily work in the field will rapidly put you in water over your head if you do not know the underlying principles.

▶ **Tips**—This book provides tips that help you to build a better foundation of knowledge or to focus your attention on an important concept that reappears later in the book. Tips are a helpful way to remind you of the context surrounding a particular area of a topic under discussion. Here is what a tip looks like:

TIP

Much of the performance of a database system comes out of a strong design. In contrast, a poor design will not perform well after it is implemented. Take the time during the initial stages of design to put together a sound foundation for the system.

▶ **Practice questions**—This section presents a short list of test questions related to the specific chapter topic. Following each question is an explanation of both the correct and incorrect answers. The practice questions highlight the areas that are most important on the exam.

The bulk of the book follows this chapter structure, but it also includes a few other elements:

▶ **Glossary**—This book provides an extensive glossary of important terms used in the book.

▶ **The Cram Sheet**—This appears as a tear-away sheet inside the front cover of this *Exam Cram* book. It is a valuable tool that represents a collection of the most difficult-to-remember facts and numbers you should memorize before taking the test. Remember, although you will be asked to surrender all personal belongings other than pencils before you enter the exam room itself, you can dump this information out of your head onto a piece of paper as soon as you enter the testing room. The Cram Sheet mainly contains facts that require brute-force memorization. You need to remember this information only long enough to write it down when you walk into the testing room.

You might want to look at the Cram Sheet in your car or in the lobby of the testing center just before you walk into the testing center. The Cram Sheet is divided with headings, so you can review the appropriate parts just before each test.

▶ **Self-Assessment**—In the introductory section of the book you will find a self-assessment that you can use to see where you are in your preparations for this exam.

Self Assessment

Before you attempt to take the exam this book covers, it is imperative that you know considerable information about SQL Server itself. Of course, because it is an implementation exam, you must also be comfortable with the operating system, hardware, and framework on which SQL Server operates. There is so much breadth to this exam that I felt it necessary to include a Self Assessment to help you evaluate your exam readiness. This Self Assessment looks at what is needed to pass the exam and to achieve additional Microsoft certifications. As you go through the Self Assessment, you will gain a good idea about your ability to take the exam.

SQL Server Implementation and Maintenance as an MCTS

To complete the Microsoft Certified IT Professional (MCITP) certification as a database developer or administrator, you have to be a well-rounded, database-aware individual. The new generation of Microsoft certifications is much more meaningful and maps more closely to the everyday work environment found in the real world. You will also likely find this particular exam quite challenging.

The 70-431 exam requires you to have at least a base level of knowledge about the entire SQL Server 2005 product. You need to know how to apply SQL Server objects and principles to everyday implementation and maintenance tasks. The exam is broad in nature and tests you across the full realm of the actual SQL Server software.

Remember that this is a Microsoft exam, and it is focused on the SQL Server product. To pass the exam, you need to know how the software interacts with both the hardware and the operating system. You need to know how to configure the software, where to store the files and data, and how to organize the placement of all the individual database elements and other application objects.

The 70-431 exam includes questions covering all SQL Server objects, including the appropriate creation and use of each object type. A business application has many supporting objects in the database management system over and above the data itself. You can expect to see questions that offer choices between a wide assortment of these objects; you need to be familiar with where each object type and technology is best implemented.

You can get all the information you need from the material presented in this book. If you're willing to tackle the preparation process seriously and do what it takes to gain the necessary experience and knowledge, you can take and pass the exam. In fact, the *Exam Cram* books and the companion *Exam Prep* books are designed to make it as easy as possible for you to prepare for these exams, but prepare you must!

The Ideal MCITP Candidate

To give you some idea of what an ideal candidate is like, the following is some relevant information about the background and experience such an individual should have:

> **NOTE**
>
> For more information on the ideal MCITP candidate, consult the *Preparation Guide for Exam 70-431*, at www.microsoft.com/learning/exams/70-431.asp.

▶ Candidates for this exam may be professionals who typically pursue careers as database administrators, database developers, or business intelligence developers.

▶ Candidates can be people who do not work with Microsoft SQL Server as a part of their primary job functions but who want to show their breadth of technology experience, such as developers, system administrators, and others.

▶ Candidates can implement and maintain databases by using specific instructions and specifications.

▶ Candidates for this exam should be expert in tools usage, user interface navigation, wizard usage, writing code in the appropriate language (Transact-SQL, CLR language, and other scripting languages), code debugging or syntactic issue resolution, and troubleshooting and accomplishing specific focused tasks by using code or user interface navigation.

You should also have at least one year's experience implementing relational databases.

Put Yourself to the Test

The following questions and observations are designed to help you figure out how much work you'll face in pursuing SQL Server certification and what kinds of resources you can consult on your quest. Be absolutely honest in your answers, or you'll end up wasting money on an exam you're not ready to take. There are no right or wrong answers, only steps along the path to certification. Only you can decide when you are ready.

Two things should be clear from the outset, however:

▸ Even a modest background in logic and reasoning is helpful.

▸ Hands-on experience with designing, coding, testing, documenting, and fine-tuning on SQL Server tools used to handle complex database systems is an essential ingredient for success.

Educational Background

1. Were you strong in mathematics—in particular, algebra—in school? (Yes or No)

2. Do you enjoy solving logic puzzles? (Yes or No)

3. a) **Development Track:** Have you every taken any classes dealing with programming a computer in any language? (Yes or No)

   If you answered yes to any of the three previous questions, then you will likely be able to grasp most of the concepts presented that require the writing of SQL code.

   If you answered yes to all three, then you will be very comfortable with most of the concepts dealing with logic and syntax.

   If you answered no to these first three questions, then you may struggle with some of the development concepts and might want to do some preparatory reading or take a course to learn about some basic programming concepts.

   This site provides a good starting point for programming skills specific to SQL: www.w3schools.com/sql/sql_intro.asp.

   This Microsoft instructor-led course is an easy-to-understand look at programming for beginners: www.microsoft.com/learning/syllabi/en-us/2667Afinal.mspx.

b) **Administration Track:** Do you have a background with SQL? (Less general coding theory is required, but a basic coding background in SQL is helpful.) (Yes or No)

This site provides a good starting point for programming skills specific to SQL: www.w3schools.com/sql/sql_intro.asp.

4. Are you comfortable with databases and table relationships? (Yes or No)

5. Have you ever used Microsoft Access, dBASE, or any other database package? (Yes or No)

6. Are you comfortable using spreadsheet packages such as Microsoft Excel? (Yes or No)

If you answered yes to any or all of the previous three questions, then you have the base knowledge to get started right away.

If you answered no to these three questions, than you might want to look into some simple database management systems information. You can find many resources on the Internet if you search for "Introduction to Database." The following site is an online course that you can take for free to become more comfortable with the topic: www.sqlcourse.com.

7. Do you have a copy of SQL Server that you can practice with?

8. Do you have access at school or work to a server that you can use to help in your studies?

If you answered yes to either or both of these questions, then you have solved one of the initial hurdles. Trying to pass an exam like this without getting regular practice with the software is next to impossible. If you answered no, then you can order a CD or download a 180-day evaluation copy of the product from www.microsoft.com/sql/downloads/trial-software.mspx.

Hands-On Experience

Perhaps the most important key to success on any certification exam is hands-on experience. If I leave you with only one realization after taking this Self Assessment, it should be that there's no substitute for time spent performing tasks and working with the product.

TIP

You can obtain the exam objectives and practice questions, and you can get other information about the new generation of Microsoft certification exams from Microsoft, at www.microsoft.com/learning/mcp/newgen/.

> **TIP**
>
> If you have the funds or your employer will pay your way, consider taking a class led by a professional instructor. This is a good idea particularly for those just starting out or with limited knowledge or access to state-of-the-art computer systems. Microsoft has designed very good courses that can be taken in most communities.

Testing Your Exam Readiness

Whether you attend a formal class on a specific topic to get ready for an exam or use written materials to study on your own, some preparation for the certification exams is essential. You pay for your exam attempts whether you pass or fail, so you want to do everything you can to pass on your first try. Not only can failed attempts be very expensive, but they can also be very discouraging.

Each chapter in this book includes practice exam questions, and Chapters 10, "Practice Exam 1," and 12, "Practice Exam 2," include practice exams. So if you don't score well on the chapter questions, you can study more by taking the practice exams.

For any given subject, you should consider taking a class if you've tackled self-study materials, taken the practice test, and failed anyway. If you can afford the privilege, the opportunity to interact with an instructor and fellow students can make all the difference in the world. For information about systems auditing classes, visit the Certification Program page at www.microsoft.com/learning/mcp.

You will find it helpful if you have taken certification exams before. Regardless, practice exams are helpful in determining readiness. Answer the following question:

1. Have you taken a practice exam on your chosen test subject? (Yes or No)

   If you answered yes to the previous question and you scored 90% or better, you're probably ready to tackle the real thing. If your score isn't above that crucial threshold, keep at it until you break that barrier. If you answered no, go back and study the book some more and repeat the practice tests. Keep at it until you can comfortably break the passing threshold.

> **TIP**
>
> There is no better way to assess your test readiness than to take a good-quality practice exam and pass with a score of 90% or better. When I'm preparing, I shoot for 95%+, just to leave room for the "weirdness factor" that sometimes shows up on Microsoft exams.

One last note: Hands-on experience using the actual product within the context of the exams is important. As you review the material for the exams, you'll realize that hands-on experience with database design concepts and best practices is invaluable.

Let's Get to It!

After you've assessed your readiness, undertaken the right background studies, obtained the hands-on experience that will help you understand the products and technologies at work, and reviewed the many sources of information to help you prepare for a test, you'll be ready to take a round of practice tests. When your scores come back positive enough to get you through the exam, you're ready to go after the real thing. If you follow this assessment regimen, you'll not only know what you need to study, but you'll also know when you're ready to take the exam. Good luck!

CHAPTER ONE

Installing and Configuring SQL Server 2005

Terms you'll need to understand:

- ✓ Shared memory
- ✓ Named pipes
- ✓ Multiprotocol
- ✓ TCP/IP
- ✓ Virtual Interface Adapter (VIA)
- ✓ RAID
- ✓ Remote server
- ✓ Linked server
- ✓ Stored procedure
- ✓ SQL Profiler
- ✓ Index
- ✓ View
- ✓ Group
- ✓ Role

Techniques you'll need to master:

- ✓ Utilizing Books Online
- ✓ Recognizing tools and utilities
- ✓ Defining and recognizing SQL objects

Microsoft's new stream of products brings with it a new type of Microsoft certification. Beginning with the release of Visual Studio 2005, SQL Server 2005, and BizTalk 2006, Microsoft is redefining the development and database environments, as well as the related certifications. There are new exams, new certifications, and a whole new set of standards. For SQL Server–related certification, there are now five different exams, of which 70-431 is the starting point along the certification path. This chapter explains how to install and configure SQL Server 2005 in preparation for 70-431. (For more information about the other exams and certification changes, consult this book's Introduction.)

Installing and Configuring SQL Server 2005

The first step in preparing to use SQL Server is to properly install Microsoft SQL Server 2005. Not so coincidentally, this is also the first exam subtopic. Before installing SQL Server, you need to select of the appropriate hardware and operating system configuration. You should expect to see questions that not only pertain specifically to the Microsoft SQL Server 2005 software but also the surrounding environment.

Within the broader topic of installing SQL Server, there are really two separate issues: performing a new installation and upgrading an existing installation. In performing a new installation, you have to consider the hardware compatibility, hardware configuration, operating system, and software requirements. When upgrading an existing installation, you must also consider the compatibility issues surrounding existing data and applications.

As explained in this book's Introduction, many of the topic areas overlap between the set of SQL Server–related exams. This particular exam focuses on the basics of hardware layout, operating system integration, and related requirements for installation.

This chapter focuses on the installation topics covered on the 70-431 exam, but for the complete picture, particularly if you plan on taking other SQL Server–related exams, you will need to know more about how to install SQL Server. In Appendix A, "Suggested Readings and Resources," you can find a list of additional resources that provide more in-depth coverage.

Installation Requirements

The Microsoft SQL Server 2005 software dictates a number of requirements for installation. Appropriate hardware, operating system, and support software are needed to successfully deploy the product.

EXAM ALERT

On all Microsoft exams, watch for questions that provide a choice of configurations for appropriate deployment. In most instances, all but one of the answers will include something that is not possible. On this exam, you are unlikely to see any questions regarding 64-bit deployments.

There are six different editions of SQL Server, each with varying requirements:

- Express Edition
- Workgroup Edition
- Developer Edition

- Standard Edition
- Enterprise Edition
- Mobile Edition

The exam primarily focuses on the high-end Enterprise Edition, but you should review the other editions to become familiar with their requirements, features, and appropriate applications. All editions have similar hardware requirements, except, of course, for the mobile edition, which is a separate platform for use on mobile devices. You need not worry about studying the Mobile Edition for the exam as its application is out of the exam scope. (The Mobile Edition is also beyond the scope of this book and therefore is not mentioned from this point forward.)

Hardware Requirements

The Express and Workgroup Editions do not support the 64-bit platform, and the requirements for those editions relate solely to a 32-bit deployment. The requirements that follow would not represent the typical configuration for most production servers. Most production equipment exceeds not only the absolute minimum requirements but for performance capacity and availability reasons contains hardware far beyond the recommended minimums.

All editions require a minimum 600MHz Pentium III processor (1GHz or better recommended) for the 32-bit deployment. The 64-bit editions require a minimum 1GHz AMD Opteron, AMD Athlon 64, Intel Xeon with Intel EM64T support, or Intel Pentium IV with EM64T support processor. The Developer, Standard, and Enterprise Editions also support deployment on 1GHz Itanium processors.

The Express Edition sets its minimum memory levels at 192MB, with the recommended being 512MB or higher. All other editions require 512MB minimum, with 1GB or more memory recommended. The disk space needed to install SQL Server (not including user databases) is the same for all editions: 350MB minimum or 425MB if Books Online and sample databases are installed.

Operating System Requirements

The first of the software requirements for installing SQL Server involves the host operating system, which varies slightly from edition to edition. Table 1.1 shows the editions and their correlating supported platforms.

TABLE 1.1 Microsoft SQL Server 2005 Operating System Support

SQL Server 2005 Edition	Windows XP, SP2	Windows XP X64, SP2	Windows 2000 Professional, SP4	Windows 2000 Server, SP4	Windows Server 2003 Standard, SP1	Windows Server 2003 Enterprise, SP1	Windows Server 2003 Datacenter, SP1	Windows Server 2003 Web, SP1	Windows Small Business Server 2003, SP1	Windows Server 2003 Standard X64, SP1	Windows Server 2003 Enterprise X64, SP1	Windows Server 2003 Datacenter X64, SP1
Express	X		X	X	X	X	X	X	X			
Workgroup	X		X	X	X	X	X		X			
Standard 32-bit	X		X	X	X	X	X		X			
Standard 64-bit		X								X	X	X
Developer 32-bit	X		X	X	X	X	X		X			
Developer 64-bit		X								X	X	X
Enterprise 32-bit				X	X	X	X		X			
Enterprise 64-bit										X	X	X

Support Software Requirements

Besides the host operating system, a couple other software components are required before you can install SQL Server. Internet Explorer 6.0, SP1, or later is a requirement for installation. If you plan on implementing SQL Server Reporting Services, you will also need Internet Information Server 5.0 or later and ASP.NET 2.0.

The network software requirements are the same for all editions. SQL Server 2005 supports the following network protocols:

- Shared memory
- Named pipes
- TCP/IP
- Virtual Interface Adapter (VIA)

SQL Server no longer supports Banyan VINES Sequenced Packet Protocol, Multiprotocol, AppleTalk, or NWLink IPX/SPX. Any existing installation that has clients connecting with these protocols must select one of the supported protocols.

Each of the protocols should be applied in different instances. The VIA protocol works specifically with VIA hardware. Named pipes is used for communications on local area networks (LANs) as an alternative to TCP/IP.

Shared memory is the simplest protocol, with no settings. Clients use shared memory to connect to an instance running on the same computer. You can use shared memory to troubleshoot when other protocols are not functioning.

TCP/IP is the most popular protocol used. It allows access to SQL Server through an associated port number that can be configured through SQL Server

Configuration Manager in the SQL Server 2005 Network Configuration. By default, SQL Server uses port 1433, but you can configure it to be a different value, if desired.

The Installation Process

Installing SQL Server is pretty straightforward, but there are a few options available during the setup. It is important to go through the installation process a few times, both because of the functionality provided by having a couple installations and also to hit a couple more exam points in the installation process.

The installation process varies slightly, depending on the edition you are installing and the options you select for the editions. A significant number of additional features are available, and during the installation process, you must select whether these are available and, if so, how they are to be set up. This chapter discusses the options available in the Enterprise Edition because it is the focus of the 70-431 exam.

Besides the database engine itself, a full array of additional products ship with SQL Server:

► Analysis Services

► Integration Services

► Notification Services

► Reporting Services

► Service Broker

These products provide additional functionality to augment the data services.

NOTE

Microsoft has made these products optional as an additional security precaution even though they provide useful functionality. They should be implemented carefully, within the scope of network security.

Some of the more advanced exams in the certification paths deal in more depth with the attributes of the installation and configuration. For the 70-431 exam, you need to concentrate on only a few of the additional products that ship with SQL Server. For this reason, the text that follows discusses only the topics needed for this exam.

Installation Preparations

To help ensure a successful installation, you can use several tools to aid in discovering potential problems. You can use the System Configuration Checker (SCC) and SQL Server Migration Assistant to smooth the installation process in a new or upgraded installation.

EXAM ALERT

You are expected to know the appropriate use of both the SCC and SQL Server Migration Assistant tools for the exam. You use the SCC to pinpoint conditions that prevent installation. You use the Migration Assistant to migrate from other systems, such as Access or Oracle.

You can use the SCC to scan the computer where SQL Server will be installed. The SCC checks many parameters and then provides remedies to enable a successful installation. The SCC checks Com+, requirements for Performance Monitor, the Windows Management Instrumentation (WMI) service requirement, the Microsoft XML Core Services (MSXML) required by some SQL Server components, the minimum operating system requirements, the minimum hardware and software requirements, and whether the system has a pending reboot. The SCC also ensures that the user has sufficient privileges to perform the installation.

The Migration Assistant is available for free download from Microsoft's website. You can perform migrations from other products by using this tool. An excellent presentation of its use is available from www.microsoft.com/sql/solutions/ssm/ssmademo.mspx.

While you are preparing for the installation, you must also consider the physical layout of the hardware on the server. You are unlikely to see the minimum requirements used on a server in a production environment. Depending on the load, you want to use a multiple-processor system for your database server. One processor is fine with a low-end server, if it is 1GHz or above, but two processors are better, and four or more processors are preferred. SQL Server is designed to work best in a symmetric multiprocessor environment.

Given the price of RAM today, it doesn't make sense to skimp in this area in order to lower costs. You should put as much RAM into the machine as your hardware and budget can handle. Increasing the memory of a server is the most cost-effective change you can make to achieve better performance on an existing machine. I am reluctant to put a low end on RAM, but I suggest 1GB for starters, and don't be afraid to move up a considerable distance from there.

The disk system is also very important. For a strong server, you should use a minimum of 5 drives. A 3-drive RAID 1 array would be used to store data, and the other 2 drives would mirror each other and store the operating system and application programs. The more drives you can add to the array, the better the performance and the greater the capacity available to store data. This peaks out at about 10 drives, which is a little overboard anyway; a 5-drive array performs very well for most implementations.

> **EXAM ALERT**
>
> You are likely to run into at least one question that deals with the concept of RAID storage devices. You must understand the differences between the varieties of RAID implementations and how the operating system interacts with the physical components.

RAID (redundant array of independent/inexpensive disks) is a technology in which two or more disk drives can be configured to provide the following:

- **Larger volumes**—Space on multiple disks is combined to form a single volume.

- **Improved performance**—The user can interact with more than one physical disk at a time (disk striping RAID 1).

- **Safeguarding of data**—You can provide mechanisms (mirroring or parity) for redundant data storage (RAID 5, which is not recommended for high-performance systems).

Even though you need to understand software implementations of RAID in order to pass certification exams, and even though they are found in production systems, they are not regarded as being as reliable as hardware RAID. For any high-volume, mission-critical application, you should set up data redundancy mechanisms at the hardware level. You should configure a gigabit backbone for the network around the server. It is even worth considering multiple network cards connected to the server to increase the bandwidth available to the machine.

If you are looking at the very high end, two sets of small RAID arrays of three drives, each on two separate controllers, can provide some additional performance gain and flexibility with data and index placement. It is also often recommended that you keep the log files separated from the data in order to improve performance and reduce disk contention.

> **TIP**
>
> Keeping the log files separate from the data can help improve performance and reduce disk contention.

When you're considering where to put the files for the database server, you need to think about the operating system files, the application program files, and the database files—both data files and log files.

It is also worth considering separating indexes because you can realize some performance gains if the indexes are stored on a drive other than the one on which the data is stored. You do this through the use of filegroups. When the index is created on a different filegroup, each group can make use of different physical drives and their own controllers. Multiple disk heads can then read data and index information in parallel.

In an ideal configuration, you might want to separate the operating system from its page file. You would then place the log onto its one drive, separate from the data, with the data configured over a RAID 1 volume. You would then separate the seldom-used data (column or table data) from data that will be accessed more frequently. After placing the indexes on their own volume as well, for about $150,000–$200,000 you would have the optimum performance in a database server.

Remember that the database management system (DBMS) relies heavily on the file system. SQL Server uses a set of files to store the data, indexes, and log information for a database. A primary file also has some header information in it, providing SQL Server with necessary information about a database. Each database has a minimum of two files associated with it: one for the data and one for the log. It is also possible to create multiple files for each of these purposes, as described in the following paragraphs. File placement and object placement within these files play an important role in the responsiveness of SQL Server. A database consists of two or more files, with each file used for only a single database. A single file cannot be shared by multiple databases.

Additional Considerations for Installation

You really cannot begin to deploy a database server into a production environment without knowing a lot about the applications that are going to use the server. The physical components of the server change dramatically for different applications. It is not enough to simply apply the software to a framework that is not specifically set up for the application that will be used.

Some of the implementation aspects that may affect the physical attributes of the server include the following:

- ▶ Partitioning of tables, indexes, and views
- ▶ Data mirroring, replication, clustering, and log shipping
- ▶ Division of application load or alteration of schema to address load issues
- ▶ Physical adjustments for slow-running applications

Changes to the environment will no doubt occur over time. It is rare for a production server to maintain the same configuration over prolonged use. You should be prepared to adjust the configuration as needed.

Postinstallation Procedures

If you have used previous versions of SQL Server, one of the first things you will notice is that the SQL Server Enterprise Manager has been renamed and revamped so that it has a lot of new functionality. The new SQL Server Management Studio is a powerful tool that allows for much more than administration and data query capabilities. You can use this new integrated environment to access, configure, manage, administer, and develop all components of SQL Server. SQL Server Management Studio includes the many features to ease database development and administration.

After you have installed SQL Server, you need to perform a number of different processes to set up connections to the data sources you will be accessing. If you have multiple instances of SQL Server installed on the same computer, or if you administer multiple machines in the same company, you will likely find it easiest to connect to and register the machines within SQL Server Management Studio.

> **NOTE**
>
> Installing two instances of SQL Server on the same computer allows you to test the most possible scenarios with a minimum of hardware and effort. Many features require two instances, and having them both on one machine will make your exam preparation easier.

From SQL Server Management Studio, you can connect to any SQL server in the enterprise. You can also connect to instances of Reporting Services, Integration Services, Analysis Services, and Mobile Edition. This is helpful in an organization where more advanced features of the environment are utilized, but it is not discussed further in this book because it is beyond the scope of the 70-431 exam.

Linked Server Configuration Options

When designing applications that use multiple data sources, you need to be able to integrate these data sources. Linked servers allow you to execute commands against data sources on remote servers. They offer a number of advantages, without requiring you to migrate data to a single server. By configuring linked servers, you can access a remote server and issue distributed queries, updates, commands, and transactions against the data sources. The data sources can be created from almost any product from Microsoft or another company. By using OLE DB and/or ODBC technologies, you can access and handle diverse data sources in a similar fashion.

After you have configured linked servers, you access them in the same manner you would if the data were located locally on the server. However, you must use four-part names when querying the data. A four-part name refers to the components needed to uniquely define the location and name of an object:

```
ServerName.DatabaseName.Owner.ObjectName
```

As you can see in Figure 1.1, when you use a linked server, you can easily query and manipulate the data when it is properly qualified in this manner.

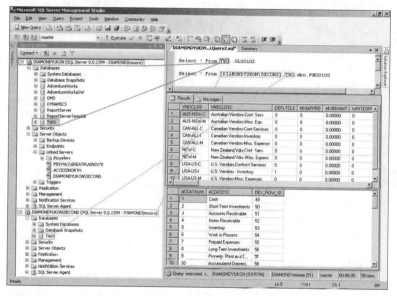

FIGURE 1.1 Using four-part names when querying a linked SQL server.

When you define a linked server, you must supply a number of criteria to use for the connection to the data. When you create a linked server object, you must define the security and optionally define any special handling of the connection and/or the format of the data.

When using linked servers, you must connect to data using the security requirements of the server hosting the data. In most cases, you must use a valid login. Additional options are not tested on the 70-431 exam, but you need to know the security-related options needed to set up logins. Several of the available options utilize the login and indicate how users are related between the systems. The security context could be any of the following:

- ▶ Current local login

- ▶ Remote login same as local

- ▶ Mapped login from list

- ▶ Singular remote login for all locals

- ▶ Impersonated login

- ▶ Restricted access to nonmapped logins

EXAM ALERT

The 70-431 exam topics dealing with linked servers focus on security and appropriate use of four-part names. Keep in mind that remote servers, although available as objects themselves in previous versions of SQL Server, are now configured using linked server objects.

When you create a linked server that will connect to an OLE DB data source, you supply a name for the server to use inside your applications. This becomes the server portion of the four-part name. Although this is similar to an alias, there is an important differentiation. An alias can be used in a query expression as an alternative name for a table or column. An alias can also be an alternative name for a server when you configure data connectivity for clients through the SQL Server Configuration Manager at the server and ODBC DSN (Data Source Name) on client machines.

Logins and security are of course an important part of working with links to other data sources. Connections must be made from one server to the other, and these connections must be validated to ensure appropriate access to the data. The configuration setup for the login sets up the security context in which the connection will operate. You can configure a mapping of local logins to remote logins and then set up the method for connecting any logins that are not mapped.

You can set logins to impersonate (also known as *delegation*) to allow SQL Server 2005 to connect to another instance of SQL Server under the context of an authenticated Windows user. With delegation, the instance of SQL Server to which a user has connected by using Windows authentication impersonates that user when communicating with another instance of SQL Server or a SQL Server provider.

NOTE

For user impersonation to be successful, the instance being connected to must be on the same computer, a remote computer within the same Windows domain, or a remote computer within a trusted Windows domain.

Enabling impersonation for distributed queries may involve configuration changes within Microsoft Active Directory as well as configuration of the user mapping within SQL Server. In Windows Server 2003, you can grant rights to be trusted for constrained delegation, which allows administrators to specify exactly which services can be accessed when using an impersonated user's security context. This configuration is the preferred, more secure, configuration in domains that have full Windows Server 2003 functionality. SQL Server 2005 also supports the ability to impersonate another principal by using the EXECUTE AS statement or clause on modules; this aspect of impersonation is discussed in Chapter 3, "Implementing Database Objects."

If you do not provide a local login with impersonation, you must supply the remote login and password that is to be used to connect to the linked server. As shown in Figure 1.2, the DYNSA local login will use impersonation, and the other two accounts will be mapped to logins on the remote system.

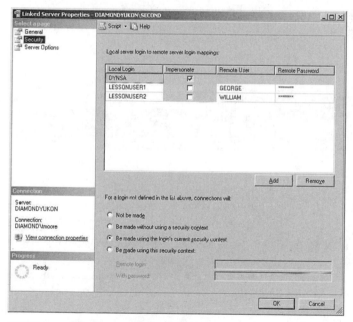

FIGURE 1.2   Remote server login mappings.

Note that at the bottom of the Linked Server Properties dialog box, you indicate the security context that the non-mapped logins will use. This determines whether any non-mapped logins can connect and under what security the connections are made. Of course, you have to know the login information on both machines before you configure linked servers for operation.

SQL Server Login Security

When connecting to SQL Server, you do so using an account that allows a level of access defined by the login information stored in SQL Server. Logins are the basis for the security context of any operation you perform. Logins are stored in SQL Server and can originate from SQL Server or from Windows user accounts and groups.

A login can belong to specialized SQL Server roles at the server or database level. Each role has a specific set of tasks that define what can and cannot be done on the server and within the database. Security granularity at this level is beyond the scope of this exam and is therefore not discussed in this book. You can find more information about each of the roles in SQL Server Books Online and on the Microsoft website.

New to SQL Server are credential objects, which allow users who connect to an instance of SQL Server by using SQL Server authentication to connect to Windows or other resources outside the instance of SQL Server. A *credential* is a record that contains the authentication information. Most credentials are made up of a Windows login and password.

> **EXAM ALERT**
>
> Don't spend a lot of time studying security for the exam. All you really need to know about the topic is how to define a role, how to use application roles, and how to create logins based on Windows groups.

To make permissions easier to administer, you should always assign them at the group or role level. Because you can add Windows groups as logins, you can leverage groupings that the network administrator has already created. You can easily allow all employees in the company access by adding the Domain Users group, but you should do this with caution in instances if that group contains external entities. You should never assign access to the Everyone group because doing so is deemed insecure and opens a hole in which data tampering can occur.

After a login ID is created, you can assign access to a resource to the login ID. Within a database, a User object exists for each login that has access to the database. The Guest user within a database should be removed in most cases. This User object gives anyone who can connect to the server access to a database, even when that person has not been explicitly granted the access. To disable guest access, you simply remove the user from the database.

Every user becomes a member of the Public role within a database. You cannot assign or remove users from this role. You can use this role to set a base level of permissions to every user in the database. You should never deny permissions to the role because in doing so, you would be denying the permissions to all users. Instead, you should simply not assign permissions at all to the role unless it is a permission you want to give to all users.

Other database roles can be created for any desired purpose. After they are created, users can be added to the roles, and permissions can be assigned to the roles accordingly. If application roles are used and activated, other users' related permissions are not in effect while the application role is active. This prevents users from performing tasks outside an application's scope.

Exam Prep Questions

1. You need to install Microsoft SQL Server 2005 Enterprise Edition for test purposes and have moderate storage capabilities. Which of the following systems suits your needs without requiring you to perform any alterations?

   ○ **A.** Pentium 400, 1GB RAM, Internet Explorer 5

   ○ **B.** Pentium 400, 512MB RAM, Internet Explorer 6

   ○ **C.** Pentium 600, 256MB RAM, Internet Explorer 6

   ○ **D.** Pentium 600, 512MB RAM, Internet Explorer 6

2. You are about to install Microsoft SQL Server 2005 Enterprise Edition on one of the servers in the company. Which of the following systems can you use without needing to upgrade? (Choose all that apply.)

   ○ **A.** Windows 2000 Server, SP4

   ○ **B.** Windows Small Business Server 2003 SP1

   ○ **C.** Windows 2000 Server, SP3

   ○ **D.** Windows Server 2003 Web Edition SP1

   ○ **E.** Windows Server 2003 Standard Edition SP1

3. You have just installed Microsoft SQL Server 2005 Enterprise Edition for use in the company. You need to set up security to allow access to the server to the employees of the company. The server will contain several databases, some of which contain sensitive information. How do you configure access to the server? (Choose two answers.)

   ○ **A.** Allow access to the Domain Users group and assign users to appropriate applications roles

   ○ **B.** Allow access to the Everyone group and assign appropriate permissions to associated SQL logins

   ○ **C.** Allow access to Active Directory groups that have been created according to company roles and assign permissions according to those groups

   ○ **D.** Disable guest access and assign minimal permissions to the Public role in the sensitive databases

   ○ **E.** Disable guest access and deny permission to the Public role in the sensitive databases

4. On an existing Microsoft SQL Server 2005 Enterprise Edition instance, you need to prevent non-management individuals from accessing the server. How do you configure access to the server?

○ **A.** Disable guest access; grant access to a network group containing the management individuals; deny access to the Public group in each database

○ **B.** Disable guest access and grant access to a network group containing the management individuals; ensure that no other access has been granted to other groups

○ **C.** Disable guest access and grant access to the Domain Users group; deny database access to anyone not in management

○ **D.** Disable guest access and grant access to a network group containing the management individuals; grant access to all other network groups and assign them to the db_denydatareader role in all databases

5. You are about to install Microsoft SQL Server 2005, and you want to ensure that the configuration is suitable for the installation. Which tool would you use?

○ **A.** System Configuration Checker

○ **B.** SQL Server Analysis Services

○ **C.** SQL Server Migration Assistant

○ **D.** SQL Server Profiler

6. You are attempting to set up the disk drives to attain the best performance while retrieving data. How would you configure the drives that are being used by the data files?

○ **A.** Use RAID 0

○ **B.** Use RAID 1

○ **C.** Use RAID 5

○ **D.** Use NTFS (no RAID)

7. You need to configure access to a second SQL server for an application that will be using the data for a single query. How would you implement the configuration and query? (Choose two answers.)

○ **A.** Set up an alias for the server

○ **B.** Set up the server as a remote server

○ **C.** Set up the server as a linked server

○ **D.** Use a four-part name in the query

○ **E.** Use a union query

○ **F.** Use a join query

Answers to Exam Prep Questions

1. **D.** To install SQL Server, you need a minimum of a Pentium 600, 512MB of RAM (although more is recommended), and Internet Explorer 6 or above. See SQL Server Books Online for more information.

2. **A, B, E.** As shown in Table 1.1 in the chapter, you need Service Pack 4 for Windows 2000 Server, and the Web Edition of Windows Server 2003 supports only the Express Edition of SQL Server.

3. **C, D.** You should never deny permissions to the Public role because, in essence, you would be denying the ability for any user. Instead, you should assign a minimal, base level of permission to this role. You can leverage Active Directory groups to ease administration, but you need to be cautious in using the Domain Users group, which in this example would be invalid. You should never use the Everyone group.

4. **B.** You should never deny permissions to the Public role because, in essence, you would be denying the ability for any user. Instead, you should assign a minimal, base level of permission to this role. You can leverage existing Active Directory groups to ease administration, as long as they contain the appropriate individuals.

5. **A.** The System Configuration Checker (SCC) can pinpoint conditions that will prevent a successful installation. The Migration Assistant, on the other hand, is used to migrate from other systems such as Access or Oracle. SQL Server Analysis Services provides online analytical processing (OLAP) and data mining functionality. SQL Server Profiler is for monitoring an existing instance of the database engine or Analysis Services.

6. **A.** Although other forms of RAID offer fault tolerance, the implementation of the fault tolerance will have an associated performance cost. No RAID at all does not provide performance as good as you can achieve by using multiple drives in a RAID 0 configuration.

7. **C, D.** You need to configure a linked server to provide access to data from the second source. Within the query, you address the second source by using four-part names.

2

Creating Database Objects

Terms you'll need to understand:

- ✓ Table
- ✓ View
- ✓ Trigger
- ✓ Function
- ✓ User-defined function (UDF)
- ✓ Table-valued function
- ✓ Scalar-valued function
- ✓ Aggregate
- ✓ Stored procedure
- ✓ Constraint
- ✓ Index
- ✓ Clustered index
- ✓ Nonclustered index
- ✓ Type and user-defined type (UDT)

- ✓ Full-text search
- ✓ Full-text index
- ✓ Full-text catalog
- ✓ Cascading action
- ✓ Data Manipulation Language (DML)
- ✓ Data Definition Language (DDL)
- ✓ Common language runtime (CLR)
- ✓ Partitioning
- ✓ Unique index
- ✓ Identity column
- ✓ Assembly
- ✓ Rule
- ✓ Default

Techniques you'll need to master:

- ✓ Defining database objects
- ✓ Viewing and creating objects using SQL Server Management Studio

- ✓ Creating objects using Transact-SQL

Chapter 1, "Installing and Configuring SQL Server 2005," describes the server installation and setup. Installation and setup are major SQL Server 2005 events. However, the 70-431 exam doesn't focus much on installation and setup. It does, however, focus on objects, which are the key components of databases. This chapter covers the objects stored on the server, which are, as noted, a meaty part of the 70-431 exam.

Many different types of objects are maintained in a SQL Server environment. Objects are a complex topic and can be confusing if you try to approach everything at once. For this reason, this chapter divides the topic into two separate categories: basic database objects and programmability objects.

First this chapter looks at the *what*s and *how*s of database objects. It simply looks at how to define and create objects, without delving too deeply into the reasons behind object selection and implementation. Chapter 3, "Implementing Database Objects," discusses objects, associates object selection with specific applications, covers some of the coding aspects behind the Transact-SQL (T-SQL) language and tasks, and looks more into the *where*s, *when*s, and *why*s of objects.

> **EXAM ALERT**
>
> Expect to see questions about not only individual objects but also the interactions between objects. Often, alterations of objects have a chain reaction and affect other objects. At other times, you might need to disable some objects to allow changes to others.

Creating and Defining Databases

The first object to be concerned with is the database itself. Creating a database from the SQL Server Management Studio is a simple task. In most cases, all you need to do is provide a name for the database and then click OK. When initializing a database, you should also think about the location of the data and log files. Other than that, initial database creation is somewhat lackluster, particularly if you have a well-configured logical data model.

In the default database creation process, you see a list of the properties present in the model system database. The model is essentially a template database for each new database created. It is a good idea to review the properties of the model database; you will likely want to change the recovery model option to Full so that every database created is set up for full recovery.

As you create databases and other objects, information about the objects is maintained inside the master database. The master database contains a set of system tables that track most of the objects on the server. Objects not stored in the master pertain to the automation objects that fall under the control of the SQL Server Agent. The automation objects controlled by the SQL Server Agent are maintained instead in the msdb database.

On the 70-431 exam, the database itself is considered a moot point. It exists, and it has predictable settings, but the exam includes no questions that involve creation of a database over and above the default scenario. It is worth looking at the CREATE and ALTER DATABASE statements, however, because they are used to create and alter most objects.

Using T-SQL to Create and Alter a Database

The T-SQL CREATE DATABASE statement allows for the creation of a new database and the files used to store the database. A database can also be created by attaching a database to the server from the files of a previously created database. The CREATE statement is also used to create a database snapshot.

After you create a database, you can use the ALTER DATABASE statement to modify it. You can make changes to the files and filegroups associated with the database, add or remove files and filegroups, change the attributes of the database or its files and filegroups, change the database collation, and set any of the database options.

> **NOTE**
>
> In previous releases of SQL Server, you could use sp_dboption to programmatically set any of the database options. The sp_dboption stored procedure will be removed in a future version of Microsoft SQL Server. You should therefore use ALTER DATABASE to set any of the options previously set through sp_dboption.

To retrieve current settings for database options, you use the sys.databases catalog view within a standard query. The sp_dboption stored procedure is still available and can be used for immediate information in this release. If desired, you can run sp_dboption as a query from SQL Server Management Studio, but sp_dboption is not recommended for any coded solution.

The Makeup of a Database

A database is made up of a variety of objects and information. The data is stored in files in a manner that allows the database engine to access the objects and information in an effective manner. Often, the database is thought of as a container for data and nothing more. However, the purpose of a database is to support applications. To this end, a variety of objects provide useful functionality to these applications, as described in this chapter.

You can use the SQL Server Management Studio to quickly view all the objects associated with a database. The Database Diagram tool and the objects it creates allow you to quickly display a group of tables and their properties and to print out the information. For documentation purposes, however, this tool significantly lacks features that database designers use, such as logical data modeling and data dictionary development.

The remaining objects are far more useful than the diagram objects, and they support the database. By opening the tree, as shown in Figure 2.1, you can get a quick glance at the various objects that SQL Server uses.

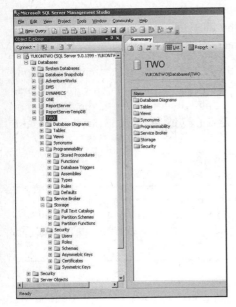

FIGURE 2.1 A database object tree within SQL Server Management Studio.

From a data perspective, the main object that the database maintains is the table, an object consisting of rows and columns that is used to store data. The columns represent an attribute, and the rows represent a set of attributes for one distinct occurrence of the data item. A table contains or is directly associated with a set of objects of its own. We look more closely at tables and their related objects later in this chapter, in the section "Defining SQL Server Tables."

SQL tables act as the actual data stores within the database environment. A *view* is a virtual table whose information is defined by an SQL query. Defined as a virtual table, a view does not normally hold any data itself. Like a table, a view is a set of columns and rows. But the data for the view is stored in the underlying tables of the database. Unless it is indexed, a view does not store data values. Views are versatile and can be used in many situations where a table is used.

Standard Views, Indexed Views, and Partitioned Views

A view can be a simple SQL query that filters the number of columns and rows in a single table to provide a more meaningful and useful display of the data. A standard view can be a little more complex and combine multiple tables in JOIN relationships or UNION relationships. In this respect, the complexity of displaying information can be hidden from the user, and the appearance of a singular set of records simplifies information handling.

The standard view is a powerful tool. It can be used in place of a table for most data query operations. Through horizontal and vertical filtering, it helps improve performance and efficiency by limiting the data sent across the network. It can efficiently process and organize data on the server to then be sent to reporting applications at the client for attractive display.

Views provide many benefits and are therefore common throughout an enterprise database environment. The number-one reason a view is created is to protect data from inquisitive eyes. This means that the developer has to worry only about allowing access to the view and further restricting the rows that are returned. Views provide many other benefits as well, including the following:

- ▶ **Make querying easier**—Views enable a user to execute specific SELECT statements over complex structures without requiring the user to provide a more detailed SELECT statement each time it executes.

- ▶ **Hide irrelevant data**—Views enable users to use SELECT to choose only the data that is needed or is of interest.

- ▶ **Enforce security**—Users can view only what you let them see. This may be a set of rows or columns or both. This feature is especially important when sensitive information is involved, such as salary and credit card information. Views provide a more efficient data retrieval process and easier security management than complete data store structures because permissions are checked and maintained at only one level.

A standard view can also make data import and export more easy to perform. Selecting just the correct data in the correct sequence and then putting the data into a form that is ready to use can be very helpful. Spreadsheets, accounting packages, and interactive websites can all make use of data that is quickly export-ed into other formats through the use of views.

> **NOTE**
>
> Views that produce aggregated data (for example, SUM, COUNT, MAX), use four or more tables in join operations, contain subquery operations, perform complex calculations, or operate through cascading table relationships can produce a significant amount of overhead.

Beyond the standard view lie some interesting tangents that you can implement to improve performance and capacity within a database. A standard view can be a significant amount of processing overhead due to the production of aggre-gates, the joining of data, or other hierarchical table issues. There may be a more efficient method of performing a view than dynamically building the data every time the view is called. In views that are frequently used by the application accessing the data, you can often improve performance by storing data within a standard view and creating an indexed view.

Using Indexed Views

Indexed views can help improve performance in systems where views are fre-quently used to return large amounts of data. To create an indexed view, you can add a unique clustered index on the view. In this style of view, the data is stored within the database, just like a table. Because the data no longer has to be dynamically prepared when the view is executed, performance is drastically improved. Indexed views are best applied in situations in which data is infre-quently updated. As data in the underlying tables changes, SQL Server must update the correlating data within the indexed view. If the data is changed often, the maintenance cost of the view may outweigh any performance gain.

When an indexed view is created, the SQL Server Query Optimizer can make use of its existence. If the Query Optimizer recognizes that the data to resolve a query is contained within the view, it might deem it more efficient to pull data from the view than to pull it directly from the tables. The Query Optimizer can perform these activities even when the view is not directly referred to in the query.

A considerable number of settings must be in place to implement indexed views:

- ▶ ANSI_NULLS must be ON when you create tables referenced by the view.

- ▶ ANSI_NULLS, ANSI_PADDING, ANSI_WARNINGS, CONCAT_NULL_YIELDS_NULL, and QUOTED_IDENTIFIER must be ON when the view is created.

- ▶ When you create an index, the IGNORE_DUP_KEY option must be OFF.

To configure these settings, you use a SET command, specify the option that you are setting, and specify the setting state as either ON or OFF, as in the following example:

```
SET ANSI_NULLS ON
```

EXAM ALERT

There are many restrictions in terms of what elements cannot be used in an indexed view. You might want to read more about the use of indexed views, but other than those on the basic designs and use of indexed views, there are not a lot of questions on the 70-431 exam about the setup and coding of views. You need to know the options for creation, how to use SCHEMABINDING, and advantages and disadvantages of the use of indexed views.

You can use the SCHEMABINDING clause when creating a view to create a relationship between the view and the underlying tables. When binding is in place, you cannot alter any object that is bound to the view. Let's look at an example of creating an indexed view. First, you need to create a database to use as an example:

```
USE MASTER
GO
CREATE DATABASE ONE
GO
```

You must set the environment options for the table, view, and index to use. The following example uses the previously created database and creates a table, view, and associated index on the view:

```
USE ONE
GO

SET ANSI_NULLS On
SET QUOTED_IDENTIFIER On
SET ANSI_PADDING On
SET ANSI_WARNINGS On
SET CONCAT_NULL_YIELDS_NULL On
SET NUMERIC_ROUNDABORT Off
GO

CREATE TABLE dbo.GLAccts(
    ActIndex int NOT NULL,
    ActNumber_1 char(9) NOT NULL,
    ActNumber_2 char(9) NOT NULL,
    ActNumber_3 char(9) NOT NULL,
    ActAlias char(21) NOT NULL,
    ActType smallint NOT NULL,
```

```
   ActDesc char(51) NOT NULL,
   ROW_ID int IDENTITY(1,1) NOT NULL,
 CONSTRAINT PKGL00100 PRIMARY KEY NONCLUSTERED(ActIndex ASC)
   WITH (IGNORE_DUP_KEY = OFF) ON [PRIMARY]
) ON [PRIMARY]
GO

CREATE VIEW dbo.v_AccountList WITH SCHEMABINDING AS
SELECT ActNumber_1, ActNumber_2, ActNumber_3, ActDesc FROM dbo.GLAccts
GO

CREATE UNIQUE CLUSTERED INDEX i_AList
   ON v_AccountList(ActNumber_1, ActNumber_2, ActNumber_3)
GO
```

Note that when you are creating a view, you use the SCHEMABINDING clause to create a relationship between the view and the underlying tables. With binding, a view or function is connected to the underlying objects. Any attempt to change or remove the objects fails unless the binding has first been removed. Once the SCHEMABINDING clause is in place, you cannot alter any object that is bound to the view. In this example, you would be able to add a column to the table, delete a column not related to the view, or change any of the columns not contained in the view.

You cannot make changes to four field definitions (ActNumber_1, ActNumber_2, ActNumber_3, and ActDesc) unless you first drop the view. After you complete the creation, you should check your results in SQL Server Management Studio. Figure 2.2 illustrates what the Object Explorer would now show for the ONE database.

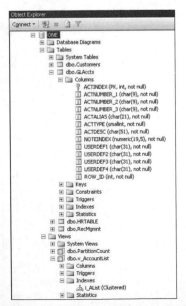

FIGURE 2.2 The ONE database object tree, showing Table, View, and Index attached to View.

You do not necessarily use the SCHEMABINDING clause only for indexed views. You can use it any time you want to attach an underlying table definition to a view or user-defined function. When you use it, however, it significantly changes the functionality.

Using Partitioned Views

A partitioned view can span a number of physical machines. Partitioned views fall into two categories:

- ▶ **Local**—Local partitioned views are available only for backward compatibility with previous versions of SQL Server. The preferred method for partitioning data locally using SQL Server 2005 is through partitioned tables. We will look more closely at local partitioning of tables later in this chapter, in the section "Defining SQL Server Tables."

- ▶ **Distributed**—Distributed partitioned views span multiple SQL Server instances.

A distinction is also made between views that are updatable and those that are read-only. The use of partitioned views can aid in the implementation of federated database servers, which are multiple machines set up to share the processing load. With federated server implementations, multiple server operations balance the load so that updates are potentially separated from queries and so query load can be spread across multiple machines. Federated servers are beyond the scope of the exam and therefore this book as well. However, for more information on federated server implementations, see SQL Server Books Online, "Designing Federated Database Servers."

Partitioned views drastically restrict the underlying table designs and require several options to be set when indexes are used. Constraints need to be defined on each participating server so that only the data pertaining to the table(s) stored on that server is handled. To use partitioned views, you horizontally split a single table into several smaller tables, and you make sure each has the same column definitions. You set up the smaller tables to accept data in ranges. You can enforce the data entry into each ranged server by using constraints. Although constraints are not needed to return the correct results, they enable the Query Optimizer to more appropriately select the correct server to find the requested data.

Then you can define the distributed view on each of the participating servers. To do so, you add linked server definitions on each of the member servers. The following is an example of a distributed view definition:

```
CREATE VIEW AllProducts AS
    Select * FROM Server1.dbo.Products9999
```

```
UNION ALL
        Select * FROM Server2.dbo.Products19999
UNION ALL
        Select * FROM Server3.dbo.Products29999
```

Partitioning attempts to achieve a balance among the machines being used. Data partitioning, as mentioned previously, involves the horizontal division of a single table into a number of smaller tables, each dealing with a range of data from the original and split off onto separate servers. Attempting to ensure that the correct query goes to the appropriate server also helps to improve performance while minimizing bandwidth use.

Designing for partitioned views requires appropriate planning of front-end applications to ensure that, whenever possible, data queries are sent to the appropriate server. Middleware, such as Microsoft Message Queue or an application server or other third-party equivalents, should attempt to match queries against data storage. When preparing for data communication with the front-end application, the operating system settings of the server affect the server's interaction with the application.

Miscellaneous SQL Server Objects

A number of SQL Server objects not discussed so far are also important: tables, the Service Broker, programmability, and security objects. Each of these topics is very hefty in its own right. These topics are therefore broken into their own sections in the remainder of the chapter.

As you peruse a database using the Object Explorer in SQL Server Management Studio, you might notice a few objects that are new to SQL Server. Many of the objects are not tested on the 70-431 exam. To be thorough, however, this chapter does discuss them. Although these objects may provide some useful functionality, you are unlikely to find them on the exam:

▶ **Synonyms**—A synonym is an alternative name for a schema-scoped object. It is a single-part name to reference a base object. A synonym is similar to an alias, but it replaces a two-part, three-part, or four-part name.

▶ **Database diagrams**—A database diagram is a graphical design of a table or set of tables that can be used to illustrate the tables and relationships within a database.

▶ **Statistics**—Stored within a table, statistics are automatically created and optionally supplemented histograms.

▶ **Assemblies**—An assembly references a managed application module (DLL file) that was created in the .NET Framework common language runtime (CLR).

▶ **Proxies**—In the msdb context, a proxy defines security context and provides the SQL Server Agent access to credentials for a Windows user.

Defining SQL Server Tables

There are two basic categories of tables in SQL Server: user created and system defined. Tables are generally used to store data, but each database contains a number of tables other than those used to store data. These tables store information that enables SQL Server to keep track of objects and procedures within a database. The sysobjects and syscomments system tables maintain entries containing the object definitions and other tracking information for each object. Various other tables also exist to maintain information about specific objects.

For more information regarding system tables, refer to SQL Server Books Online. System tables are used whenever SQL Server needs object information. You should never alter system tables directly; instead, you should allow SQL Server to manipulate the entries as needed. Many stored procedure and system views have been created to minimize the need to query the tables directly.

> **EXAM ALERT**
>
> Querying system tables is not the preferred method for obtaining system data. Using store procedures and dynamic management views are preferred methods.

In many systems, prior to creating tables (or any object, for that matter), you must determine the purpose of the table. If it is to hold data that is frequently accessed, the file placement of the table should take that into consideration. Tables that hold archive data and other less frequently accessed data require less maintenance than more volatile tables and don't have to be as responsive to user queries, so you should consider that as well.

Keep in mind when assigning objects to files that you can place some objects away from the mainstream data by using filegroups. You can select the object placement from Table Design Properties in the Enterprise Manager or through the use of an ON clause in a CREATE/ALTER statement. SQL Server enables you to place the following table objects:

▶ Tables

▶ Indexes

▶ `text`, `ntext`, or `image` data

You don't necessarily always move objects around. Most applications are not large enough to justify these measures. You need to move objects around only in very large database systems.

When you create a table, you define the structure of the rows and columns (or records and fields, if you prefer) of the table. The objects associated with a table are actually considerably more than just column definitions. In SQL Server 2005, six types of objects are associated with a table definition

▶ **Columns**—These are the fields or attributes of the records in a table.

▶ **Keys**—Keys are primary or secondary identifiers of a table and table relationship.

▶ **Constraints**—A constraint is a regulation placed on data in a table.

▶ **Triggers**—Triggers are actions that automatically occur as additions, changes, and deletions of data occur.

▶ **Indexes**—An index is an object that controls the viewing of data in a particular sequence.

▶ **Statistics**—Statistical information helps the SQL Server Query Optimizer resolve queries in the most efficient manner possible.

Each of these objects plays an important role in a table. The objects are all closely related. In most cases, a setting in one of the objects causes an action or a reaction to occur in another object. Most of this activity occurs at the time of data entry. As additions, changes, and deletions are performed against the data, activities can be configured to aid in keeping the system functional and reliable.

When a table is created, you assign each column in the table a number of attributes that make up the column definition. The minimum requirements for column attributes are a name for the attribute and a data type.

Using Types and Schemas

The data types in SQL Server 2005 span more than just numbers, letters, and special characters. Table 2.1 summarizes the available data types.

Table 2.1 SQL Server 2005 Data Types

Data Type	Type	Byte Size	Notes
bigint	Exact numeric	8 bytes	
binary	Binary string	1 byte per character	
bit	Exact numeric	1 byte per 8 or less in table	
char	Character	1 byte per character	
cursor	Transact SQL cursor	N/A	Cannot be assigned as a column data type
datetime	Date and time	8 bytes	
decimal	Exact numeric	5, 9, 13, or 17 bytes (depending on the precision)	Equivalent to numeric
float	Approximate numeric	4 or 8 bytes (depending on the precision)	
image	Binary string	2TB maximum	
int	Exact numeric	4 bytes	
money	Exact numeric	8 bytes	
nchar	Unicode character	2 bytes per character	
ntext	Unicode character	2 bytes per character and 1TB maximum	
numeric	Exact numeric	5, 9, 13, or 17 bytes (depending on the precision)	Equivalent to decimal
nvarchar	Unicode character	2 bytes per character	
real	Approximate numeric	4 bytes	
smalldatetime	Date and time	4 bytes	
smallint	Exact numeric	2 bytes	
smallmoney	Exact numeric	4 bytes	
sql_variant	Undetermined/ any	Varies with content	Can store any data type except text, ntext, image, timestamp, and sql_variant
table	SQL Server table	N/A	Cannot be assigned as a column data type

Table 2.1 *Continued*

Data Type	Type	Byte Size	Notes
text	Character	1 byte per character and 2TB maximum	
timestamp	Auto-generated	8 bytes	Auto-generated value
tinyint	Exact numeric	1 byte	
varbinary	Binary string	1 byte per character	
varchar	Character	1 byte per character	
uniqueidentifier	GUID	16 bytes	Globally unique identifier
xml	XML document	2GB maximum	

When you select the data type for any given column, you should keep in mind the maximum content of the column. You should also consider the presence or absence of a key field or a column in an index because these should be kept as small as possible.

User-Defined Types (UDTs)

There are two types of UDTs: standard and CLR UDTs. In the simplest form, UDTs simply remap system data types and apply some limits. More advanced UDTs can execute code to provide more diverse types. Some potential implementations of UDTs include those that use date, time, currency, and extended numeric types in a manner other than is offered by default data type behavior. Applications that utilize nonstandard data where system types can't be applied, such as geographical or other complex graphical data, are good candidates for UDTs. Also, if you use encoded or encrypted data, you can use UDTs.

UDTs are stored as database objects and are based on any of the system data types. UDTs can be used when several tables must store the same type of data in a column and you must ensure that these columns have exactly the same data type, length, and nullability.

Using UDTs can help you create tables more quickly and can also help you control the data in a predictable manner. Often, a UDT is created in the model database; it then exists in all new user-defined databases created.

The 70-431 exam might include questions that deal with the selection of the most appropriate or most efficient data type. You can use the byte sizes listed in Table 2.1 to help determine the correct type. You might also get questions in which you must differentiate between standard UDT use and CLR UDTs. You might also need to decide between the use of UDTs and user-defined functions (UDFs).

CLR UDTs

UDTs are programmability database objects that can take advantage of the CLR provided in SQL Server 2005. These CLR objects are programmed against an assembly created in the Microsoft .NET Framework. The ability to execute CLR code is set to OFF by default. You can enable CLR code by using sp_configure or via SQL Server Surface Area Configuration for Features.

EXAM ALERT

With the CLR being the latest and greatest thing to hit SQL Server, you can bet that you will see a question or two on the topic. Remember, just because it's possible to use other languages doesn't mean that doing so is the best solution. With a standard data task, T-SQL is more efficient than the CLR. If a task is a little out of the ordinary and requires an extra level of processing capabilities, you can effectively use the CLR.

Something that has always been a problem with UDTs in the past is the inability to encompass business logic into the type definition. With use of the CLR in complex processing scenarios, however, anything is possible. Although it is possible, though, you should not try to throw the CLR at every problem. T-SQL still handles data issues more effectively than the CLR.

You should use the CLR only when necessary because there is a considerable amount of overhead associated with using CLR types. Most data-checking mechanisms should be performed by other features of the database system, where they are performed in a more efficient and effective manner. One potential use of the CLR would be in situations where data types are set up in class/subclass scenarios.

XML Schema Collections

SQL Server provides for storage of a full XML document within a single column through the xml data type. You can associate XSD schemas with XML data through the association of an XML schema collection. The XML schema collection stores imported schemas. You can use these imported schemas to validate XML data or to apply type information for the XML data as it is stored in the database. XML is such an intricate part of SQL Server databases that this book provides a whole chapter on it. Refer to Chapter 4, "Supporting the XML Framework," for more information on using XML and XSD.

Other Attributes

You can set the NULL or NOT NULL property when you define a column. If a column is set to NULL, it allows empty entries. If a column is set to NOT NULL, the column must have an entry during entry or alteration of row data. If a column is to be included as the primary key or as a portion of the primary key, then it is set to NOT NULL and cannot be altered.

You might want a column to have a default value. The best way to achieve this is to use the DEFAULT option of the CREATE and ALTER TABLE statements. For backward compatibility, you can programmatically create and bind a DEFAULT object, but you should not do this because it will not be supported in future versions of SQL Server.

Using Columns with Automated or Calculated Values

Many types of columns achieve their resulting values through calculations or other internally automated mechanisms. Several of these column types are defined in the following sections, and each is used for a specific reason.

Computed Columns

When a column is defined, it can be defined so as to get its results from the result of a calculation. This type of column is referred to as a *computed column*. You might want to use a computed column in a denormalized data framework to avoid having to do complex or frequently repeated calculations within an application. In this case, the calculation is performed when the data is entered or when the data the formula is based on changes.

A computed column is calculated based on an expression that can use other columns in the same table. The expression can be a noncomputed column name, constant, function, variable, or any combination of these, connected by one or more operators. About the only restriction is that the expression cannot be a subquery.

Identity Columns

Another type of field that has its value automatically calculated and entered is an *identity column*. If you select a column to be used as an identity column, the value is calculated based on a seed starting point for the table, and an incremental value is added each time the calculation occurs.

Identity columns are useful when you want to achieve unique column content in an increasing (or decreasing) manner. Identity columns are often candidates for the primary key because they contain unique values.

Columns with `timestamp` Data Types

The `timestamp` data type is a binary data type. Oddly enough, everyone seems to assume that it is a time-valued variable, but `timestamp` has no time-related values, at least not from a calendar or clock perspective. The content is derived through the fact that each database has a counter that is incremented for each insert or update operation performed. This counter is the database timestamp. A table can have only one column that uses the `timestamp` data type. Each generated timestamp is guaranteed to be unique within the database. The `timestamp` data type is useful for concurrency logic—that is, for detecting whether a row has been updated since it was last read.

Maintaining Order by Using Indexes

Putting data into sequence to accommodate quick retrieval and to provide meaningful and usable output for an application usually requires that a variety of indexes be defined. A *clustered index* provides the physical order of the data being stored, whereas a *nonclustered index* provides an ordered list with pointers to the physical location of the data.

You can most easily understand indexing if you compare the data and index storage of a database to that of a book. In a book, the data itself is placed on the pages in a sequence that is meaningful if you read the book sequentially from cover to cover. An index at the back of the book enables you to read the data in a different order. You can locate a topic by looking through a list of topics that is accompanied by a physical page reference to the place where the topic can be found. To read a single topic, you need not skim through the entire book; you simply need to use the index to find the topic. In a similar manner, data in a database can be handled randomly or in sequence. You can locate a single record in the database by looking it up in the index rather than reading through all the rest of the data. Conversely, if a report is to be generated from all the data in a database, you can read the data sequentially, in its entirety.

Index storage in SQL Server has a B-tree storage structure. The indexes are maintained in 8KB pages classified as root, intermediate, and leaf-level pages. In a clustered index, the leaf level is the data itself, and all other levels represent index pages. In a nonclustered index, all pages contain indexes (see Figure 2.3).

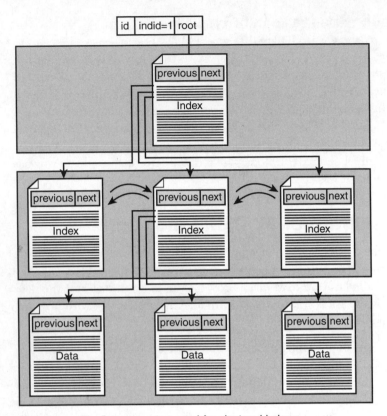

FIGURE 2.3   The B-tree structure used for clustered indexes.

If a clustered index has not been defined for a given table, the data is stored in a *heap*. A data heap does not maintain data in any particular order; it simply stores the data in the order in which it is entered. In some applications, in which data is never retrieved in any particular order on a regular basis, this might actually be advantageous.

You can create indexes by using the T-SQL CREATE INDEX command. When creating indexes, it is good practice to leave space for later insertions of data. The following example creates a compound, nonclustered index that is 75% full:

```
CREATE INDEX IXProductItem
ON ProductOrderLine (OrderMateKey, ProductLineKey)
WITH FILLFACTOR = 75
```

The two different organizations of indexes, *clustered* and *nonclustered*, provide for the ordering of data in two ways: either through physically rearranging the data, as in a clustered index, or through the use of data pointers, as in a nonclustered index. If the organization is not specified, as in the previous example, nonclustered is the default behavior.

Indexing Through Reordering: Clustered Indexing

Selecting the appropriate column(s) on which to base a clustered index is important for several reasons. As previously mentioned, a clustered index represents the order in which data is physically stored on the disk. For this reason, you can define only a single clustered index for any table. If you choose not to use a clustered index in a table, the data on disk is stored in a heap. A clustered index, if present, has clustering keys that are used by all nonclustered indexes to determine the physical location of the data.

The basis for the index is usually determined by the order in which the majority of applications and queries want their output. The clustered index values are also present in other indexes, and the size of the defined index should be kept as small as possible. When you select a clustering key, you should try to utilize a numeric data type because character types cause index storage to occupy much more space.

You should always define a clustered index before you define any nonclustered indexes. If you do these tasks in reverse order, all nonclustered indexes rebuild themselves when the clustered index is created.

Indexing Through Data Pointers: Nonclustered Indexing

Nonclustered indexes provide a means of retrieving data from a database in an order other than that in which the data is physically stored. The only alternative to the use of these indexes is to use a sort operation, which would place undue overhead on the client system and might not produce the desired response times. A data sort implementation is usually performed for one-time operations only or for applications that will have very limited usage.

Although creating indexes increases performance and saves resources in a lot of cases, you should avoid creating indexes that will rarely be utilized. Each time a record is added to a table, all indexes in the table must be updated, and this might also cause undue system overhead. Therefore, it is important to carefully plan index usage.

One-of-a-Kind Indexing: Unique Indexing

When you create indexes, it is important to guarantee that each value is distinctive. This is particularly important for a primary key. SQL Server automatically applies a unique index to a primary key to ensure that each key value uniquely defines a row in the table. You might want to create additional unique indexes for columns that are not defined as the primary key.

Leaving Room for Additions in Indexes

The *fill factor* is the percentage at which SQL Server fills leaf-level pages upon creation of indexes. Provision for empty pages enables the server to insert additional rows without performing a page-split operation. A page split occurs when a new row is inserted into a table that has no empty space for its placement. As the storage pages fill, page splits occur, and they can hamper performance and increase fragmentation.

You normally find that queries (which read existing data) outweigh data updates by a substantial margin. Providing the extra room slows down the query process. Therefore, you might not want to adjust the FILLFACTOR setting at all in static systems where there are small numbers of additions.

On the other hand, setting the fill factor too low hampers read performance because the server must negotiate a series of empty pages to actually fetch the desired data. It is beneficial to specify a fill factor when you create an index on a table that already has data and will have a high volume of inserts. If you do not specify the fill factor when creating an index, the server default FILLFACTOR setting is chosen. You set the fill factor for a server through the Enterprise Manager or by using the sp_configure stored procedure.

The percentage value for the fill factor is not maintained over time; it applies only at the time of creation. Therefore, if inserts into a table occur frequently, it is important to take maintenance measures for rebuilding the indexes to ensure that the empty space is put back in place. You can rebuild a specific index by using the CREATE INDEX T-SQL command with the DROP EXISTING option. You can also defragment indexes by using the DBCC INDEXDEFRAG command, which also reapplies the fill factor.

The PADINDEX setting is closely related to the FILLFACTOR setting, to allow space to be left in non-leaf levels. You cannot specify PADINDEX by itself; you can use it only if you supply a fill factor. You do not provide a value for this setting; it matches the setting given for the fill factor.

Primary/Foreign Keys and Relationships

A table key is an attribute that is used to identify a particular row of a table. Both primary and foreign keys are defined in the form of constraints. These keys work together to accommodate table relationships. A *foreign key* refers to the primary key in the parent table, forming a one-to-one or one-to-many relationship. A many-to-many relationship is really two one-to-many relationships using a joining table.

When multiple tables maintained in a database are related to each other, you need to take some measures to ensure that the reliability of these relationships stays intact. To enforce referential integrity, you create a relationship between two tables. You can do this through the database diagram feature of the

Enterprise Manager or by using the CREATE and ALTER TABLE T-SQL state-ments. Normally, you relate the referencing or foreign key of one table to the primary key or other unique value of a second table.

The PRIMARY KEY Constraint

A PRIMARY KEY constraint enforces entity integrity in that it does not permit any two rows in a table to have the same key value. This enables each row to be uniquely defined in its own right. Although a primary key should be created when a table is initially created, you can add or change a primary key at any time after table creation. You could add a primary key upon table creation as shown here:

```
CREATE TABLE Suppliers
( supid id NOT NULL
    CONSTRAINT [UPKCL_supind] PRIMARY KEY  CLUSTERED,
  lname varchar (40) NOT NULL ,
  fname varchar (20) NOT NULL ,
  phone char (12) NOT NULL ,
  address varchar (40) NULL ,
  city varchar (20) NULL ,
  state char (2) NULL ,
  zip char (5) NULL ,
  active bit NOT NULL ) ON [PRIMARY]
```

A primary key cannot have any duplicate values. SQL Server automatically cre-ates a unique index to enforce the exclusiveness of each value. If a primary key is referenced by a foreign key in another table, the primary key cannot be removed unless the foreign key relationship is removed first.

Although it is not a requirement of the SQL Server database environment, a pri-mary key should be defined for each table. A primary key helps records maintain their identities as unique rows of a table and also provides a means of relating tables to other tables in the database to maintain normal forms. A foreign key is defined in a subsidiary table as a pointer to the primary key or another unique value in the primary table to create a relationship.

Table keys can be set up in several different types of relationships:

▶ **One-to-many relationships**—The most common relationships are one-to-many relationships, in which the unique value in one table has many subsidiary records in the second table.

▶ **One-to-one relationships**—Another form of relationship, which is nor-mally used to split a table with an extraordinary number of columns, is a one-to-one relationship. You can use one-to-one relationships to split a table and associate a single unique value in one table with the same unique value in a second table.

▶ **Many-to-many relationships**—You can also define a many-to-many relationship, but this form of referencing requires three tables and is really two separate one-to-many relationships.

Utilizing referential integrity guidelines helps maintain the accuracy of data entered into a system. A database system uses referential integrity rules to prohibit subsidiary elements from being entered into the system unless a matching unique element is in the referenced table. The system also protects the data from changes and deletions, assuming that cascading actions have been carefully and properly implemented. (Cascading actions are discussed later in this chapter, in the section "Using Cascading Actions.")

The FOREIGN KEY Constraint

A FOREIGN KEY constraint is defined so that a primary and subsidiary table can be linked together by a common value. A foreign key can be linked to any unique column in the main table; it does not necessarily have to be linked to the primary key. It can be linked to any column that is associated with a unique index.

You can define a foreign key and its relationship when creating or altering a table definition. The following example defines a relationship by using T-SQL:

```
CREATE TABLE PurchaseOrderDetails
    ( DetailsID          smallint,
      OrderID            smallint
        FOREIGN KEY (OrderID) REFERENCES PurchaseOrders(OrderID),
      SupID              smallint
        FOREIGN KEY (SupID) REFERENCES Suppliers(SupID),
      QtyOrdered bigint,
      WarehouseLocation  smallint
    )
```

With a foreign key defined, you cannot add a value to the foreign key column if a matching value is not present in the primary table. If a child entry with an ID is not found in the parent table, this is known as an *orphan child* and is a breach of referential integrity rules.

Using Cascading Actions

Cascading actions affect update and delete activity when an existing foreign key value is changed or removed. You control cascading action by using the CREATE and ALTER TABLE statements, with clauses for ON DELETE and ON UPDATE. You can also select these features by using the Enterprise Manager.

In a cascading update, when you change the value of a key in a situation in which a foreign key in another table references the key value, those changed values are reflected in the other tables. Something similar happens with a delete operation: If a record is deleted, all subsidiary records in other tables are also deleted. For example, if an invoice record is deleted from an invoice table that has invoice details stored in another table and referenced by a foreign key, the details are also removed.

A series of cascading actions could easily result from the update or deletion of important keys. For example, the deletion of a customer could cause the deletion of all that customer's orders, which could cause the deletion of all the customer's invoices, which in turn could cause the deletion of all of the customer's invoice details. For this reason, careful system design is important, and you should consider archiving data through the use of triggers.

In the case of multiple cascading actions, all the triggers to be fired by the effects of the original deletion fire first. AFTER triggers then fire on the original table, and then the AFTER triggers in the table chain subsequently fire. As discussed in the following section, SQL Server 2005 has two different styles of triggers:

▶ Data Manipulation Language (DML) triggers are familiar to most SQL Server technicians.

▶ Data Definition Language (DDL) triggers are new to SQL Server.

Using DML and DDL Triggers

A DML trigger is like a stored procedure in that it contains a set of T-SQL statements saved for future execution. The big difference is that, unlike stored procedures, DML triggers are executed automatically, based on data activity in a table. A DML trigger may fire based on UPDATE, INSERT, or DELETE operations.

DDL triggers, also referred to as database triggers, fire procedures in response to DDL statements. DDL statements start with CREATE, ALTER, and DROP. DDL triggers can be used for administrative tasks such as auditing and regulating database operations. DDL triggers fire after an event has occurred. You cannot define an INSTEAD OF operation on a DDL trigger. In SQL Server, DML triggers can be fired *after* an operation completes (the SQL Server default) or *instead of* the triggering operation. You can use an AFTER trigger to archive data when it is deleted, to send a notification that the new data has been added or changed, or to initiate any other process you might want to automate based on data activity. You can use an INSTEAD OF trigger to perform more advanced activities such as advanced data checking, to enable updates in a view to occur across multiple tables, or to perform many other functions that might be necessary in place of a triggering activity.

Triggers represent a mechanism in which code can be executed based on activity in the data.

Partitioning Tables

To support the partitioning of tables, you must be running SQL Server 2005 Enterprise Edition. Only the Enterprise Edition of SQL Server supports partitioning.

As discussed earlier in this chapter, tables store information about an entity, such as products or sales. Each table has attributes that describe only that entity. While a single table for each entity is the easiest to design and understand, such tables are not necessarily optimized for performance, scalability, and manageability, particularly as the tables grow larger.

Partitioning of data could allow data to be always available, even during periods of scheduled maintenance. By dividing the data into partitions, you can implement the maintenance process such that data on one partition is available while maintenance occurs on another.

When maintenance operations are performed, many costly effects can occur, such as degrading performance and data blocking problems. System and database backups—although being performed when the database is still online—could affect the overall performance of a server. There are also space, time, and operational costs associated with most maintenance activities. All this can negatively affect overall scalability of a server.

Partitioning Strategies

Partitions can be designed in a symmetric or asymmetric fashion, and although it is most useful to design symmetrically, the access requirements of a lot of systems necessitate an asymmetric design.

A *symmetric design* is one in which all related data is placed on the same server so that most queries do not have to cross network boundaries to access the data. It is also easier to manage data if the division of tables can be performed in such a manner that each server has the same amount of data. In most real-world applications, data is accessed in a random fashion that can make the designer lean toward an *asymmetric implementation*. The design can be configured so that one server has a larger role and/or contains more data than the others. You can improve performance if you weigh each server's use and make one server work harder on the partitioned applications because the other servers perform larger tasks that deal with other, unrelated processes.

Table Considerations

Table size is usually the primary factor in considering a table to be a candidate for partitioning. A table can also be considered if activities of other users or maintenance operations have a limiting effect on availability. You might want to implement partitioning in any scenario where performance is severely degraded or if a period of downtime is regularly needed for maintenance purposes.

Varying access patterns of the rows and columns within data could have an impact on the decision to partition a table. Performance could be degraded because of excessive reading of data when table scans are used to retrieve individual pieces of data.

A database doesn't necessarily have to be a large database to be problematic enough to warrant partitioning. You might want to consider partitioning any database that does not perform as desired. You also need to consider whether operational and maintenance costs have exceeded budgetary specifications.

Advantages of Partitioning

Using partitions aids in improving scalability and manageability of large tables or tables that have varying access patterns. Partitioning can help by dividing the data into smaller, more manageable sections.

If a table exists on a system that has multiple CPUs, partitioning the table can lead to better performance through execution of parallel operations. The performance of operations across extremely large data sets can benefit if operations are performed against individual subsets of the data in a parallel manner. In SQL Server 2005, related tables that are partitioned to the same partitioning key and the same partitioning function are aligned. When the Query Optimizer detects that two aligned tables are joined, it can join the data that resides on the same partitions first, and then it can combine the results with the results from other partitions.

Creating Partitioned Tables

To implement table partitioning, you follow these steps:

1. Determine what you are using as the partitioning key and how many partitions you will use. Assume here that you are to divide the data into four partitions, based on alphabetic sorting:

   ▶ First partition: A–F

   ▶ Second partition: G–M

   ▶ Third partition: N–S

   ▶ Fourth partition: T–Z

2. Create one or more filegroups. It is generally recommended that you have the same number of filegroups as partitions.

3. Use the CREATE PARTITION FUNCTION statement to create a function in the current database that maps the rows of a table or index into partitions based on the values of a specified column. The number and domain of the partitions of a partitioned table or index are determined in a partition function.

4. Use the CREATE PARTITION SCHEME statement to create a scheme in the current database that maps the partitions of a partitioned table or index to filegroups.

5. Create the tables and other objects that are going to be stored on each partition.

6. Create indexes and any other partition objects that have the same functions and create the partition scheme.

Let's first look at creating the filegroups used for data storage. To begin, you need to have created a database called ONE. You will need to add some filegroups and files to the database. You do this by using the ALTER DATABASE statement. You should probably create one filegroup/file for each partition. Depending on the actual physical storage, you might want to create multiple filegroups, each with one or more files. The following code creates four filegroups, each with a single file:

```
ALTER DATABASE ONE ADD FILEGROUP PartitionOne
ALTER DATABASE ONE ADD FILEGROUP PartitionTwo
ALTER DATABASE ONE ADD FILEGROUP PartitionTri
ALTER DATABASE ONE ADD FILEGROUP PartitionFour
GO
```

```
ALTER DATABASE ONE ADD FILE (NAME = N'PartitionOne',
    FILENAME = N'C:\PartitionData\Part1.ndf',
    SIZE = 10MB, FILEGROWTH = 5MB)
    TO FILEGROUP PartitionOne
ALTER DATABASE ONE ADD FILE (NAME = N'PartitionTwo',
    FILENAME = N'C:\PartitionData\Part2.ndf',
    SIZE = 10MB, FILEGROWTH = 5MB)
    TO FILEGROUP PartitionTwo
ALTER DATABASE ONE ADD FILE (NAME = N'PartitionTri',
    FILENAME = N'C:\PartitionData\Part3.ndf',
    SIZE = 10MB, FILEGROWTH = 5MB)
    TO FILEGROUP PartitionTri
ALTER DATABASE ONE ADD FILE (NAME = N'PartitionFour',
    FILENAME = N'C:\PartitionData\Part4.ndf',
    SIZE = 10MB, FILEGROWTH = 5MB)
    TO FILEGROUP PartitionFour
GO
```

In this example, each partition file is in the same location, `C:\PartitionData`, which is a pre-created file folder on the hard drive where the data will be stored. In a production scenario, the partition files would each likely be stored on different volumes. Each file has appropriate autogrowth properties assigned.

EXAM ALERT

Pay close attention to the order in which objects are put in place:

1. The function definition has to be present to define a scheme based on that function.
2. The filegroups have to be present before creating the scheme that will use them.
3. The scheme has to be present for table creation to know where to store data.

The first true step in the partitioning process uses the CREATE PARTITION FUNCTION statement to provide the definition of how the data is to be split among the partitions. You need to supply three parameters to the statement.

▶ The data type of the column used for determining the partitioning of the data

▶ A range boundary indicator as to whether values fall left (the default) or right of the provided values

▶ A list of the boundary values to be used in partitioning

To continue along with the example, the partition function creation would be similar to the following code:

```
CREATE PARTITION FUNCTION AlphaRangePartFun(char(30))
    AS RANGE RIGHT FOR VALUES ('G', 'N', 'T')
GO
```

Three values are provided, and using the RIGHT boundary element means that the value provided is the boundary element just to the right of the partition. In this example, G is the first letter to the right of the partition values, which will be A, B, C, D, E, and F. Also, N is the first letter to the right of G through M, and T is the first letter to the right of N through S. The final partition would hold all remaining values to T through Z. The last partition value set does not need to be defined.

When the partition function has been defined, you can proceed to define the scheme on which storage will be performed, using the previously defined function to divide the data into partitions. In defining the scheme, you use the CREATE PARTITION SCHEME statement and supply the name of the partition function to use as well as the names of the filegroups that hold the data for each partition. For this example, the code would be as follows:

```
CREATE PARTITION SCHEME AlphaRangePartSch
    AS PARTITION AlphaRangePartFun
    TO (PartitionOne, PartitionTwo, PartitionTri, PartitionFour)
GO
```

Finally, you create the tables and any other objects you want to assign to the partitions. Notice in the following example that both the table and the index that are partitioned will be stored on AlphaRangePartSch, and the storage is based on the CUSTNAME field of the table:

```
CREATE TABLE dbo.CUSTOMERS(
    CUSTNMBR char(15) NOT NULL,
    CUSTNAME char(30) NOT NULL
     CONSTRAINT AlphaCheckCon
       CHECK (CUSTNAME >= 'A' AND CUSTNAME <= 'ZZZ'),
    CNTCPRSN char(31),
    ADDRESS1 char(31),
    ADDRESS2 char(31),
    ADDRESS3 char(31),
    COUNTRY char(21),
    CITY char(31),
    STATE char(29),
    ZIP char(11),
    PHONE1 char(21),
    PHONE2 char(21),
    INACTIVE tinyint NOT NULL
  CONSTRAINT [PKCUSTMR] PRIMARY KEY NONCLUSTERED
   (CUSTNAME ASC) WITH (IGNORE_DUP_KEY = OFF)
    ON AlphaRangePartSch(CUSTNAME))
  ON AlphaRangePartSch(CUSTNAME)
GO
```

After you finish creating the partitioned table, data begins to be stored across the partitions, based on the function you defined. You can then see the PARTITION FUNCTION and PARTITION SCHEME objects within the Storage folder of the ONE database within SQL Server Management Studio. The appropriate scheme then shows up as the storage location in both the table properties and the index properties.

Using $PARTITION in Queries

With a partitioned table, you can perform queries against the entire table in a normal manner. If you prefer to make a query against only a single partition, you can also easily perform that or any other similar query by using the $PARTITION function. You use this function to return the partition number. When you use it in combination with the other functions or aggregates, you can return some very useful information.

> **EXAM ALERT**
>
> $PARTITION is a function that returns a number that corresponds to the partition where the data is or would be. You can use this function in a number of ways whenever you need to know how data is dispersed.

You can use the $PARTITION function to test the function and scheme of any partitioned table. Even if a table has no data, you can find out which partition would be used by running a test similar to this:

```
USE ONE
GO
SELECT $Partition.AlphaRangePartFun ('Brown')
SELECT $Partition.AlphaRangePartFun ('Jones')
SELECT $Partition.AlphaRangePartFun ('Smith')
SELECT $Partition.AlphaRangePartFun ('Zachary')
GO
```

You can substitute any name in the single quotes. The value returned tells in which partition a record would be stored if it were inserted in the table. You can also use $PARTITION to easily track the record content of each partition. For example, the following query would return the number of records found in each of the partitions:

```
USE ONE
GO
SELECT $Partition.AlphaRangePartFun(CUSTNAME) AS Partition,
    COUNT(*) AS Count FROM Customers
    GROUP BY $Partition.AlphaRangePartFun(CUSTNAME)
    ORDER BY Partition
GO
```

In combination with grouping, in this manner you can get a good summary of the number of records stored within each partition. This is a useful view to set up in a production environment; you can easily convert the procedure to a view as follows:

```
CREATE VIEW PartitionCount AS
    SELECT $Partition.AlphaRangePartFun(CUSTNAME) AS Partition,
        COUNT(*) AS Count FROM Customers
        GROUP BY $Partition.AlphaRangePartFun(CUSTNAME)
GO
SELECT * FROM PartitionCount
    ORDER BY Partition
GO
```

SQL Server Programmability Objects

A set of objects stored within a database are of particular interest to a database developer. These objects allow coders to add their own capabilities and functionality to a database. These SQL Server 2005 objects offer state-of-the-art functionality (compared to rules and defaults, which are being phased out).

The coding environment in SQL Server 2005 is much more like what programmers expected than that in previous versions of SQL Server. CLR support, which is new to this version, offers techniques through which SQL procedures and functions can be written in languages other than T-SQL.

Stored Procedures

An important execution element that is stored within the context of a database is a stored procedure. A *stored procedure* is a set of T-SQL statements that can be saved as a database object for future and repeated executions. With stored procedures, you can enable a lot of the development and processing to be performed on the server, producing much more efficient and lightweight front-end applications. Any commands that can be entered via SQL Query tools can be included in a stored procedure.

Many system-stored procedures have already been created and are available when you install SQL Server. Extended stored procedures, which enable DLL files to be accessed from the operating system, are created upon installation and are present in the `master` database.

Extended stored procedures, like many of the system-stored procedures, are loaded automatically when you install SQL Server. Extended stored procedures access DLL files stored on the machine to enable the calling of the functions contained in the DLLs from within a SQL Server application. You can add to this set of procedures stored in the `master` database by using the `sp_addextendedproc` procedure, as shown here:

```
sp_addextendedproc 'MyFunction', 'MyFunctionSet.DLL'
```

Stored procedures and views can both be used as part of a broader security plan.

Creating CHECK Constraints

A `CHECK` constraint is one of several mechanisms that can be used to prevent incorrect data from entering a system. You can apply restrictions on data entry at the table or column level through the use of a `CHECK` constraint. You might also apply more than a single check to any one column, in which case the checks are evaluated in the order in which they were created.

A `CHECK` constraint represents any Boolean expression that is applied to the data to determine whether the data meets the criteria of the check. The advantage of using a check is that it is applied to the data before it enters the system. However, `CHECK` constraints have less functionality than mechanisms such as stored procedures or triggers.

One use for a `CHECK` constraint is to ensure that a value entered meets given criteria, based on another value entered. A table-level `CHECK` constraint is defined at the bottom of the `ALTER/CREATE TABLE` statement, unlike a `COLUMN CHECK` constraint, which is defined as part of a column definition. For example, when a due date entered must be at least 30 days beyond an invoice date, you could define a table-level constraint this way:

```
(DueDate - InvoiceDate) >= 30
```

You might use a column-level check to ensure that data is within acceptable ranges, as in the following:

```
InvoiceAmount >= 1 AND InvoiceAmount <= 25000
```

You can also use a check to define the pattern or format in which data values are entered. You might, for example, want an invoice number to have an alphabetic character in the first position, followed by five numeric values, in which case the check might look similar to the following:

```
InvoiceNumber LIKE '[A-Z][0-9][0-9][0-9][0-9][0-9]'
```

Finally, you might want to apply a check when an entry must be from a range of number choices within a list. An inventory item that must be one of a series of category choices might look similar to this:

```
ProductCategory IN ('HARDWARE', 'SOFTWARE', 'SERVICE')
```

A COLUMN CHECK (or other constraint) is stated as a portion of the column definition itself and applies only to the column where it is defined. A TABLE CHECK (or other constraint), on the other hand, is defined independently of any column, can be applied to more than one column, and must be used if more than one column is included in the constraint.

The following is an example of a table definition that is to define restrictions to a single column (for example, minimum quantity ordered is 50), as well as a table constraint (for example, the date on which a part is required must be later than when it is ordered):

```
CREATE TABLE ProductOrderLine
      (ProductLineKey  BigInt,
       OrderMatchKey   BigInt,
       ProductOrdered  Char(6),
       QtyOrdered      BigInt
         CONSTRAINT Over50 CHECK (QtyOrdered > 50),
       OrderDate       DateTime,
       RequiredDate    DateTime,
         CONSTRAINT CK_Date CHECK (RequiredDate > OrderDate))
```

Usually, a single table definition provides clauses for key definition, indexing, and other elements that have been left out of the previous definition to focus more closely on the use of CHECK constraints.

As you can see, constraints come in all shapes and sizes, and they control table content, inter-table relationships, and validity of data. The following sections tie up a few loose ends in order to give a full perspective on objects.

Creating Your Own Functions

Microsoft SQL Server 2005 has a variety of types of UDFs. A *UDF* is a single statement or routine that can accept parameter information, perform a defined process, and return the result of the process. The return value can either be a single scalar value or a result set.

A UDF has a two-part header/body structure. The header of the function defines the function name, input parameter, and return parameter. The body defines the activity that the function is to perform. When you create the function, the header is everything leading up to the AS keyword. The body is the trailing portion of the CREATE FUNTION statement that follows the AS keyword.

The following function definition (which calculates the cubed value for any number that is input) illustrates the components of a function definition:

```
CREATE FUNCTION dbo.Cubit        -- function name
(@Numb int)                      -- input parameter name and data type
```

```
RETURNS int                              -- return parameter data type
AS
BEGIN                                    -- begin body definition
DECLARE @Result int                      -- declaration of any variables
SELECT @Result = @Numb*@Numb*@Numb       -- action performed
RETURN @Result                           -- Answer returned from call
END                                      -- end body definition
```

The function call would look like this:

```
SELECT dbo.Cubit(4)
```

A UDF can be scalar valued or table valued:

- ▶ **Scalar-valued function**—A scalar-valued function defines a single piece of data in the RETURNS clause. For an inline scalar function, the function body is the result of a single statement. For a multistatement scalar function, the function body is defined in a BEGIN...END block. The data returned from the function cannot be a Text, Ntext, Image, Cursor, or Timestamp value.

- ▶ **Table-valued function**—A table-valued function uses the TABLE data type in the RETURNS clause. The function returns a set of records or more than one result line.

English Query Capabilities with Full-Text Catalogs

Full-Text Search is a program that runs as a service to SQL Server. You can use Full-Text Search in conjunction with all sorts of information from all the various Microsoft BackOffice products. Full-text catalogs and indexes are not stored in a SQL Server database; they are stored in separate files managed by the service.

Full-text indexes are special indexes that efficiently track the words you're looking for in a table. They help in enabling special searching functions that differ from regular indexes. Full-text indexes are not automatically updated, and they reside in a storage space called the full-text catalog.

EXAM ALERT

Full-Text Search questions have always been a favorite topic in Microsoft database exams. Expect to see one or two questions about the use of Full-Text Search and the command language surrounding the feature on the 70-431 exam.

With a full-text index, you can perform wildcard searches (using Full-Text Search) to locate words in close proximity. All full-text indexes are by default placed in a single full-text catalog. Each server, at its apex, can store 256 full-text catalogs.

The full-text catalog files are not recovered during a SQL Server recovery. They also cannot be backed up and restored by using the T-SQL BACKUP and RESTORE statements. The full-text catalogs must be resynchronized separately after a recovery or restore operation. The full-text catalog files are accessible only to the Microsoft search service and the Windows NT or Windows 2000 system administrator.

To enable full-text searches, you can run the Full-Text Indexing Wizard, which enables you to manage and create full-text indexes. Note that you can create full-text indexes only on columns that contain just text. Full-text indexes are not automatically updated, which means you need to automate the process of updating by setting a job or performing a manual administrative task.

Objects with Security Context

Permissions can be granted for object use or denied, for that matter, to anyone who connects to the server. Logins are created or denied at the server level. A login to the server has the level of permission determined by the groups, roles, and permissions allocated to the login. A login gains access to any database that has a user associated with the login, that has the guest user enabled, or that has a role that permits access directly or through an application.

Server roles exist to identify processes at the server level and allow logins to be associated with performing the processes allocated to a role. Individuals or groups can be associated to the roles to privileges associated to the role. Server roles are fixed; that is to say, you cannot create your own roles and role definitions.

Database roles are similar but have scope solely within the database in which they exist. Database roles are not fixed. Roles can be created for any purpose you want. You can create a special kind of database role, the application role, to gain more control over permissions that exist while performing operations through specific applications.

Credentials, new in SQL Server 2005, contain authentication data to connect to a resource outside the server. A credential is usually a Windows login and its associated password. Users who connect using SQL Authentication can use credentials to connect to other resources outside the server that might be needed for some SQL Server processes. A credential can be mapped to one or more SQL Server logins, but a login can be mapped to only one credential.

Exam Prep Questions

1. An existing sales catalog database structure exists on a system in your company. The company sells inventory from a single warehouse location that is across town from where the computer systems are located. The product table has been created with a nonclustered index, based on the product ID, which is also the primary key. Nonclustered indexes exist on the product category column and also the storage location column. Most of the reporting done is ordered by storage location. How would you change the existing index structure?

   ○ **A.** Change the definition of the primary key so that it is a clustered index.

   ○ **B.** Create a new clustered index, based on the combination of storage location and product category.

   ○ **C.** Change the definition of the product category so that it is a clustered index.

   ○ **D.** Change the definition of the storage location so that it is a clustered index.

2. You are designing an application that will provide data entry clerks the capability of updating the data in several tables. You would like to ease entry and provide common input so the clerks do not need to enter data into all fields or enter redundant values. What types of technologies could you use to minimize the amount of input needed? (Select all that apply.)

   ○ **A.** Foreign key

   ○ **B.** Cascading update

   ○ **C.** Identity column

   ○ **D.** Default

   ○ **E.** NULL

   ○ **F.** Primary key

   ○ **G.** Unique index

3. You are the database developer for a leasing company. Your database includes a table that is defined as shown here:

```
CREATE TABLE Lease
(Id Int IDENTITY NOT NULL
   CONSTRAINT pk_lease_id PRIMARY KEY NONCLUSTERED,
Lastname varchar(50) NOT NULL,
FirstName varchar(50) NOT NULL,
SSNo char(9) NOT NULL,
Rating char(10) NULL,
Limit money NULL)
```

Each SSNo must be unique. You want the data to be physically stored in SSNo sequence. Which constraint should you add to the SSNo column on the Lease table?

- ○ **A.** The UNIQUE CLUSTERED constraint
- ○ **B.** The UNIQUE UNCLUSTERED constraint
- ○ **C.** The PRIMARY KEY CLUSTERED constraint
- ○ **D.** The PRIMARY KEY UNCLUSTERED constraint

4. You are preparing a new index on a table that has 1,500 rows. 10 rows are added to this table every day. The table already has a primary key, and the new index does not represent the order in which data in the table is to be stored. Updates to the table occur periodically but are infrequent. Which type of index would you create under this situation?

- ○ **A.** Use a clustered index with a high FILLFACTOR setting
- ○ **B.** Use a clustered index with a low FILLFACTOR setting
- ○ **C.** Use a nonclustered index with a high FILLFACTOR setting
- ○ **D.** Use a nonclustered index with a low FILLFACTOR setting

5. You have a database that contains several FOREIGN KEY and CHECK constraints. Users are having problems with data entry on the database because the data they are adding is constantly in violation of the CHECK constraints. Corporate policy regarding database design prevents you from modifying the current constraints, so you decide to implement your changes via a trigger. Which types of triggers would be best suited for this task?

- ○ **A.** UPDATE, DELETE, and INSERT triggers
- ○ **B.** Just UPDATE and INSERT triggers
- ○ **C.** INSTEAD OF triggers
- ○ **D.** Triggers cannot be used in this circumstance.

6. You have an accounting SQL Server database application that is accessed by 50 users on your company network. When a user inserts or updates a record, you want to make sure that all the required columns have appropriate values. Which of the following would be best for this situation?

- ○ **A.** A stored procedure and a trigger
- ○ **B.** A batch and a trigger
- ○ **C.** An UPDATE trigger and an INSERT trigger
- ○ **D.** One trigger by itself

7. You have a development environment in which a number of individuals create databases regularly. You would like to log the database creation activity so that the username, time, date, and details of the creation are recorded. How would you implement this?

- ○ **A.** Use a DDL trigger.
- ○ **B.** Use a DML trigger.
- ○ **C.** Use a constraint.
- ○ **D.** Use a UDF.

Answers to Exam Prep Questions

1. **D.** Because the majority of the reporting is going to be performed by using the storage location, it would be the likely candidate. The clustered index represents the physical order of the data and would minimize sorting operations when deriving the output. For more information, see the section "Maintaining Order by Using Indexes."

2. **B, C, D, E.** All these options have activities that provide or alter data so that they do not have to be performed as entry operations. In the case of NULL, data does not need to be provided, possibly because the column contains noncritical information. For more information, see the section "Defining SQL Server Tables."

3. **A.** To obtain the physical storage sequence of the data, you must use a clustered constraint or index. Although a primary key would also provide for the desired level of uniqueness, it is not the appropriate key for this table. For more information, see the section "Maintaining Order by Using Indexes."

4. **D.** The primary key is usually the clustered index of a table. The clustered index indicates the physical order of the data. A low fill factor leaves more room for updates. For more information, see the section "Maintaining Order by Using Indexes."

5. **C.** INSTEAD OF triggers are required for this task because you must check for constraint violations before the update occurs. If there are constraint violations, AFTER triggers will not fire. Most likely, you need to implement INSTEAD OF INSERT or INSTEAD OF INSERT and UPDATE triggers. When trigger actions are listed, such as an INSERT trigger, you cannot know for sure whether it is an INSTEAD OF or AFTER trigger, but you should assume that it is a FOR or AFTER trigger if not specifically mentioned. For more information about the order in which triggers and constraints are applied see the information on sp_settriggerorder in SQL Server Books Online.

6. **D.** A single trigger can be used to perform validation on more than one event, such as INSERT and UPDATE. For more information about the differences between trigger types, see the section "Using DML and DDL Triggers."

7. **A.** You can use a DDL trigger applied to the creation of the database to have this information recorded. See the section "Using DML and DDL Triggers."

CHAPTER THREE

Implementing Database Objects

Terms you'll need to understand:

- ✓ SELECT command
- ✓ INSERT command
- ✓ UPDATE command
- ✓ DELETE command
- ✓ Transaction
- ✓ COMMIT statement
- ✓ ROLLBACK statement
- ✓ Index
- ✓ FROM clause and WHERE clause
- ✓ GROUP BY clause and HAVING clause
- ✓ LEFT JOIN or RIGHT JOIN
- ✓ INNER JOIN
- ✓ OUTER JOIN
- ✓ BETWEEN keyword
- ✓ ISNULL statement
- ✓ NULL value
- ✓ TABLESAMPLE clause
- ✓ Catalog
- ✓ CONTAINS command and CONTAINSTABLE command
- ✓ FREETEXT command and FREETEXTTABLE command

Techniques you'll need to master:

- ✓ Performing queries to extract data and produce reports
- ✓ Inserting data, updating data, and disabling objects during insertion
- ✓ Writing procedures that utilize transactions
- ✓ Setting up and using full-text queries

Although it is important to get tables and other objects in place, all that is really just the beginning of a database. With database applications, you put raw data in and attempt to gain information in return. Although every system is different, there are five basic functions that every system must support:

▶ Adding new data to the system

▶ Changing the existing data

▶ Removing obsolete or unwanted data

▶ Allowing user viewing of queries and data

▶ Reporting the data in a meaningful and useful manner

The server side does not necessarily perform the implementation of all these processes. In fact, most front-end applications provide the basics of these operations. The 70-431 exam does not focus a great deal on the actual writing of complete processes; its focus is more on individual situations where, as an administrator, you might perform the activities using some form of scripting.

This chapter is organized into individual scenarios that you may see on the exam and the operations you would perform to accommodate each situation.

Data Querying and Reporting

After data is in a database, it is likely to need to be accessed, changed, and reported on. To perform these basic operations, you need to apply the programming constructs of SQL, specifically Microsoft's implementation, referred to as Transact-SQL (T-SQL). Traditional applications can be completely centered on the four basic SQL commands: SELECT, INSERT, UPDATE, and DELETE. Essentially, these statements handle every operation that needs to be performed against the data. The most common of these constructs—the SELECT statement—is the basis for getting data out of the system.

SELECT statements can be complex and can include the use of options that can join many tables together and functions that can calculate and summarize data at the same time. However, a SELECT statement can be as simple as one line of code that retrieves the requested data. The complete SELECT syntax is involved, with many optional portions. You can find the complete syntax reference in SQL Server Books Online, under "SELECT, SELECT (described)." Many of the options are used only under special circumstances.

Listing the Contents of a Table

You will often be retrieving all the data from a particular table. Even if the final query is not intended to get all the data, you can often begin the data analysis by examining all the rows and columns of data in a particular table. The following example retrieves the customer data from the ONE database created in Chapter 2, "Creating Database Objects":

```
SELECT * FROM YUKONTWO.ONE.dbo.Customers
```

Note that the * is used to obtain all columns from the Customers table. It is also worth noting the use of the four-part name (*Server.Owner.Database.Object*). This name includes the server name YUKONTWO, database name ONE, the owner name dbo, and the name of the table itself, Customers.

Four-part names are used to perform queries when the one-part name of a table does not sufficiently qualify the table being queried. If you are executing a query within the scope of the server itself with the ONE database in use, and you are the owner or the owner is dbo, the four-part name is not necessary. There are therefore several valid variations on queries for the Customers table. Each of the following will produce the same results:

```
SELECT * FROM Customers
SELECT * FROM dbo.Customers
SELECT * FROM ONE.dbo.Customers
SELECT * FROM ONE..Customers
```

Although queries often go after all the data in a table, there are a considerable number of options available for a query statement. You can choose some of the columns of a table, provide record-level conditions to limit the number of rows returned, put the output into groups, provide group-level conditions to selectively choose the groups, put the output into sorted order, or produce calculated results. You can also get into some complex queries through the use of JOIN, UNION, and subquery operations.

> **TIP**
>
> The clauses of a SELECT query must be provided in the correct order to have valid syntax. As a mechanism for remembering the order, you can use the following acronym and phrase: SIFWGHOC (Some Infinitely Funny Winos Get High On Champagne), for SELECT, INTO, FROM, WHERE, GROUP BY, HAVING, ORDER BY, COMPUTE (BY).

You do not need to formulate complex queries for the 70-431 exam, so this chapter covers only the basic theory of the use of the queries, which is what the exam focuses on.

You can optionally supply column headers to give a user-friendly listing of the data. By default, the column headers that are displayed in the result set are the same as the columns specified in the column select list, such as CUSTNMBR and CNTCPRSN.

Making a Report More Presentable

Why not change a result set's column header to something more readable? You can change the name of a result set column by specifying the keyword AS. (This is the traditional SQL-92 ANSI standard.) Changing the column name by adding an equals sign (=) or implied assignment is also an alternative syntax choice. (Of course, you would normally use only one of these three techniques, and the industry standard is SQL-92 ANSI.) The following example illustrates the use of column aliasing:

```
SELECT CUSTNMBR AS 'Customer Number',
       'Customer Name' = CUSTNAME,
       CNTCPRSN 'Contact Person',
       FROM Employees

SELECT CUSTNMBR AS 'Employee ID',
       CUSTNAME AS 'Customer Name',
       CNTCPRSN AS 'Contact Person',
       FROM Employees
```

Notice that the previous column aliases have been enclosed in single quotation marks. This enclosure is necessary when the column alias includes a space. The alias name must be enclosed within brackets when the alias is a reserved SQL Server keyword.

Sometimes you need to combine two columns together to show the two columns as one. When you do this, you are using a method called *string concatenation*. You can think of concatenation as joining strings together, just as you can combine words into phrases. The operator used to perform the concatenation is the plus sign (+).

Using TRIM to Remove White Space

To create a single name column, you combine the last name and first name values. If there are leading or training blanks within the data, you might want to polish the output a little bit, by using the functions LTRIM (left trim) and RTRIM (right trim). These functions remove leading spaces (LTRIM) or trailing spaces (RTRIM). The resulting code would then look like this:

```
SELECT LTRIM(RTRIM(Address1))
 + ' ' + LTRIM(RTRIM(Address2))
 + ' ' + LTRIM(RTRIM(Address3)) 'Full Address'
FROM Customers
```

You can create your own function, which you could name TRIM, to eliminate both left and right spaces. This would be a handy feature to have in the product, and here is how it would look:

```
CREATE FUNCTION dbo.TRIM(@CHARSTRING NVARCHAR(255))
 RETURNS NVARCHAR(255)
 AS
  BEGIN
   RETURN (RTRIM(LTRIM(@CHARSTRING)))
  END
```

Returning TOP Rows

The TOP clause limits the number of rows returned in a result set to a specified number or percentage at the top of a sorted range. Here are two examples:

▶ SELECT TOP 50 returns the top 50 rows.

▶ SELECT TOP 50 PERCENT returns the top 50% of the rows.

As an alternative to TOP, you can also limit the number of rows to return by using SET ROWCOUNT N. The difference between this keyword and TOP is that the TOP keyword applies to the single SELECT statement in which it is specified. For example, SET ROWCOUNT stays in effect until another SET ROWCOUNT statement is executed (for example, SET ROWCOUNT 0 to turn off the option).

You can optionally specify that the TOP keyword is to use the WITH TIES option. In this case, any number of records can possibly be displayed. WITH TIES displays all records that are equivalent to the last matching element. If you are looking for the top 10 employees and two employees tie for 10th, 11 or more records are displayed. If the tie is for 9th or a higher position, only 10 records are listed.

Of course, after you begin placing data in the desired order, you then need to group the output and perform calculations based on the groups. As discussed in the following section, grouping allows the production of subtotals and also provides more usable output in applications that require grouped output.

Displaying Groups in Output

You can use the GROUP BY clause of the SELECT statement to create groups within data. You can then use these groups to display data in a more orderly fashion or produce more meaningful results through the use of aggregate functions.

The GROUP BY clause specifies the groups into which output is to be shown and, if aggregate functions are included, calculations of summary values are performed for each group. When GROUP BY is specified, either each column in any non-aggregate expression in the select list should be included in the GROUP BY list, or the GROUP BY expression must match exactly the select list expression.

> **EXAM ALERT**
>
> The GROUP BY option of the SELECT statement is often coupled with a HAVING clause to provide a condition against all groups. Also, the ORDER BY clause is almost always present with GROUP BY to ensure that functions operate correctly.

It is important to note that if the ORDER BY clause is not specified, groups returned using the GROUP BY clause are not in any particular order. It is recommended that you always use the ORDER BY clause to specify a particular ordering of data. Data will still be collected into groups. See the following example:

```
SELECT Country, Count(DISTINCT City) AS 'Number of Cities'
 FROM Customers GROUP BY Country
```

In this example, countries are collected together and are placed in the order chosen by SQL Server (usually ascending). The number of unique cities is counted and displayed beside the related country. By supplying the ORDER BY clause, as in the following example, you sort data into descending sequence, placing the country with the greatest number of unique cities at the top:

```
SELECT Country, Count(DISTINCT City) AS 'Number of Cities'
 FROM Customers GROUP BY Country
 ORDER BY Count(DISTINCT City) DESC
```

You might not want all groups to be included in the output. To exclude groups from the recordset, you can utilize the HAVING clause, which operates against the groups of data in the same way that the WHERE clause acts against the individual rows. In the example shown in Figure 3.1, the listing has been narrowed down through the elimination of countries with fewer than three unique cities.

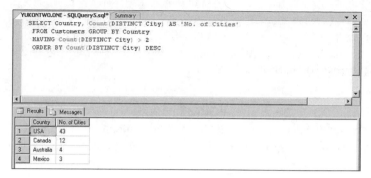

FIGURE 3.1 An example of GROUP, HAVING, and ORDER used together.

The HAVING clause is similar to the WHERE clause. In a SELECT statement, these clauses control the rows from the source tables that are used to build the result set. WHERE and HAVING are filters: They specify a series of search conditions, and only those rows that meet the terms of the search conditions are used to build the result set. To address how these clauses are used, you must understand the conditions that can be applied within these clauses.

Querying a Sampling of the Data Stored

In some cases, you don't want to run a query against all the data in a table. In such a situation, you can use the new TABLESAMPLE clause to limit the number of rows that any query processes. Unlike TOP, which returns only the first rows from a result set, TABLESAMPLE returns rows selected randomly by the system from throughout the set of rows processed by the query.

NOTE

TABLESAMPLE requires a sufficient amount of data to operate properly. In small tables, where all the data fits onto a single data page, the only possible returns are all (100%) and none (0%).

EXAM ALERT

To get the results provided by TABLESAMPLE in previous versions of SQL Server, you have to create complex routines to read random records. With TABLESAMPLE, the reading of random records is controlled by SYSTEM, which is currently the only keyword option. There may be additional functionality in future releases to add other options. The keyword SYSTEM is optional on the queries.

You can specify the conditions of the random selection by percentage or by number of rows, as in the two following examples:

```
SELECT * FROM Customers TABLESAMPLE(10 PERCENT)
SELECT * FROM Customers TABLESAMPLE(10 ROWS)
```

Selecting Rows Based on NULL Values

A NULL value is a value given to a field that that has no value. Many people confuse NULL values with zero-length strings or the value zero, but they are not the same. NULL is basically a fancy word for a value that is unknown. In SQL Server, you can select the desired NULL values or reject them by using ISNULL, as shown in the following query:

```
SELECT * FROM ONE.dbo.Customers
    WHERE ISNULL(StreetAddress, '#') = '#'
```

The ISNULL function operates on the basis of substitution. In the previous example, if a value for StreetAddress is not known for a particular customer, then within the query, it is replaced by and treated as the '#' character, which matches the condition of the WHERE clause and returns customers with NULL addresses. NULL values frequently show up as the result of JOIN operations that formulate derived tables.

Relating Data from Multiple Tables

Joins and derived tables figure prominently in the 70-431 exam. Joins are the backbone of relational databases; they actually put the "relation" in relational databases. They can be used in all the main SQL statements (SELECT, INSERT, UPDATE, and DELETE). They are important. Also, derived tables tend to be overlooked, and they're perceived as complicated even though they're not; so they are also likely to show up on the 70-431 exam.

Joining tables is a natural occurrence in a relational database system. Many of the queries performed on a regular basis involve multiple tables. Whenever you query data from two tables, you need to find some way to relate the two tables. Connecting one table to another requires a common element of the tables. You would use a JOIN operation in this manner whenever you want to see a result set that includes columns from several tables.

You can use three basic join types, as well as a union operation, to connect tables:

▶ **Inner join**—An inner join shows results only where there are matches between the elements. An inner join leaves out all the records that don't have matches.

▶ **Outer join**—An outer join can show all the records from one side of a relationship, records that match where they are available, and NULL values for records that do not have matches. An outer join shows all the same records as an inner join, plus all the records that don't match.

▶ **Cross join**—The cross join is less often used than the other two types of joins because it returns all possible combinations of rows between the two sides of the join. The number of records in the result set is equal to the number of records on one side of the join multiplied by the number of records on the other side of the join. No correlation is attempted between the two records; all the records from both sides are returned.

Again, cross joins are less frequently used than inner and outer joins. With an outer join, you are guaranteed to have all records returned from one side or the other. With inner joins, the only rows returned are those that match in the joined tables. It is easier to contemplate the overall processes if you consider join operations first. What you put in the WHERE clause and other clauses is applied after the joins are processed. So bear in mind that when a join returns a specified set of records, the SQL statement may or may not return all those records, depending on what you have specified in the WHERE clause.

Now let's look at each of the different join operators: INNER JOIN and OUTER JOIN.

Outputting Only Matches: INNER JOIN

The INNER JOIN statement is the easiest and most often used join operator. For this reason, when an inner join operation is performed, the INNER portion of the syntax is optional. A rowset is returned from the operation for the records that match up based on the criteria provided through the ON clause. A one-to-many relationship is handled inside an application with the inner join. To show all orders for a particular customer, you could use the following join operation:

```
SELECT Orders.* FROM Orders
 JOIN Customers
  ON Orders.CustomerID = Customers.CustomerID
```

The results from this query may appear a little on the unusual side because no sorting is performed. Typically, an order is specified or information is grouped to make the output more usable.

Returning Output Even When No Match Exists: OUTER JOIN

You can use an outer join when you want to return all of one entire list of rows from one side of the join. There are three types of outer joins: left, right, and full.

The terms *left* and *right* are used based on the positioning of the tables within the query. The first table is the right; the second is the left. You may find it easiest to draw a picture to represent the table when you are first learning outer joins. A right outer join, often abbreviated as *right join*, returns all the rows belonging to the table on the right side and only the matching rows on the table on the left side. Conversely, a left outer join returns all the rows from the table on the left side. A full outer join returns all the rows from both sides that have correlations.

Left and right outer joins, for all intents and purposes, are the same operations; they are simply a matter of the position of the tables within the queries. Therefore, the following examples use only the left outer join syntax, which is the one typically used. In the current ANSI standard, RIGHT is the table name on the right side of the JOIN keyword, and LEFT is the table being joined. The following query produces a listing of all customers and their orders:

```
SELECT * FROM Customers AS C
 LEFT JOIN Orders AS O
 ON C.CustomerID = O.CustomerID
```

Customers that have never placed an order would still be in the listing, accompanied by NULL for the OrderID.

A cross join, also known as a Cartesian join, is rarely used because it connects every element in one table with every other element of another table. This has some bearing in statistical operations but is not relevant in most business processing.

Applying Conditional Data Filtering

You apply filtering to data to determine the data to be selected based on conditional requirements. Essentially, all conditions come down to one of three possible outcomes. If two values are compared, the result is positive, negative, or equal (greater than, less than, or equal to). Actually, filters always evaluate to a Boolean result, either True or False. BETWEEN 10 and 20 is either True or False. Even numeric tests, such as month > 0 and Price > 10.00, are either True or False.

BETWEEN, IN, and LIKE

With the help of the BETWEEN keyword, you can specify ranges when using the WHERE clause. Simply put, BETWEEN provides a range of values within which the data should lie; otherwise, the data does not meet the condition. BETWEEN is inclusive, meaning that the range includes the lower value specified and the upper value specified. For example, the following query would have the values 10 and 20 as a possibility in the results:

```
SELECT * FROM Products WHERE UnitPrice BETWEEN 10 AND 20
```

If the intent is to exclude the value 20, the query would be written like this:

```
SELECT * FROM Products WHERE UnitPrice BETWEEN 10.00 AND 19.99
```

You can also incorporate something known as a *list* when using the WHERE clause. Essentially, a list specifies the exact values a column may or may not take. If the record does not contain the value for the column specified in the IN list, it is not selected. IN determines whether a given value matches a set of values listed. Here is an example:

```
SELECT * FROM Customers WHERE Country IN ('UK', 'USA')
```

This example limits the values of Country to only UK and USA. Customers who live in the countries mentioned in the IN list are the only ones listed.

You can retrieve rows that are based on portions of character strings by using the LIKE predicate. The LIKE predicate determines whether a given character string matches a specified pattern. The data types a LIKE statement can work with are char, varchar, nvarchar, nchar, datetime, smalldatetime, and text. A pattern specified in the LIKE predicate can include regular characters and wildcard characters. During pattern matching, regular characters must exactly match the characters specified in the column value. Wildcard characters can be matched with any character or set of characters, according to the wildcard character used, as shown in Table 3.1.

TABLE 3.1   Wildcard Characters Allowed in T-SQL

Character	Meaning
[ ]	Any single character within the specified range (for example, [f-j]) or set (for example, [fghij])
_ (underscore)	Any single character
%	Any number of zero or more characters
[^]	Any single character not in the specified range or set

If an application repeatedly calls the LIKE predicate and performs numerous wildcard searches, you should consider using the MS Search facility if it is installed and in use on the server. Consider the value of the response time over the storage resources that the MS Search service and full-text search capabilities require. MS Search service is required to use a full-text search. Full-text searching enables a variety of powerful wildcard searches. You should avoid LIKE searches that have a % wildcard at both the beginning and the end. The following example shows how the LIKE clause uses the % wildcard to select all customers whose CustomerID begins with the letter A:

```
SELECT CustomerID, ContactName FROM Customers
 WHERE CustomerID LIKE 'A%'
```

You can also use the NOT keyword with the LIKE predicate to simply retrieve a query that does not contain records matching the specified elements in the LIKE clause. With character matching, it is sometimes more efficient to exclude characters by using NOT.

Data Querying Using Full-Text Indexes

Full-text indexes are special indexes that efficiently track the words you're looking for in a table. They help in enabling special searching functions that differ from regular indexes. Full-text indexes are not automatically updated, and they reside in a storage space called a *full-text catalog*. Full-text indexes are stored in the file system, not in the database. They are, however, administered through the database.

Full-text catalog files are not recovered during a SQL Server recovery. They also cannot be backed up and restored by using the T-SQL BACKUP and RESTORE statements. The full-text catalogs must be resynchronized separately after a recovery or restore operation.

Creating and Populating a Catalog

Before you can begin using full-text capabilities, you must create and populate a catalog on the server. The catalog will be stored in the file system. Full-text catalogs must be created on a local hard drive. You should store the catalog in a folder created solely for that purpose. It is recommended that you set up a secondary filegroup for the catalog storage. You could use the following to create the filegroup and catalog:

```
ALTER DATABASE AdventureWorks ADD FILEGROUP FullTextCat
GO
ALTER DATABASE AdventureWorks ADD FILE (NAME = N'FullTextCatalog',
    FILENAME = N'C:\FullTextCatalogs\FTCat.ndf',
    SIZE = 10MB, FILEGROWTH = 5MB)
    TO FILEGROUP FullTextCat
GO
CREATE FULLTEXT CATALOG ftCatalog
 ON FILEGROUP FullTextCat
 IN PATH 'C:\FullTextCatalogs'
 AS DEFAULT
GO
```

With the storage location set up, you can begin defining and creating the indexes to be used. These indexes can be set up on any text-based data stored in the database, including `varbinary` data that stores a document. The T-SQL syntax for creating these indexes has changed since SQL 2000 and is now similar to the following:

```
CREATE FULLTEXT INDEX
 ON Production.Document(
 Title, FileName, DocumentSummary, Document TYPE COLUMN FileExtension)
 KEY INDEX PK_Document_DocumentID
GO
```

After you create an index, you need to administer the population. It is recommended that you begin with a full population (the default upon creation) and then schedule population updates periodically afterward. The frequency of the schedule depends on the frequency of changes within the data and the latency requirements of the system. You can use `ALTER FULLTEXT INDEX` to perform the repopulation.

> **EXAM ALERT**
>
> The 70-431 exam could present you with several different scenarios about setting up and using full-text indexes. You need to know how to create the catalog and the index. Remember that you cannot configure the system database for full-text use.

You can now perform queries by using `CONTAINS` to search within a single column or `CONTAINSTABLE` to search through the entire table. You can use a variety of specialty search capabilities, including looking for various word forms or proximate searches for multiple words and other forms of fuzzy searches. The basic form of a query would look similar to the following:

```
SELECT * FROM Production.Document
 WHERE CONTAINS(DocumentSummary, 'safety')
GO
```

You can also use `FREETEXT` or `FREETEXTTABLE` for more free-form queries. When you use either of these two commands, you can perform a fuzzy search for matches to phrases.

Using System Tables and Views

SQL Server tracks information and maintains data about every object in the system. This information is maintained in system tables that can be queried like any other tables. Of course, it helps to know which table to query because sifting through the information in the system tables can be an arduous task. Microsoft has already gone to the effort of preparing some of the most desired information. You can see this information by querying views. You can produce still other information from recordsets of data displayed by executing system stored procedures.

If you look behind the scenes into these views and procedures, you are likely to see nothing more than the system tables being queried and the information being presented in a more readable fashion.

TIP

If you are just starting out with T-SQL, you might find it helpful to look at what is already in the system. If you select any of the system views or stored procedures and then select the modify option, you can see the code behind the process. You can learn a lot when you look at how these views and processes are put together.

Still, nothing beats a little bit of know-how or, in this case, know-*where*. There are some useful system tables that you might want to query from time to time to double-check definitions.

Getting Information from System Tables

We have already discussed most of the actual object definitions, and if you look into the master database, you can find the storage area for these definitions. Querying the master database allows you to get information from the system. Views have replaced system tables and are prefixed with sys stored object definitions. There are many system views, but the ones described in Table 3.2 are the most commonly accessed and useful for development purposes.

TABLE 3.2   Common System Views/Tables

Current View/ Table Name	Old View/ Table Name	Description
Common System Views/Tables in Every Database (Including master):		
sys.columns	syscolumns	Contains a row for every column in every table, for every view, and for each parameter in a stored procedure.
sys.indexes, sys.partitions, sys.allocation_units, and sys.dm_db_partition statssys	sysindexes	Contains a row for each index and table in the database.

TABLE 3.2 *Continued*

Current View/ Table Name	Old View/ Table Name	Description
Common System Views/Tables in Every Database (Including `master`):		
`sys.sql_modules`	`syscomments`	Contains entries for each view, rule, default, trigger, constraint, and stored procedure. The text column contains the original SQL definition statements.
`sys.objects`	`sysobjects`	Contains a row for each object created within a database. In `tempdb` only, this table includes a row for each temporary object.
`sys.types`	`systypes`	Contains a row for each system-supplied data type and each user-defined data type.
`sys.database_principals`	`sysusers`	Contains a row for each user or role in the database.
Common System Views/Tables Additionally Found in the `master` Database Only:		
`sys.server_principals`	`syslogins`	Contains a row for each login.
`sys.messages`	`sysmessages`	Contains a row for each system error or warning that can be displayed to the user.
`sys.databases`	`sysdatabases`	Contains a row for each database on the server.
`sys.dm_exec_connections`, `sys.dm_exec_sessions`, and `sys.dm_exec_requests`	`sysprocesses`	Holds information about processes running on the server.
`sys.remote_logins`	`sysremotelogins`	Contains a row for each remote user allowed to call remote stored procedures on the server.
`sys.servers`	`sysservers`	Contains a row for each server that the current server can access as an OLE DB data source.

In SQL Server 2005, each of the tables now maps to a system view that can be queried in place of the table. Although it is possible through some advanced configuration, the system tables should not be changed directly. You should never try to modify system tables by using DELETE, UPDATE, or INSERT statements or user-defined triggers.

In SQL Server 2000 and earlier versions, these views were system tables. For backward compatibility, they are still available. Each view, however, has a replacement system view that you should use going forward. For each of the previously mentioned system tables/views, there is a replacement, as shown in Table 3.2.

It is possible to write a database management application that uses some of the information from these tables. The information from these tables is more reliable than what can be found in other resources. Many of the columns in system tables are not documented, and you should only apply those whose supporting documentation is known, so you need to be sure to refer to the documentation. You should not write applications to directly query undocumented columns.

Instead of trying to retrieve information stored in system tables, you can create applications that access the information via system stored procedures, T-SQL statements and functions, SQL Server Management Objects (SMO), Replication Management Objects (RMO), or Database API catalog functions. These components make up a published API for obtaining system information from SQL Server.

> **EXAM ALERT**
>
> The information provided in this section is the official Microsoft stance. If you see exam questions asking you where to access reliable information and apply that to applications that will be supported in the future, you should select system stored procedures, T-SQL statements and functions, SMO, RMO, or Database API catalog functions.

Microsoft maintains compatibility of these alternative components from version to version. The format of the system tables depends on the internal architecture of SQL Server and may change from release to release. The supporting procedure and functions, however, still accommodate the required information. Applications that directly access the undocumented columns of system tables may have to be changed in a future release.

Information Retrieval from System Stored Procedures

Many stored procedures can provide information about the state of objects. The following are some of the most common procedures to gain this information from the database engine:

- ▶ **sp_help**—Provides a list of objects if no parameters are supplied. If you supply an object name or ID, it provides information about the object.

- ▶ **sp_help*objecttype*** or **sp_help_*objectytpe***—Provides information about a specified type of object. You can replace *objecttype* with just about any SQL Server object.

- ▶ **sp_table_validation**—Provides checksum or row count for a table. If you provide the checksum or row count, the procedure will validate the table against the supplied value.

- ▶ **sp_settriggerorder**—Specifies the first or last trigger to fire if multiple triggers have been defined. The order of other triggers between the first and the last cannot be set or guaranteed.

- ▶ **sp_lock**—Reports information about current locks that are in place.

- ▶ **sp_configure**—Displays or alters server configuration settings.

- ▶ **sp_who**—Provides information about a user's current logins, sessions, and processes.

- ▶ **sp_updatestats**—Updates the statistics for every table in the current database.

Keep in mind that there are somewhere in the neighborhood of 1,500 stored procedures that can be used within SQL Server. Because this chapter cannot cover every one of them, the proceeding list contains the ones you are most likely to see on the 70-431 exam and/or use on a regular basis as a database administrator.

EXAM ALERT

There are a lot of commonly used stored procedures. You can expect some of them to be correct answers on 70-431 exam questions. Others might be distracters or red herrings. When you see sp_ as one of the answers, you should read the question carefully and understand what each procedure will and will not provide before selecting it as the answer.

Using Dynamic Management Views and Other System Views

SQL Server provides many dynamic management views and functions. These views and functions return server state information. The best use for these views and functions is in monitoring and determining the health of a server instance. They can be useful in diagnosing problem situations and providing information to assist in performance tuning.

> **EXAM ALERT**
>
> All dynamic management views are specific to the version of SQL Server. There is no guarantee that the current views will be supported in future releases. Therefore, you should find the equivalent stored procedures to get the desired information for something that will be in prolonged use.

All dynamic management views and functions exist in the sys schema. The naming for these views and functions follows the dm_* convention. Each database contains almost 100 different dynamic management views and functions. Because of the naming convention, you can find categories of the dynamic management views by using a query of sysobjects similar to the following:

```
SELECT * FROM sysobjects
    WHERE NAME LIKE 'dm_db%'
SELECT * FROM sysobjects
    WHERE NAME LIKE 'dm_db_index%'
SELECT * FROM sysobjects
    WHERE NAME LIKE 'dm_fts%'
```

Some of the most important categories and their common views and functions are detailed in the following list:

▶ **dm_db_index_operational_stats**—Reports current locking and access, by partition.

▶ **dm_db_index_usage_stats**—Specifies a count of index operations and times of last occurrences.

▶ **dm_db_index_physical_stats**—Provides index fragmentation information.

▶ **dm_fts_index_population**—Displays status information on the index population.

▶ **dm_fts_active catalogs**—Reports any population activity in progress.

- ► **dm_fts_populations_ranges**—Specifies the memory address ranges in use.

- ► **dm_exec_query_stats**—Specifies performance statistics for cached query plans.

- ► **dm_exec_query_plan**—Displays the XML show plan for the cached query plan.

- ► **dm_exec_cached_plans**—Specifies the currently cached execution plans held by the server.

The first time you look, the views and the results returned by the functions look peculiar at best. However, with time and experience, the views will appear normal.

Inserting Data

You must be able to accurately get data into a system, and it needs to be organized for efficient retrieval. Although initial data loading is performed by other means as time passes, new data will no doubt need to be inserted individually or in small groups of records.

Although there are many ways to insert data into an existing table, the primary coding method is by using the INSERT statement. This statement causes the data values to be inserted into an existing table as one or more rows.

Data must meet all rules and constraints that have been defined in the table schema. The type of data being inserted must be suitable input for the data types within the table definition. Data types can themselves have control mechanisms or, with the advent of common language runtime (CLR) user-defined types (UDTs), can be complete processes for checking and manipulating data as it enters the system.

Using UDT and the CLR to Control Data Input

UDTs and the CLR component offer functionality not previously available in SQL Server. In previous releases, UDTs were only a mapping of existing data types that you could place rules and defaults onto, but little else.

EXAM ALERT

The CLR allows you to encapsulate business logic within a data type itself. It is possible to write assemblies that contain the processing to represent, persist, and manipulate complex numbers.

The functionality of CLR UDTs is powerful but should not be overused. There is a significant amount of overhead associated with CLR use. The CLR is disabled by default in a new SQL Server installation, and to use it to its full extent, you must write the .DLL assembly in a format defined by UDT standards.

Using the CLR Within Stored Procedures

In many respects, the CLR is a wonderful thing. It opens up the opportunity to use other programming languages, such as C#, Visual C++, Visual Basic, and others, to create procedures executed within the database engine. The CLR is implemented through the use of assemblies that are referred to as *managed code*. Managed code is executed in the CLR environment rather than directly by the operating system.

The ability to use CLR objects within SQL Server is disabled by default upon SQL Server installation; this is partially because of the overhead involved in its use. The CLR need not be enabled in the majority of database environments. The deployment of CLR is not likely to achieve widespread use, at least initially.

The CLR will be more efficient than T-SQL in many instances. Managed code will outperform T-SQL in situations where there is use of procedural code, computation, and string manipulation. The CLR will perform better than T-SQL in any process that is computing intensive. The CLR should not be used to perform data access; T-SQL, which is specifically designed for interaction with the database engine, performs data access more efficiently than the CLR.

EXAM ALERT

You should use CLR procedures and managed code for processes that involve complex calculations but do not perform standard data interactions. You should use T-SQL procedures for processes that are standard database activities with minimal complex calculations.

Not all calculations perform better in a CLR environment than with T-SQL. Managed code is moderately slower than built-in SQL Server aggregate functions, but it outperforms any cursor-based aggregation.

Inserting Individual Records

Data inserted must meet the parameters defined by the table structure. This means that NOT NULL columns must have data provided either through input or through the use of column definitions that provide for their own values. A column can obtain its input value through a DEFAULT, IDENTITY, formula, timestamp, or default object.

> **EXAM ALERT**
>
> Watch for column definitions that are NOT NULL. These fields must get data during an insert. This data can be supplied either through a value or via IDENTITY, DEFAULT, a computed column, or a timestamp.

When inserting data, you specify the VALUES keyword to supply the data. VALUES is required unless you are using INSERT/SELECT, SELECT INTO, or EXECUTE. The following example shows the addition of a single record, using VALUES for each field:

```
INSERT INTO Customers
     VALUES('H99999', 'Jillier and Jergenson', 'Special',
               'John Smith', NULL, NULL, '123 Mill Street',
               NULL, NULL, 'US', 'Miami', 'FL', '27622',
               '292-782-6378', NULL, NULL, NULL, 0, NULL)
```

Many of these fields have no value supplied, and it might be easier and neater to provide a field list with INSERT, as follows:

```
INSERT INTO Customers
               (CUSTNMBR, CUSTNAME, CUSTCLAS,
               CNTCPRSN, ADDRESS1, COUNTRY,
               CITY, STATE, ZIP, PHONE1, INACTIVE)
     VALUES('H99999', 'Jillier and Jergenson', 'Special',
               'John Smith', '123 Mill Street', 'US',
               'Miami', 'FL', '27622', '292-782-6378', 0)
```

These two statements have the same result when adding a single record to the table.

Using a Query to Insert Complete Recordsets

The SELECT INTO statement can perform a data insertion and create the table for the data in a single operation. The new table is populated with the data provided by a FROM clause. The SELECT INTO statement creates a new table with a structure identical to that of the columns provided in the query. It then copies all data that meets the WHERE condition into this newly created table. It is possible to combine data from several tables or views into one table, and you can use a variety of sources. The following example creates a new table within a database that contains only two columns:

```
SELECT FirstName + ' ' + LastName
     AS 'Employee Name',
               Title
     INTO HRTable
     FROM Employees
```

The INTO clause creates a table, so it is important that the table does not exist when you're using the command. If you want to add data to an existing table, you must perform an INSERT INTO operation. You can use a SELECT statement within the INSERT statement to add values to a table from one or more other tables or views. Using a SELECT subquery is another mechanism that enables more than one row to be inserted at one time. This type of INSERT statement is often used to insert data into a separate table from some other table or data source. In this manner, the data can be copied or just separated for handling of exceptions or specialty tasks.

For example, imagine that you would like to copy all your current employees into a customer table to enable them to make purchases and, of course, allow for an employee discount. The query to perform this operation might look similar to the following:

```
INSERT INTO Customers
        SELECT EmployeeID, 'TOMORA Systems',
                'Employee', FirstName + ' ' + LastName,
                'N/A', 'INTERNAL', Address, NULL, NULL,
                Country, City, Region, PostalCode,
                HomePhone, NULL, NULL, NULL, 0, NULL
        FROM Employees
```

The SELECT list of the subquery must match the column list of the INSERT statement. If no column list is specified, the SELECT list must match the columns in the table or view being inserted into, as in the example. Note that NULL has been provided for several fields as a placeholder for columns in which there is no data.

You can use the INSERT SELECT statement to insert data from any viable source. This includes SQL Server tables and views, as well as sources outside SQL Server. Often, the operation is used in more involved procedures to move data to and from temporary tables or table variables.

Temporary tables exist only during the duration of the procedure, so they need to be loaded during the process and offloaded before the procedure ends. A temporary table is defined using the # prefix for local temporary tables that are accessible only to the immediate scope/batch or ## for global temporary tables that are accessible outside the current batch. These are used less often because SQL Server now has a table data type that can be used for this purpose.

Disabling Functionality During Data Insertion

At times, you might want to disable indexes, triggers, constraints, and other objects to improve performance and prevent errors from occurring while loading data. This is particularly useful when loading large amounts of data in a bulk or batch format.

Disabling Indexes

Disabling an index puts the index to sleep and prevents the system from accessing it until it is enabled again. The index definition remains in the system catalog. To see the status of an index, you can query the is_disabled column in the sys.indexes catalog view. The DISABLE INDEX feature is new to SQL Server 2005 and is therefore very likely to be on the exam.

It really makes sense to disable only nonclustered indexes. Disabling a clustered index prevents access to the data. The data remains in the B-tree and must be dropped or rebuilt to correct the situation. Disabling an index on a view physically deletes the data associated with the index.

If a table is in a transactional replication publication, you cannot disable any indexes that are associated with primary key columns. These indexes are required by replication. To disable an index, you must first drop the table from the publication.

You use the ALTER INDEX REBUILD statement or the CREATE INDEX WITH DROP_EXISTING statement to enable an index. You cannot rebuild a disabled clustered index when the ONLINE option is set to ON. For more information, see the information on DISABLE INDEX in SQL Server Books Online.

Disabling Trigger Firing

Disabling a trigger does not drop the trigger. The definition of the trigger still exists as an object in the current database. A disabled trigger does not fire when any T-SQL statements on which it was programmed are executeds. This applies to both DDL and DML triggers.

To disable a trigger, you simply use the DISABLE TRIGGER statement. To turn it back on again, you use ENABLE TRIGGER.

Disabling Constraint Checking

You can use ALTER TABLE with the NOCHECK CONSTRAINT clause to disable a constraint. While a constraint is disabled, the system allows for an insertion of data that would typically violate the constraint. You might want this in rare situations, but it would corrupt most systems.

Using ALTER TABLE with CHECK CONSTRAINT turns the constraint back on again.

Changing What Is Already Stored

You alter data through the use of UPDATE. Just as with the input of data, any alterations made to the data are subject to the rules and constraints defined in the table schema. Any data modifications made that do not meet these defined standards result in errors that the front-end application may have to trap and control.

Updating a Single Record

There are three different techniques for updating a single record:

▶ **Filtered update**—This technique is no different than changing a number of records. The difference is that the criteria used need to be something unique, such as a primary key or an identity.

▶ **Positioned update**—This technique is a programmatic solution. Essentially, you set up a procedure that scrolls through the data. When the record pointer (that is, cursor) is on the record to be updated, you issue the UPDATE command with the WHERE CURRENT OF clause.

▶ **Computed column**—You can update a single record by using a computed column. In this case, when the computation involves a field whose value changes, the result of the computation is affected and the field will change.

Doing Updates That Affect Multiple Records

Most data modifications are based on a conditional operation or are in-place updates of the current record. The following is a basic UPDATE statement that adjusts data based on the criteria given:

```
UPDATE Customers
  SET Region = 'South America'
  WHERE Country IN ('Argentina', 'Brazil', 'Venezuela')
```

Obviously, an update performed with a broad condition will affect a number of records. Records in other tables could be affected. In the event of cascading updates, if a referenced row has its key altered, those changes would ripple down to the related rows of the subsidiary table.

Performing Transaction Processing

Updating data within a transaction gives you a chance to undo changes before they are actually saved to the database. This usually comes into play when there are a number of steps needed for the data alteration to be valid. If any of the steps within the process fails, you can roll back everything that has been done, which leaves the system as if no change had ever occurred.

The key to handling transactions is to know when to commit the change and when to roll it back. You usually execute the ROLLBACK statement as part of a conditional operation that checks for lack of success in the process. If an error occurs in a transaction, you roll back the transaction. If the user decides to cancel the transaction, you roll back the transaction. If a portion of a required process cannot be completed, you roll back the transaction.

A ROLLBACK statement backs out all modifications made in the transaction. This statement returns the data to the state it was in at the start of the transaction. When errors occur, you should use COMMIT or ROLLBACK. You use COMMIT if you want to ensure that changes are saved to the point of the error, and you use ROLLBACK to cancel all changes.

One effective tool for handling errors, including those in transactions, is the new T-SQL TRY/CATCH construct, illustrated here:

```
BEGIN TRY
    -- Attempt the desired processing
    COMMIT
END TRY
BEGIN CATCH
    -- An error occurred, handle it or
    ROLLBACK
END CATCH;
GO
```

Normally, ROLLBACK would occur during the CATCH operation; however, if desired, a COMMIT could be coded there as well to save the changes instead of abandoning the operation.

Upgrading Data from Previous Releases of SQL Server

If you have worked with SQL Server for a while and are comfortable with the four-part naming convention for addressing objects, you will be comfortable working with the new object schemas, which also uses a four-part name for addressing objects:

```
Server.Catalog.Schema.Object
```

The *Schema* portion historically was addressed as the object owner. All objects on previous instances of the server were generally owned by dbo. That makes the most common schema for upgraded databases the dbo schema. For comparison purposes, you can visit the Microsoft website, at www.microsoft.com/sql/downloads/2005/default.mspx, and install the sample databases Pubs, Northwind, and AdventureWorks and compare the object naming conventions.

Removing Unwanted Data

Over time, data becomes obsolete and needs to be removed. You remove data by using the DELETE statement. It is extremely important to provide a condition when performing data deletions because it is easy to remove all data if you do not exercise caution. The following command removes all records from the specified table:

```
DELETE FROM Customers
```

If you would like to delete all rows, you can use the fast, nonlogged method TRUNCATE TABLE. This immediately frees all space used by indexes and data by that table. On the other hand, DELETE should be used when partial data removal is desired. Although both TRUNCATE TABLE and a DELETE statement with no WHERE clause remove all rows in a table, TRUNCATE TABLE is faster and uses fewer system and log resources. The DELETE statement removes rows one at a time, recording an entry in the transaction log for each row.

TRUNCATE TABLE removes data by deallocating the data pages used to store the table's data, and only the page deallocations are recorded in the log. TRUNCATE TABLE removes all rows from a table, but the table structure and its columns, constraints, and indexes remain intact. The counter used by any identity columns is reset to the seed value for the column. If you want to retain the identity counter, you should use DELETE instead.

Directly Removing Records from a Table

The DELETE statement removes one or more records from a table, based on a condition in the WHERE clause. The following is a simplified sample DELETE statement:

```
DELETE FROM Products
   WHERE Discontinued = 1
```

In a fashion similar to that used to remove a single record via a positioned update, you could also create a procedure that performs a positioned deletion by using the DELETE statement with the WHERE CURRENT OF clause as part of a CURSOR operation.

Indirectly Removing Data from a Table

Removing data from a table can affect other tables if cascading deletions have been specified for a relationship. This could mean the removal of other records based on a single DELETE operation. Also, a relationship definition may prevent the deletion of data and return an error condition to the operation. Triggers, restore operations, and stored procedures are other processes that could indirectly delete records.

Escalating Privileges to Allow Deletion

You often need to have an application remove data from a database on the user's behalf. In cases where users with limited permissions need to delete data in a special circumstance, it is best to do so through a controlled and logged procedure.

You could create a stored procedure to perform the deletion and optionally log information about who is performing the task, when, and why the deletion occurred. If the user does not have the rights to delete records, the procedure could be executed under a user ID or role that has that permission.

Normally, during a session, permission checks are performed based on the user currently logged in. When an EXECUTE AS statement is run, the context of the session changes. This change lasts for the duration of the immediate scope. After the switch, permissions are checked against the login used in the EXECUTE AS operation. In essence, the user or login account is impersonated for the duration of the batch or module execution. This allows operations to be performed that the user context would not normally allow.

IMPERSONATE permissions must be granted to the individual running the process with the EXECUTE AS operation. If the user logged into the system is the database owner or a member of the sysadmin role, these permissions are inherited. In this respect, the owner or administrator can test processes with a reduced level of permission to ensure that security measures that are in place are functioning as expected.

Controlling Privileges by Using GRANT, DENY, and REVOKE

Permissions on objects in a database can be assigned to users and roles either directly, using the graphical tools, or programmatically, through the use of scripting. Groups and logins can be associated with users and roles and thus have permissions affect them within the database. Permissions can also be assigned directly to logins within the server that affect the systemwide functions that can be performed.

The T-SQL GRANT, DENY, REVOKE statements can be executed within a procedure to deal with permissions through process execution. DENY is the strongest of the three permissions; when assigned, it takes precedence over all other permissions. Therefore, you need to be careful never to deny permission to a resource for the public role because doing so effectively blocks everyone from using the resource.

Exam Prep Questions

1. In preparation for a major system upgrade, multiple data changes are going to be made on a system. You would like to implement various changes without disturbing any of the existing data. Which of the following operations do not affect any of the existing data values? (Select all that apply.)

   ○ **A.** INSERT

   ○ **B.** UPDATE

   ○ **C.** Changing column name

   ○ **D.** Increasing column length

   ○ **E.** Decreasing column length

2. You would like to produce a grouped report of sales, by city. You only want included on the report groups that have sales within the last calendar year (2005). Which of the following query elements would you use to solve the problem? (Select all that apply.)

   ○ **A.** GROUP BY

   ○ **B.** WHERE

   ○ **C.** HAVING

   ○ **D.** BETWEEN

   ○ **E.** NOT ISNULL

   ○ **F.** JOIN

3. You would like to produce a report from a random selection of records within a database. There are 10,000 records in the table, and you would like to include 1,000 of them in the process. How would you implement the process?

   ○ **A.** Use CURSOR and process every 10th record.

   ○ **B.** Use the TOP clause to get 1,000 records.

   ○ **C.** Set the ROWCOUNT to 1000.

   ○ **D.** Use TABLESAMPLE to get 10% of the records.

   ○ **E.** Use the RND function to achieve random records.

4. You would like to add an additional column to a table. The new column will be used to hold a seven-character serial number for assets and will be a mandatory element of data in the future. How would you implement the process? (Select two answers, each of which represents part of the solution.)

   ○ **A.** Create a new NOT NULL column.

   ○ **B.** Set a default value of N/A.

   ○ **C.** Create the new column as an identity column.

   ○ **D.** Enter serial numbers for all existing records.

   ○ **E.** Set a default value of NewID().

5. You need to add a column to a table that will hold a unique value. Which of the following would accommodate the situation? (Select all that apply.)

   ○ **A.** An identity column with an `integer` data type

   ○ **B.** A `timestamp` data type

   ○ **C.** A `numeric` data type with a default of `RND()`

   ○ **D.** A user-defined `character` data type with a CLR that assigns a random set of characters

   ○ **E.** A `uniqueidentifier` data type with a default value of `NewID()`

   ○ **F.** A column set as the primary key

   ○ **G.** A column with a unique index attached

6. You are creating a procedure that will update two tables within a transaction. The code looks similar to the following (line numbers are included for reference only):

```
1 BEGIN TRANSACTION
2
3  BEGIN TRY
4      UPDATE . . .
5
6  END TRY
7
8  BEGIN CATCH
9       IF . . .
10
11  END CATCH
12
```

In most common situations, where would you put the ROLLBACK statement?

   ○ **A.** Line 2

   ○ **B.** Line 5

   ○ **C.** Line 7

   ○ **D.** Line 10

   ○ **E.** Line 12

7. You are building a scientific application that will store data in a SQL Server 2005 database. The application does not store data until a final process is complete. One of the procedures you are currently working with performs many processor-intensive calculations. Which of the following would accommodate the situation? (Select all that apply.)

   ○ **A.** A standard T-SQL stored procedure

   ○ **B.** A T-SQL stored procedure that uses a cursor

   ○ **C.** A CLR-integrated stored procedure

   ○ **D.** A CLR-integrated stored procedure that uses a cursor

Answers to Exam Prep Questions

1. **A, C, D.** The purpose of the UPDATE command is exactly what you want to avoid. You should be able to increase the data storage size and alter a column name without affecting the internal data. However, a decrease in the data storage size results in data truncation or loss. INSERT, used appropriately, adds data but does not alter any existing values. For more information, see the section "Inserting Data."

2. **A, B, D.** You want to exclude sales records from all but the last year before the grouping. This requires a WHERE clause, not HAVING. A HAVING condition would be needed if you were limiting to a total value of sales last year. BETWEEN would be used for the date range condition. There is no multiple-table scenario that we know of that would need a JOIN. There is also no mention or need for checking for NULL values.

3. **D.** Processing a random sample of records is exactly what TABLESAMPLE accomplishes. The answer for previous SQL Server versions may have been B, as using the TOP clause to get 1,000 records would sort of accomplish the goal. Answers A, B, and C would not give you truly random selection, although they would be able to limit the output to 1,000 records. RND is a random number generator and would not accomplish random selection of records. For more information, see the section "Querying a Sampling of the Data Stored."

4. **A, B.** The best solution would involve creating a new NOT NULL column because this is a mandatory data element. You cannot create such a column in a table that has existing data without supplying a value for the field. N/A would supply that value until a correct one can be entered. NEWID() would generate a value too large to go into the field, and the value would be meaningless. Using an identity column would not be a valid way to initialize a serial number field.

5. **A, B, E, F, G.** A random number generator will produce duplicates on a regular basis and will not always be unique. The CLR routine could work if it also has some method of checking uniqueness. Every other option produces unique content or does not allow duplicates.

6. **D.** The purpose of the CATCH block is to isolate error handling. Within the CATCH, code is placed that reacts to errors that may have occurred while executing the code in the TRY block. Normally, this reaction would be a rollback of anything that had occurred. For more information, see the section "Using the CLR Within Stored Procedures."

7. **C.** Because there is no data access in the process, a cursor is unnecessary. Any process with a set of complex mathematical operations to perform will probably operate more efficiently by using a CLR procedure. For more information, see the section "Using the CLR Within Stored Procedures."

CHAPTER FOUR

Supporting the XML Framework

Terms you'll need to understand:

- ✓ Extensible Markup Language (XML)
- ✓ XML schema definition (XSD)
- ✓ XQuery
- ✓ XML document
- ✓ Schema
- ✓ Element
- ✓ Attribute
- ✓ Node
- ✓ FOR XML
- ✓ ELEMENTS

- ✓ XSINIL
- ✓ value()
- ✓ nodes()
- ✓ query()
- ✓ exist()
- ✓ modify()
- ✓ replace value of
- ✓ insert
- ✓ delete
- ✓ XML index

Techniques you'll need to master:

- ✓ Writing queries that return XML
- ✓ Using the xml data type

- ✓ Using xml data type methods
- ✓ Creating XML indexes

The language of business communication, in particular between data storage systems, is Extensible Markup Language (XML). SQL Server 2005 leverages XML with many features that implement XML functionality. This chapter looks at the breadth of XML coverage within the application. You can expect XML coverage on the 70-431 exam to encompass much of this functionality.

There are a variety of methods for storing XML, from using the data type itself to variations of standard types, which may actually be preferred in most instances. When XML is stored, indexing the XML is important for perform-ance and quick response times. There has been much advancement in terms of data queries in SQL Server as well.

This chapter covers a lot of ground when it comes to the integration of XML within SQL Server. You don't need to be an XML expert to work with it, but you definitely have to know how to operate with XML within a SQL Server database.

Managing XML Data

In general, XML is a data storage format that can be used to define and store data. An XML document is a data storage medium that lays out the data into ele-ments and attributes in much the same way that a database has rows and columns. An XML schema defines the complete data structure and business rules similarly to how a table definition defines the columns, their types, and the constraints to which data must conform.

XML is much more portable than a database and is quickly becoming the stan-dard for data exchange among websites, applications, and other implementa-tions that require exchange of data. XML is derived from HTML, which was designed to provide an application-independent, character-set–independent method of transferring data, especially transaction-oriented data, across systems.

> **NOTE**
>
> XML can easily be viewed in Internet Explorer. You simply save well-formed XML into a text file with an .xml extension, and you can then view the XML within Internet Explorer.

One of the primary uses for XML is the transfer of data between disparate sys-tems. Through XML's definition techniques, when the data is sent, the complete definition accompanies the data. This means that the data is always within con-text and can more easily be mapped to other definitions of the same data.

> **NOTE**
>
> SQL Server had support for XML already, but prior to SQL Server 2005, it was somewhat difficult to work with. This kept many systems away from its use because it was too cumbersome and complex to deal with. One of the biggest issues was the minimal support for XML documents, which is the heart of what XML is all about.

Newly Supported XML Features

In SQL Server 2005, XML features have grown by leaps and bounds. The new functionality, including an XML data type, XQuery standards-based query capability, XQuery extensions to allow for modifications, enhanced functionality of the FOR XML clause, indexing capabilities over XML data, and a SOAP endpoint for better XML transfers over the Internet.

Using the xml Data Type

The new xml data type provides the previously lacking support for the storage of XML documents and fragments without dealing with text conversion issues. You can now store an XML document in its entirety in one field. You can store the accompanying schema as well, to provide for data definition. XML instances stored using the xml data type can be associated with an XML schema definition (XSD) to provide the definition and validation. The xml data type can be used in columns, in variables, or as parameters for stored procedures and functions.

Using XQuery with XML

XQuery is a language for querying XML data. When data is stored using the xml data type, you can use XQuery to dissect the data and pull the required information out for use in procedures. The SQL Server 2005 implementation of XQuery is based on working drafts of the World Wide Web Consortium (W3C).

Using Larger XML with xarchar(max)

Another new feature is related to storing XML documents. The new varchar(max) and varbinary(max) declarations of database fields and procedure variables allow for increased XML storage. Previously, developers were limited to 8000 bytes, and because many XML documents are larger than that, text fields were used. Now, with varchar(max), developers can store XML of virtually any size in a field. This is more useful if there is not a need to run XQuery against it.

Using XML DML

The new XML Data Manipulation Language (XML DML) extends the current definition supplied by the W3C. The current working draft of XQuery does not include the ability to modify XML documents. In SQL Server 2005, XQuery is extended to include the capability of inserting, updating, and deleting directly in XML documents or document fragments.

Using FOR XML with PATH

In SQL Server 2005, you can nest FOR XML statements to create a hierarchy of documents. The addition of the PATH parameter provides an alternative to the cumbersome EXPLICIT clause. The results of a FOR XML statement can be stored directly in the xml data type, which leads to easier transfers of data.

The XML data stored in a system is much more efficiently queried if it has indexing capabilities. Documents and fragments stored in the xml data type can have indexes defined for more effective processing and quicker response times.

Using XML Document Returns

You can configure HTTP endpoints or addresses to which requests based on the SOAP standard can be sent. SQL Server can now receive the packets directly, with no need for middle-tier processing and redirection. The results of queries sent to an HTTP endpoint are returned as an XML document. HTTP endpoint configuration and use are discussed fully in Chapter 6, "Database Maintenance."

The 70-431 exam objectives require you to know how to retrieve and send data from SQL Server for exchange with other systems. You also need to know how to index XML data and how to utilize and manipulate the new xml data type and its associated methods, and you need to know how to configure HTTP endpoints.

> **EXAM ALERT**
>
> Expect several questions about the SQL Server implementation of XML. Expect questions related to new features, including the ability to index XML, xml data type methods (nodes, query, value, exist, modify), and XML document handling and HTTP endpoints.

There is a considerable amount of new XML functionality in SQL Server. To understand its use, you also have to understand the layout and architecture behind XML documents.

XML: The Basics

An XML document consists of one or more elements, which are bound between angle brackets (< >). The first word that appears inside the angle brackets is the name of the element. The rest of the element consists of element attributes. For example, here's an element:

```
<Customer ID="9" First="Danny" Last="Thomas"/>
```

The name of this element, or the element type, is `Customer`. The element has attributes such as `ID`, `First`, and `Last`, which all have values. The element ends with a forward slash and an angle bracket, indicating the end of the element.

An element can also contain other elements, as shown here:

```
<Customer ID="9" First="Danny" Last="Thomas">
<Sales Qty="4"/>
<Sales Qty="3"/>
</Customer>
```

In this case, the `Customer` element contains two `Sales` elements. Notice that on the first line, there isn't a slash before the ending bracket; the matching slash for this element is on the last line. This is how objects are nested in XML.

Outputting Data in XML Format

To output data in XML format, you use the `SELECT` statement with the `FOR XML` operator. This tells SQL Server that instead of returning a rowset, it should return an XML document. There are four different options for generating the XML: `RAW`, `AUTO`, `EXPLICIT`, and `PATH`.

> **EXAM ALERT**
>
> Where is the XML schema? To produce XML output that also contains the schema information for the XML, you must tack the `XMLDATA` qualifier to the end of the `FOR XML` clause.

In `AUTO` mode, SQL Server returns the rowset in an automatically generated, nested XML format. If the query has no joins, it doesn't have a nesting at all. If the query has joins, it returns the first row from the first table and then all the correlated rows from each joined table as a nested level. For example, the following query shows order details nested inside orders:

```
SELECT O.OrderID, O.CustomerID, OD.ProductID, OD.UnitPrice, OD.Quantity
 FROM Orders AS O
JOIN [Order Details] AS OD ON O.OrderID = OD.OrderID
 WHERE O.OrderID < 10251
 FOR XML AUTO
<O OrderID="10248" CustomerID="VINET">
<OD ProductID="11" UnitPrice="14.0000" Quantity="12"/>
<OD ProductID="42" UnitPrice="9.8000" Quantity="10"/>
<OD ProductID="72" UnitPrice="34.8000" Quantity="5"/></O>
<O OrderID="10249" CustomerID="TOMSP">
<OD ProductID="14" UnitPrice="18.6000" Quantity="9"/>
<OD ProductID="51" UnitPrice="42.4000" Quantity="40"/></O>
<O OrderID="10250" CustomerID="HANAR">
```

```
<OD ProductID="41" UnitPrice="7.7000" Quantity="10"/>
<OD ProductID="51" UnitPrice="42.4000" Quantity="35"/>
<OD ProductID="65" UnitPrice="15.8000" Quantity="15"/></O>
```

Note that the alias for each table becomes a row identifier within the XML output.

> **NOTE**
>
> XML results as shown in the previous query need a unique opening and closing tag, known as the root tag (that is, `<root>` and `</root>`), to be well formed. Well-formed XML can be displayed within Internet Explorer for ease of viewing.

When you run the query, the actual XML comes out all on one line, as a stream of data. XML output does not use linefeeds or make things readable in any fashion. The easiest way to write queries for XML is to write them with the FOR XML clause left out, make sure that they are returning the data you want, and then add the FOR XML back onto the end of the query. This eliminates the need for a lot of extra formatting.

The use of the RAW mode of XML output is best suited for situations in which minimal formatting is desired. In RAW mode, each row is returned as an element with the identifier row. Here's an example of the same query you just saw, this time returned in RAW mode:

```
SELECT O.OrderID, O.CustomerID, OD.ProductID, OD.UnitPrice, OD.Quantity
 FROM Orders AS O
JOIN [Order Details] AS OD ON O.OrderID = OD.OrderID
 WHERE O.OrderID < 10251
 FOR XML RAW
<row OrderID="10248" CustomerID="VINET"
ProductID="11" UnitPrice="14.0000" Quantity="12"/>
<row OrderID="10248" CustomerID="VINET"
ProductID="42" UnitPrice="9.8000" Quantity="10"/>
<row OrderID="10248" CustomerID="VINET"
ProductID="72" UnitPrice="34.8000" Quantity="5"/>
<row OrderID="10249" CustomerID="TOMSP"
ProductID="14" UnitPrice="18.6000" Quantity="9"/>
<row OrderID="10249" CustomerID="TOMSP"
ProductID="51" UnitPrice="42.4000" Quantity="40"/>
<row OrderID="10250" CustomerID="HANAR"
ProductID="41" UnitPrice="7.7000" Quantity="10"/>
<row OrderID="10250" CustomerID="HANAR"
ProductID="51" UnitPrice="42.4000" Quantity="35"/>
<row OrderID="10250" CustomerID="HANAR"
ProductID="65" UnitPrice="15.8000" Quantity="15"/>
```

Notice that the XML output is in an element/attribute association in that each row of the table is returned as an element, with each column being an attribute. If you prefer, you can return everything as elements, with no attributes, using FOR XML RAW, ELEMENTS. New in SQL Server 2005, this provides the following results:

```
<row><OrderID>10248</OrderID><CustomerID>VINET</CustomerID>
<ProductID>11</ProductID><UnitPrice>14.0000</UnitPrice>
<Quantity>12</Quantity></row>
<row><OrderID>10248</OrderID><CustomerID>VINET</CustomerID>
<ProductID>42</ProductID><UnitPrice>9.8000</UnitPrice>
<Quantity>10</Quantity></row>
<row><OrderID>10248</OrderID><CustomerID>VINET</CustomerID>
<ProductID>72</ProductID><UnitPrice>34.8000</UnitPrice>
<Quantity>5</Quantity></row>
<row><OrderID>10249</OrderID><CustomerID>TOMSP</CustomerID>
<ProductID>14</ProductID><UnitPrice>18.6000</UnitPrice>
<Quantity>9</Quantity></row>
<row><OrderID>10249</OrderID><CustomerID>TOMSP</CustomerID>
<ProductID>51</ProductID><UnitPrice>42.4000</UnitPrice>
<Quantity>40</Quantity></row>
<row><OrderID>10250</OrderID><CustomerID>HANAR</CustomerID>
<ProductID>41</ProductID><UnitPrice>7.7000</UnitPrice>
<Quantity>10</Quantity></row>
<row><OrderID>10250</OrderID><CustomerID>HANAR</CustomerID>
<ProductID>51</ProductID><UnitPrice>42.4000</UnitPrice>
<Quantity>35</Quantity></row>
<row><OrderID>10250</OrderID><CustomerID>HANAR</CustomerID>
<ProductID>65</ProductID><UnitPrice>16.8000</UnitPrice>
<Quantity>15</Quantity></row>
```

Adding XSINIL to the end of the command tacks the namespace argument to the beginning of the XML.

The EXPLICIT and PATH options enable you to specify the format of the XML that will be created. Using these options makes the query more complicated to formulate, but it gives you a little more control over the output.

To answer the questions on the 70-431 exam, you really only need to know the definitions. You will want to dig in much deeper if you continue with the remaining SQL Server certification exams.

NOTE

You are not going to become an XML expert overnight, and the material presented in this book is not intended to instruct you on XML. Essentially, all this chapter has done thus far is show how to draw data out of SQL Server in XML format. It has not tried to explain XML or produce an XML reference text, but knowing the material presented in this section and the two that follow should get you through the XML portion of the 70-431 exam.

Using the FOR XML clause to view data in XML format is really easy when you get the hang of it. Getting XML data into a database is a little more tricky and not as user friendly.

The xml Data Type and Methods

The xml data type lets you store XML documents in a field within an SQL Server database or lets you store a variable within a procedure. By using the xml data type, you can store a complete document in a singular column. XML fragments are also supported. An XML fragment is similar to an XML document, but it is missing a single top-level element. There is a limit to the size of a fragment; its stored XML data cannot exceed 2GB.

XML data stored by itself is referred to as *untyped XML*. If you optionally associate an XML schema collection with the data, the XML becomes typed, meaning that the definition for the stored XML is also stored. The saved schemas in the collection are used to validate and define the XML.

The xml data type is treated in the same manner as any of the other data types. When used in a table, an XML column can have defaults assigned, can have constraints in place, and can be used as a source or result for computed columns. An XML column cannot be a primary or foreign key, and if the XML data is typed (that is, has an associated schema), the schema must be provided with the definition.

Let's look at a practical example of using an xml data type. In the following example, resumes submitted for online job applications store educational background information into a table called Education. General name and address information is stored in a table called EmployeeProspect. EmployeeProspect has an XML column named Education:

```
UPDATE ONE.dbo.EmployeeProspect
 SET Education =
  (SELECT A.*
    FROM ONE.dbo.Education A, ONE.dbo.EmployeeProspect B
    WHERE A.ProspectID = B.ProspectID
    FOR XML AUTO)
```

The easiest way to populate an XML column or variable is simply to send the results of a query by using the FOR XML clause. In this example, the results were sent to the Education table before the data was placed in an XML column, which made it easier to illustrate the use of FOR XML. However, other techniques can be used to eliminate the need for the Education table altogether, as you will see a little later in the chapter. Normally, you would receive XML from a web service or other source outside SQL Server, which would then be deposited into a field of the xml data type.

XML AUTO by itself provides untyped XML. You can produce typed data by using XML AUTO, TYPE. The enhanced OPENROWSET functionality allows you to bulk-load XML documents into the xml data type columns in the database. Chapter 5, "Data Consumption and Throughput," discusses this functionality further.

XML Method Interactions

The xml data type has several directly associated methods. The following xml data type methods allow for querying, modifying, and reporting on the xml data type:

▶ **query()**—Executes a query over XML and returns the untyped XML result of the query.

▶ **value()**—Extracts a value of SQL type from an XML instance.

▶ **exist()**—Determines whether a query returns a result.

▶ **modify()**—Is used in the SET statement or SET clause of an UPDATE command to alter the content of an XML document.

▶ **nodes()**—Helps shred XML into relational data.

xml data type methods are considered subqueries and are therefore not permitted in areas where subqueries are not allowed. Because of this, the xml data type methods cannot be used in the PRINT statement or within the GROUP BY clause.

The query() Method

By using the query() method, you can return portions of XML. In its simplest form, you supply to the query() method the path through the XML that is desired. The information returned to you is the elements from the path and any subordinate elements and attributes. The information returned is XML data. To return the entire XML set, you use a query() method and supply only the appropriate root identifier, as shown in the following:

```
SELECT Education.query('/A') FROM EmployeeProspect
```

To return a subset of the information, you continue through the XML path, providing the necessary level to produce the desired results. The following example pulls from the XML the extra curricular elements only, identified by <EXTRA>, and any subordinates:

```
SELECT Education.query('/A/EXTRA') FROM EmployeeProspect
<EXTRA>Chess Club President</EXTRA><EXTRA>Valedictorian</EXTRA>
<EXTRA>Student Body President</EXTRA>
<EXTRA>Varsity Basketball</EXTRA>
<EXTRA />
<EXTRA />
NULL
<EXTRA>Volleyball</EXTRA><EXTRA>Basketball</EXTRA>
<EXTRA />
<EXTRA>Gymnastics</EXTRA><EXTRA>Cheerleaders</EXTRA>
<EXTRA />
<EXTRA />
<EXTRA />
<EXTRA>Debating Team</EXTRA><EXTRA>Ping Pong</EXTRA>
<EXTRA />
<EXTRA />
<EXTRA />
<EXTRA />
<EXTRA />
<EXTRA>Bowling</EXTRA><EXTRA>Golf</EXTRA>
<EXTRA>Basketball</EXTRA><EXTRA>Baseball</EXTRA>
NULL
<EXTRA />
```

You can drill through more complex nested XML in the same manner. You can also get more involved and begin to implement namespace arguments, but that is beyond the scope of the 70-431 exam and therefore this book.

The value() Method

The value() method is similar to the query() method except that it returns a SQL data type instead of an xml data type. You use this method to extract values from XML data. You can specify SELECT queries that combine or compare XML data with data in non-XML columns. You can also produce standard SQL-style reports based on the XML data.

You can retrieve individual attributes by using the @ sign prior to the attribute name within the supplied path. The following query illustrates how you can display a standard SQL column report that combines information from the SQL data type columns and from within the xml data type column:

```
SELECT ProspectID, FirstName + ' ' + LastName AS Name,
  Education.value('(/A/@SCHOOL)[1]', 'varchar(40)') AS School
  FROM EmployeeProspects
ProspectID Name                      School
---------- --------------------      ----------------------------------------
ACKE0001   Pilar Ackerman            Maple Grove High
BARB0001   Angela Barbariol          Illinois Tech School
BARR0001   Adam Barr                 Wabash University
BONI0001   Luis Bonifaz              Northern CC
BUCH0001   Nancy Buchanan            Univ of IL
CHEN0001   John Chen                 NULL
CLAY0001   Jane Clayton              Elgin CC
DELA0001   Aidan Delaney             DuPage
DIAZ0001   Brenda Diaz               Roosevelt High School
DOYL0001   Jenny Doyle               Heartland CC
```

The ordinal [1] indicates that the first subordinate is to be used. If multiple schools were present in the data, only the first in each record would be returned.

The exist() Method

You can perform an existence test against data by using the exist() method. For example, the following query resolves who in the data set has a degree:

```
SELECT ProspectID, Education.exist('/A/@DEGREE')
  FROM EmployeeProspects
EmployeeID
---------- -----
ACKE0001   0
BARB0001   1
BARR0001   1
BONI0001   1
BUCH0001   1
CHEN0001   NULL
CLAY0001   1
DELA0001   1
DIAZ0001   0
DOYL0001   1
```

This method returns a 0, 1, or NULL, depending on whether data in the specified query is found, not found, or null. Our data sample would return 0 for anyone with XML present but no degree, 1 for anyone with a degree, and NULL for anyone with no associated data in the XML column.

The `modify()` Method

You use the `modify()` method to update an XML document. You can change the content of an XML type variable or column similarly to how you would change the content of any other SQL type column or variable. The `modify()` method takes an XML DML statement. XML DML provides statements to insert, update, or delete nodes from data. You use the `modify()` method in the SET clause of an UPDATE statement, as in the following example:

```
UPDATE Education
 SET Education.modify('replace value of(/A/@DEGREE)[1] with "MA"')
 WHERE ProspectID = 'DOYL0001'
```

Three different XML DML commands can be executed through the `modify()` method: `insert`, `replace value of`, and `delete`. The `replace value of` keywords are similar to the traditional SQL UPDATE statement. The `insert` keyword allows for the addition of one or more nodes or siblings, as in the following:

```
UPDATE Education
 SET Education.modify('insert
 <A SCHOOL="Univ of IL" DEGREE="MA"
  MAJOR="Speech and Communica" GPA="3.3"
  GRADYEAR="1991"><EXTRA /></A>
   after (/A)[1]')
 WHERE ProspectID = 'BUCH0001'
```

When `after` is used, the new node(s) is placed after the position of the defined query as a sibling. When `before` is used, the new node(s) is placed in front of the position as a sibling. When `into` is used, you specify `as last` or `as first`, and the new nodes are placed accordingly as descendants of the node identified by the query.

You can also specify the `delete` keyword with the `modify()` method to remove nodes from the XML:

```
UPDATE Education
 SET Education.modify('delete /A/EXTRA')
 WHERE ProspectID = 'BUCH0001'
```

The `nodes()` Method

You use the `nodes()` method to shred XML into relational data. It allows you to identify nodes that will be mapped into a new row of a recordset. The recordset contains copies of the original XML. You can retrieve multiple values from the recordset to provide a standard SQL report.

Unlike the other methods, `nodes()` is used as the source of a query in the FROM clause of the SELECT statement. You can either query directly from an XML variable or use CROSS APPLY on a table to an XML column contained within the table, as illustrated in the following example:

```
SELECT ProspectID, RTRIM(FirstName) + ' ' + Lastname AS Name,
 T.Loc.value('@SCHOOL', 'varchar(40)') AS School,
 T.Loc.value('@DEGREE', 'varchar(5)') AS Degree
 FROM Education CROSS APPLY Education.nodes('/A') AS T(Loc)
ProspectID Name                  School                    Degree
---------- -------------------- ------------------------- -------
ACKE0001   Millar Ackerman       Maple Grove High
BARB0001   Angela Barbariol      Illinois Tech School      AS
BARR0001   Adam Barr             Wabash University         BS
BONI0001   Luis Bonifaz          Northern CC               AA
BUCH0001   Nancy Buchanan        Univ of IL                BA
BUCH0001   Nancy Buchanan        Univ of IL                MA
CLAY0001   Jane Clayton          Elgin CC                  AA
DELA0001   Aidan Delaney         DuPage                    BA
DIAZ0001   Brenda Diaz           Roosevelt High School
DOYL0001   Jenny Doyle           Heartland CC              AA
ERIC0001   Gregory Erickson      Harvard University        BS
```

Other SQL Server XML Support

SQL Server 2005 has many features that utilize XML capabilities either directly or indirectly. This chapter discusses some of the primary storage and coding mechanisms that utilize XML, and you are likely to see questions covering these topics on the 70-431 exam. The exam may also cover a couple other topics; you may see the odd theory-based question centering around the XML functionality described in the following sections.

Indexing XML Data

SQL Server allows you to create indexes over XML data. xml data type instances are stored in a database as large binary objects (BLOBs). The XML can be large (up to 2GB), and without an index, querying, evaluating, and altering these columns can be inefficient and time-consuming.

If an application relies heavily on XML storage and the manipulation and querying of this data, you will find it helpful to index the XML columns. There is a significant performance hit and associated resource cost associated with such an index during data changes.

There are two types of XML indexes. A primary XML index is the first index placed on an XML column. After the primary index has been created, any of three types of secondary indexes can be created: PATH, VALUE, or PROPERTY. Secondary indexes may help improve query performance with some types of queries.

Creating Primary and Secondary Indexes

When you create a primary XML index, you assign the index name and provide the associated XML to be indexed. The primary index alone is helpful when you have queries that specify the exist() method in the WHERE clause. When you use a primary XML index, you avoid having to shred the XML at runtime. An example of the index creation would look similar to the following:

```
CREATE PRIMARY XML INDEX PXMLIndex
 ON ONE.dbo.EmployeeProspect(Education)
```

You must create the primary index before creating a secondary index. To create a secondary index, you assign either the PATH, VALUE, or PROPERTY directive and define the secondary index as being associated to the primary, as shown in the following:

```
CREATE XML INDEX IXMLPathIndex
 ON ONE.dbo.EmployeeProspect(Education)
 USING XML INDEX PXMLIndex FOR PATH
```

If your application uses queries that specify path expressions, using a PATH index may speed up searches. Having a secondary index built on the path and node values can speed up index searches. If your XML searches involve looking for specific values without knowing the element or attribute where they would be located, using VALUE indexes may be helpful. Queries that retrieve more than one value from individual XML instances may benefit from the use of PROPERTY indexes.

Native XML Web Service Support

By using Native XML Web Services, you can send requests over HTTP to an instance of SQL Server 2005 to run T-SQL batch statements (with or without parameters), stored procedures, extended stored procedures, and scalar-valued user-defined functions (UDFs).

To use Web Services in SQL Server, an endpoint must be established at the server. This endpoint is the gateway through which clients can query the server over HTTP. After an endpoint is established, stored procedures or UDFs can be made available to users through the endpoint. These procedures and UDFs are referred to as web methods, and collectively when the methods are used together, they are called a *web service*.

The endpoint definition determines the state of the endpoint, the type of authentication, whether batches are permitted through the endpoint, the Web Service Description Language (WSDL) to be used, and the processes that are exposed through the endpoint. You configure all these options by using the CREATE ENDPOINT statement, and you can change them by using the ALTER ENDPOINT statement.

EXAM ALERT

You may see endpoint configuration on the 70-431 exam. It is important to know how to start and stop an endpoint and how to configure authentication and batch use. You also need to know what processes are permitted as web methods.

The state of the endpoint can be set to one of the following:

▶ **STARTED**—Actively listens for connections.

▶ **STOPPED**—Listens for requests returning error messages to clients.

▶ **DISABLED**—Does not listen for and does not respond to requests.

You can enable or disable SQL batches to determine whether ad hoc SQL or parameterized queries are permitted. SQL ad hoc queries are disabled by default.

You can set user authentication for access to SQL Server through the endpoint to any of the following:

▶ **BASIC**—The lowest level, used as a last resort. You must run through SSL if using this setting.

▶ **DIGEST**—No support for local user accounts. Enables MD5 over Windows Server 2003 domain controllers only.

▶ **NTLM**—Challenge/response authentication where the username and password are asked for and supplied at the time the connection is made. Supported by Windows 95, 98, and NT 4.0.

▶ **KERBEROS**—Internet standard supported by Windows 2000 and later.

▶ **INTEGRATED**—Can use Kerberos or NTLM for authentication, depending on what the client supports.

Web services can be described using the WSDL format generated by SQL Server and returned to SOAP clients for any HTTP endpoints on which WSDL is enabled. If required, you can use DEFAULT to make the WSDL format a custom solution instead of one generated by SQL Server. You can also use NONE to configure the endpoint to not answer WSDL requests. You can also assign WSDL as a custom solution associated with a stored procedure to provide the functionality.

Exam Prep Questions

1. You are working with a table structure that contains a column that has the xml data type. You need to alter the contents of the column. What method of the xml data type do you use?

   ○ **A.** query()

   ○ **B.** value()

   ○ **C.** exist()

   ○ **D.** modify()

   ○ **E.** nodes()

2. You are producing a report that will combine the contents from xml data type and SQL data type columns. Which method of the xml data type do you use?

   ○ **A.** query()

   ○ **B.** value()

   ○ **C.** exist()

   ○ **D.** modify()

   ○ **E.** nodes()

3. You are trying to connect to an endpoint to perform an ad hoc SQL query. You are able to connect, but when you try a query, it fails to execute. Your endpoint creation script looks as follows:

```
CREATE ENDPOINT sql_endpoint
STATE = STARTED
AS HTTP(PATH = '/sql',
    AUTHENTICATION = (INTEGRATED),
    PORTS = ( CLEAR ),
    SITE = 'SERVER')
FOR SOAP ( WEBMETHOD 'GetSqlInfo'
            (name='master.dbo.xp_msver',
             SCHEMA=STANDARD ),
            WEBMETHOD 'DayAsNumber'
            (name='master.sys.fn_MSdayasnumber'),
    WSDL = DEFAULT,
    SCHEMA = STANDARD,
    DATABASE = 'master',
    NAMESPACE = 'http://tempUri.org/')
```

What needs to be corrected with the endpoint settings?

○ **A.** Change the authentication to Kerberos.

○ **B.** Change the WSDL to custom through stored procedures.

○ **C.** Change the state attribute.

○ **D.** Add a parameter for batches to be enabled.

○ **E.** Change the database to the correct execution database.

4. You need to store a large amount of data in an `xml` data type column of a database. The column must be indexed. You want to establish the fewest possible indexes and still provide the best performance for queries that utilize a lot of XQuery path operations. How would you set up the indexing? (Select two answers.)

○ **A.** Create a standard clustered index on the primary key field.

○ **B.** Create a primary XML index on the `xml` data type column.

○ **C.** Create a secondary XML index configured for properties.

○ **D.** Create a secondary XML index configure for paths.

○ **E.** Create a secondary XML index configured for values.

5. You are executing a query that needs to provide the results, with no attributes at all. The results should contain the namespace for the data. Which option would you use?

○ **A.** FOR XML

○ **B.** FOR XML RAW

○ **C.** FOR XML RAW, ELEMENTS

○ **D.** FOR XML RAW, ELEMENTS XSINIL

○ **E.** FOR XML AUTO

Answers to Exam Prep Questions

1. **D.** You use the `modify()` method in the SET clause of an UPDATE statement to alter the content of an XML document. `query()` is used to return untyped XML from a positioned query. `value()` returns the SQL data from within the defined XML. `exist()` determines whether XML exists to match up with the positioned query provided. `nodes()` is used as the source for a query that returns multiple pieces of data for reporting purposes.

2. **B.** `value()` returns the SQL data from within the defined XML. This would allow you to combine it with other SQL data. You use the `modify()` method within the SET clause of an UPDATE statement to alter the content of an XML document. `query()` is used to return untyped XML from a positioned query. `exist()` determines whether XML exists to match up with the positioned query provided. `nodes()` is used as the source for a query that returns multiple pieces of data for reporting purposes.

3. **D.** The default setting for SQL batches that allow for ad hoc queries is disabled. In the preceding endpoint definition, no setting is supplied, and therefore the ad hoc query capability is turned off.

4. **B, D.** To create a secondary XML index, you must first have a primary XML index created. The best secondary index in this scenario is for paths. An index configured for values would perform well in queries that do not provide path information. Queries based on multiple XML values would benefit from a properties index.

5. **D.** The ELEMENTS keyword provides all the output in element format, with no attributes. XSINIL adds the namespace prefix to the resulting XML.

CHAPTER FIVE

Data Consumption and Throughput

Terms you'll need to understand:

✓ bcp command

✓ BULK INSERT statement

✓ OPENROWSET command

✓ Format file

✓ SQL Server Integration Services (SSIS)

✓ Business Intelligence Development Studio

✓ Service Broker

✓ Synchronous model

✓ Asynchronous model

✓ Service Broker queue

✓ Service Broker dialogue

✓ Service Broker contract

✓ Service Broker service

Techniques you'll need to master:

✓ Using BCP to export data to a file

✓ Importing data by using a format file (BCP, BULK INSERT, and OPENROWSET)

✓ Creating services and contracts by using Service Broker

✓ Communicating between applications by using Service Broker

There are many ways to get data into and out of a database. Traditional tools for loading and unloading data with SQL Server are still commonly used today. In addition, newer applications and implementations continue to grow in a diverse manner. New functionality and technology continue to give us different ways of accessing data. This chapter first discusses the old tools and then progresses through SQL Server functionality by discussing some of the newest techniques and features. Everything from bulk processes to the use of the Service Broker handles aspects of maneuvering data throughout the environment.

Importing and Exporting Data

There are several ways of moving large amounts of data either within a single server or between servers. Importing and exporting tasks vary in SQL Server, and each task has an appropriate implementation. You can move data by using two techniques:

- ▶ **Connected**—Connected techniques, often called "live" updates, occur directly against the database.

- ▶ **Disconnected**—Disconnected techniques, in general, store data into a file as an intermediate step in the transfer.

One of the easier disconnected methods to use is a backup/restore that involves the backing up of data from a database and the subsequent restore to a different database or server. This technique is often used as a method of initiating replication or log shipping. This is not a selective technique, however, and other techniques are better suited to importing and exporting information. In a similar fashion, you can use the Copy Database Wizard as a connected mechanism to copy objects from one server to another, but again, this is not usually best suited to selectively importing and exporting.

The import and export of data to and from a file can use one of three basic methods: the bcp command, the BULK INSERT statement, and the INSERT ... SELECT * FROM OPENROWSET(BULK) statement. Other methods can also be used for import and export, as discussed later in this chapter. This chapter also discusses the use of bcp to export data from SQL Server. A bcp command can export data from anywhere that a SELECT statement works, including partitioned views.

TIP

You can use bcp with no options. When you do, you are prompted for the information needed for the format file. You can then optionally save the format file. The resulting files can be used as input for any of the three operations bcp, OPENROWSET, and BULK INSERT.

The following section discusses a traditional mechanism for moving data: using bcp.

Using the Bulk Copy Program (BCP)

You most often use the Bulk Copy Program (BCP) when the database can be temporarily taken out of production to import large amounts of data. Of course, BCP also allows for the export of data, in which case the database can remain online. Using BCP for importing data is extremely fast. As the name indicates, BCP is a process used to copy large amounts of data.

BCP is not a specific implementation of SQL Server. The BCP command-line tool is often used from batch files. BCP's biggest asset is its speed. It moves information into and out of a database by using data files. BCP is normally used to do the following:

- ▶ Bulk copy from a table, view, or result set into a native-mode data file in the same format as the table or view.

- ▶ Bulk copy from a table, view, or result set into a data file in a format other than the one that the table or view is in. In this instance, a format file is created that defines the characteristics of each column. If all columns are converted to character format, the resulting file is called a *character-mode* data file.

- ▶ Bulk copy from a data file into a table or view. A format file can be used to determine the layout of the data file.

- ▶ Load data into program variables and then import the data into a table or view one row at a time.

As stated earlier, BCP is best suited for quickly loading data into a database. BCP does not create tables. You must have a table set up and waiting before you run BCP. The basic syntax of the bcp command is as follows:

```
bcp <table¦query> <in¦out¦queryout¦format> filename
```

To avoid unnecessary confusion, this chapter avoids a lot of the specifics of each implementation of bcp and variation of the coding because you do not need to know about them for the 70-431 exam.

EXAM ALERT

To prepare for the 70-431 exam, you should know several standard BCP operations, as discussed in this chapter. Putting data into sequence, use of a format file, and what happens in default scenarios with no options specified are all potential topic areas for the exam.

The bcp command provides a set of switches you can use to specify the options to be used for the operation. If you do not supply any switches that define the field information, you are prompted for formatting information that you can then optionally save into a format file. The prompts ask you to define the data type for each field, the field prefix length, and the field terminator.

If you allow the defaults for the fields, the data type will default to the type supplied by the switches (-c for character, -w for Unicode, -n for native, and -N for native Unicode for character data types). A tab is the default field delimiter, and a newline (carriage return) is the default record delimiter.

When exporting data, you can easily select all data to be exported. If you want to filter horizontally (that is, only some rows), filter vertically (that is, only some columns), or save the data in a specific order within the file, you use queryout and define a SQL query to be used as the basis for the export. The column list of the SELECT statement provides the vertical filter, the WHERE clause provides the horizontal filter, and the ORDER BY statement arranges the data as desired.

Importing Data with BCP Format File

When you use BCP in a controlled fashion, the process utilizes two separate files: One contains the data and the other, the format file, contains the definition of the data. You can use the format file during an import operation to help define the properties of the data being imported. Using the bcp command with a format file would look like this:

```
BCP ONE.dbo.CustCopy IN C:\CustTwoBCP.dat -T -f C:\BCP2.fmt
```

At the top of the format file are two header rows: The first identifies the SQL version (SQL Server 2005 is version 9.0), and the second contains the number of fields stored in the file. Each field is allocated a row within the format file and includes the data type, field prefix length, field size, field delimiter, field name, and collating sequence.

Microsoft recommends that you include the collating sequence for every field. During the actual import, you have limited control over the process, but before the import, you can alter the data and format files. After you start the BCP process to import the data, the process proceeds unabated.

You can have a minimal amount of control over the reactions to an import through the use of import hints. Constraints are usually ignored during BCP imports. To ensure that data conforms to constraints, you can supply the CHECK_CONSTRAINTS hint, although it significantly slows the process. Also, the server ignores insert triggers by default during import; if you want these triggers to fire, you must specify the FIRE_TRIGGERS hint.

> **NOTE**
>
> Because constraints are by default not applied and triggers do not fire, BCP activities could affect the standard data and work flows in a production environment. Make sure you take into consideration any trigger activities that should take place. Also, pre-check imported data for errors.

You can aid in improving the performance of BCP by using the ORDER hint. This hint identifies the order of the data within the data file. It has no effect on the order of the data, and it is ignored when it cannot be of any benefit. You can also use the TABLOCK hint to change the default locking behavior from row-level locking. Table level locks perform much more efficiently than row-level locks.

For large files with more than about a couple thousand rows, you should turn on the SELECT INTO/BULKCOPY option for the database or set the database recovery mode to SIMPLE. Either of these methods disables all transaction log backups while they are turned on, and you must do a full backup to get transaction log backups to work afterward. These methods affect certain operations—that is, those involving SELECT INTO and BULK COPY—by changing how transaction logging works.

If you set the recovery mode to SIMPLE, it is recommended that when you have completed your process, you turn it back to FULL and perform a full database backup.

Using BULK INSERT as an Alternative to BCP

A closely related technique to using BCP involves the use of BULK INSERT. This is really just an extension of the BCP functionality that you can use to perform bulk operations from within a query environment without having to use the command prompt.

The BULK INSERT statement implements part of BCP inside SQL Server, so it has all the speed of BCP, but an easier-to-use interface. BULK INSERT allows for the copying of a data file into a database table or view with a user-specified format. However, the BULK INSERT statement cannot copy data from SQL Server out to a data file.

Although BULK INSERT uses most of the same options as BPC, it doesn't need to know which server to use or what security to use because you use it from within T-SQL, so it runs on that server, with the security context with which you logged in. Using BULK INSERT for importing data offers identical functionality as BCP. You could use the following, for example, to import data in a similar fashion to the way you use bcp:

```
BULK INSERT ONE.dbo.CustCopy
  FROM C:\CustTwoBCP.dat
  WITH FORMATFILE = C:\BCP2.fmt
```

Using OPENROWSET for Importing Data

You can use OPENROWSET to gain access to any OLE DB data source that will return a rowset. However, you should use it only for data that is accessed infrequently to avoid the overhead of its use. In situations in which a data source needs to be accessed repeatedly, a linked server should be defined. Besides the associated overhead, OPENROWSET does not provide the functionality of linked server definitions.

You use a format file with the OPENROWSET(BULK...) option in the same manner in which you would for a bcp or BULK INSERT operation. Here is an example:

```
SELECT A.* FROM OPENROWSET(BULK N'C:\CustTwoBCP.dat',
 FORMATFILE = 'C:\bcp2.fmt') AS A
```

In this example, the user must have appropriate permissions to access the file. When this user accesses other OLE DB data sources, he or she must provide connection information to gain access to the external data.

You can import XML data as a single document by using OPENROWSET with the SINGLE_BLOB directive. This directive causes the data to be read as a single-row, single-column result set. The data is treated as a varbinary(max) data type, which can be used as XML without conversion. This is not the same as storing the data in a field that uses the XML data type and is often a preferred technique. You could also use the SINGLE_CLOB or SINGLE_NCLOB to perform the action with character or Unicode data, which could then be cast directly into an XML variable or database column.

Large-scale importing and exporting of data are regularly recurring operations in most production environments. For repeated access to another data source, you should configure and use a linked server. For solutions that involve data extraction, transformation, and loading (ETL) on regular basis, you should use SQL Server Integration Services (SSIS), as described in the following section.

Using SQL Server Integration Services (SSIS)

Many import and export activities involve much more than reading data from one location and pushing it into another. Some form of alteration or massaging of the data is usually needed between the source and destination. In previous versions of SQL Server, this is where Data Transformation Services (DTS) came into play.

Like many of the other SQL Server features, DTS has undergone a transformation. Now known as SSIS, it has become a full-featured platform for handling data transfer. Figure 5.1 shows an example of a package saved in SSIS.

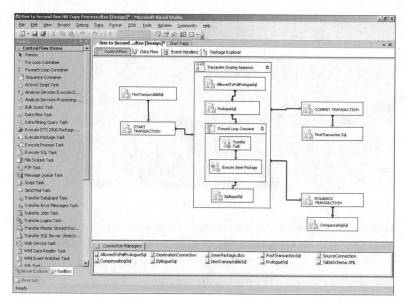

FIGURE 5.1 A sample SSIS package.

This package illustrates both the transactional and workflow capabilities of SSIS. Operations can be performed within transaction boundaries. If errors occur, then rollback processing and additional flow can be designed. In the event of successful execution, alternative processing can occur.

You can easily use SSIS to perform a number of common ETL activities. It can also assist in automating many of the data transfer tasks already discussed in this chapter. The following are some of the most common uses of SSIS:

▶ **Merging data from heterogeneous data stores**—SSIS can be used to take data from different systems, extract the data, and then merge the data into a consistent source.

▶ **Populating data warehouses and data marts**—With SSIS, updates of large amounts of data can be performed frequently.

▶ **Cleaning and standardizing data**—With SSIS, abbreviations and data structures (names and addresses) can be processed to agree with corporate conventions.

▶ **Building business intelligence into data transformation**—SSIS can be used for data summarization, conversion, or distribution based on data values.

▶ **Automating Data Transfers**—Rarely are data transfer processes a one-time thing. SSIS packages can be stored and executed when needed. They can also be scheduled using SQL Server Agent jobs.

SSIS is a diverse tool that can be applied to almost any data movement process. Most of the mechanisms that you use to import and export data by using SQL Server Management Studio now use SSIS principles. When you select to save these data transfers, you save an SSIS package.

EXAM ALERT

Although SSIS is a versatile and powerful tool for importing and exporting data, it is not a particular focus of the 70-431 exam, and you are unlikely to get any questions dealing with the specifics of its use. You need to recognize only the basics of where it would be used and what it can do.

You use the SQL Server Business Intelligence Development Studio to create and edit SSIS packages. You can use it to provide a full workflow definition as well as data flow definitions and event handlers. Anyone comfortable with DTS will see many similarities in SSIS, although the tool does have a significant amount of improved functionality.

Implementing Service Broker

Service Broker is an inter-application messaging agent that provides queuing and messaging within a single instance of SQL Server or between multiple instances. Database applications can use Service Broker to utilize an asynchronous programming model. Unlike synchronous models, where activities happen live, in real-time, asynchronous processing operates under extended delays, often waiting for secondary processes to activate the continuation of the procedure.

In a synchronous model, the application often spends its time waiting for a response. In many situations, the response is nothing more than a confirmation that an action was completed. In other situations, responses may be needed from other applications or activities, and an asynchronous model would therefore allow processing to continue without requiring a wait.

In an asynchronous model, processing can continue in situations in which the response is not a requirement for processing to continue. To shorten the interactive response time and increase overall application throughput, you can implement this type of model by using Service Broker. Service Broker provides reliable messaging between servers and their applications. Messages are the interaction tools used between the service applications that utilize Service Broker. Service Broker uses TCP/IP to exchange messages. The messages are delivered using mechanisms that help prevent unauthorized access and provide for encryption.

The next few sections illustrate some of the coding and functionality of Service Broker. In each environment, the details change significantly. For that reason, the example described here is intended solely as a mechanism to illustrate functionality. If it were to be put in place in an actual environment, several additional pieces would be needed.

Designing a Service

A Service Broker service component is composed of several elements. When designing an application that will interact with Service Broker, you need to specify the following:

- **Message types**—You define classes and provide names for the messages that will be exchanged.

- **Contracts**—You define the direction of the message flow and which types of messages are utilized within a conversation. A contract provides the service with a set of message types.

- **Queues**—These are the message stores. Queues are the vehicle that enables asynchronous communication between services to exist.

- **Services**—These are the endpoints for conversations. Messages are sent from one service to another. A service specifies a queue and the contracts for which the service is targeted.

The basis for a Service Broker application is a conversation. Two or more applications communicate by creating conversations. Conversations occur between service components. When a conversation is initiated, it allows for the exchange of messages between services.

Defining Message Types

The first portion of a service is the message type. When you create a message type, you are creating a category of message that can be used by an application. With the creation, you may also specify any validation that is to occur against the message. The message content can be checked against an existing schema or have less stringent validation rules, as is the case in the following examples:

```
CREATE MESSAGE TYPE JobPosting
 VALIDATION = VALID_XML
 WITH SCHEMA COLLECTION JobPostingSchema
GO
CREATE MESSAGE TYPE OpenPositionResponse
 VALIDATION = WELL_FORMED_XML
GO
```

```
CREATE MESSAGE TYPE ApplicationReceived
 VALIDATION = NONE
GO
```

If you are using an XML schema for validation, the schema must already exist within the database before you can create the message type.

Providing Contract Details

A contract is used to define the message types used within a conversation, and it determines which side of the conversation a message can be sent by. The initiating service specifies the contract to be used for any given conversation. The target service defines the contracts that the service accepts. You use the CREATE CONTRACT statement as follows:

```
CREATE CONTRACT JobApplication
 ( OpenPositionResponse SENT BY INITIATOR,
 ApplicationReceived SENT BY TARGET)
```

The contract can involve any number of message types. Each conversation need not use all messages that are bound to the contract.

Creating a Queue

A queue is used to store messages. When a message arrives for a particular service, Service Broker places the message in the queue that is associated with the service. Message queues can be created with a number of different mannerisms.

> **EXAM ALERT**
>
> A critical component of Service Broker functionality is the definition and use of message queues while a dialogue is taking place. You should carefully study the various options available for queues and the associated dialogues.

The queue definition that is provided at the point of creation determines how messages are handled when they reach the queue. You can make changes in the queue definition by using ALTER QUEUE, as in this example:

```
CREATE QUEUE JobApplicationQueue
 WITH STATUS = ON, RETENTION = ON,
 ACTIVATION ( STATUS = ON, PROCEDURE_NAME = ProcessResume,
            MAX_QUEUE_READERS = 1, EXECUTE AS SELF)
```

If no activation is defined, the queue must be explicitly handled and read by the services that interact with the queue. When you define activation, you provide the name of the stored procedure that will execute to handle the message. It is possible to turn the queue status on and off so that it is unavailable. If the activation status is turned off, the queue is still available, but the automated handling as messages are received does not occur.

It is not recommended that you retain messages over time. If the RETENTION setting is set to ON, messages stay in the queue after they have been received. It can degrade performance and increases maintenance on the system to periodically review and clean out messages from the queue.

When setting up the procedure execution security for a task, you can choose to execute the procedure as the owner of the queue, self (the person who created the queue), or another defined user.

Assembling Components into a Service

After all the components of a service have been created, the parts can collectively become the service. When you create a service, you assign the service to a queue and optionally provide the contract that will be used for the service communication to the queue, as in the following example:

```
CREATE SERVICE SubmitJobApplication
 ON QUEUE JobApplicationQueue(JobApplication)
```

At this point, you initiate the service by using the communication and you initiate the messages by using some front-end application. Within each application, interactions with the queues is simply a matter of sending and receiving messages.

The Communications Dialogue

A dialogue encompasses a conversation. The initiator must begin the communication via the dialogue, and the target usually handles the message and ends the communication. Messages are sent to the corresponding queue using the dialogue via the SEND statement, as in the following example:

```
Declare @dialog_handle uniqueidentifier
Declare @XMLMessageContent XML

SET @XMLMessageContent = NCHAR(0xFEFF) +
 N'<root>XML Message Content</root>'

BEGIN DIALOG CONVERSATION @dialog_handle
 FROM SERVICE SubmitJobApplication
 TO SERVICE 'ProvideApplicationResponse'
 ON CONTRACT JobApplication
 WITH ENCRYPTION = OFF

;SEND ON CONVERSATION @dialog_handle
MESSAGE TYPE OpenPositionResponse( @XMLMessageContent )
```

You read messages that are waiting in the queue by using the RECEIVE statement. When retrieving messages, a dialog need not be initiated. An example of message retrieval is as follows:

```
Declare @dialog_handle uniqueidentifier
Declare @msgtype nvarchar(256)
Declare @XMLMessageContent nvarchar(max)

;RECEIVE TOP(1) @XMLMessageContent = message_body,
 @dialog_handle = conversation_handle, @mgstype = message_type_name
 FROM ApplicationResponseQueue
```

The simple example that we have been using illustrates the functionality in a singular machine environment, using local object names. If the communication is going to occur between multiple machines, some additional setup is required. For communications over a local area network, for example, you need to create a TCP endpoint for the service broker to use, like this:

```
CREATE ENDPOINT ServiceBrokerEndPoint
 STATE = STARTED
 AS TCP ( LISTENER_PORT = 4037)
 FOR SERVICE_BROKER (AUTHENTICATION = WINDOWS)
```

To set up the security credentials that are needed to initiate a conversation with a service that is located on another machine, you need to define the credential binding to be used. You do this by using CREATE REMOTE SERVICE BINDING, as in the following example:

```
CREATE REMOTE SERVICE BINDING JobAppServBind
 AUTHORIZATION [dbo]
 TO SERVICE '//YukonTwo:80/sql/Services'
 WITH USER CertOwnerUserName, ANONYMOUS = ON
```

With this binding you can identify a specific owner of the binding by using the AUTHORIZATION clause. You can specify the USER clause to identify the owner of the certificate associated with the remote service. It is possible to define the remote access as anonymous.

If ANONYMOUS = ON, anonymous authentication is used, and operations in the remote database occur as a member of the public fixed database role. If ANONYMOUS = OFF, operations in the remote database occur as a specific user in that database.

You can set up an HTTP namespace to be used. This makes it easier to access the services on the machine from sources external to the machine. You can initiate a namespace by using the following stored procedure call:

```
sp_reserve_http_namespace N'http://YukonTwo:80/sql'
```

The name can be a machine name or can be a standard DNS name for the location of the service.

Exam Prep Questions

1. You would like to perform a bulk data load. This process will be repeated often. You will be exporting from one server and importing into the other. To speed up the process, you want to have the data imported in the primary key sequence. How do you implement this so that it will occur as quickly as possible? (Select the best answer.)

   ○ **A.** Import using BCP with an order hint.

   ○ **B.** Import using BULK INSERT with an order hint.

   ○ **C.** Import using OPENROWSET with ORDER BY.

   ○ **D.** Export using BCP with ORDER BY.

   ○ **E.** Export using BULK INSERT with ORDER BY.

2. A small manufacturing company has a considerable number of data sources because no standardization has occurred across any platform. One of the database servers has SQL Server installed; the others come from various vendors. For a project you are working on, you need to gather data from the SQL Server machine and merge it together with data from two other sources. You then need to bring the data into Excel to do some charting. How would you accomplish this task? (Select the best answer.)

   ○ **A.** Export the data from the other sources into a comma-delimited file. Then export from SQL Server the data that is to be imported into Excel.

   ○ **B.** Export the data from all three sources so that it can be imported into Excel.

   ○ **C.** Use SSIS to transfer all the data from all sources directly into Excel.

   ○ **D.** Use Excel to transfer data from all three sources into a spreadsheet.

3. You are implementing a portion of the corporate extranet. You want to make the server accessible for web services over HTTP. You also want to use the asynchronous features of Service Broker. How would you accomplish this task? (Select the best answer.)

   ○ **A.** Create a TCP endpoint.

   ○ **B.** Create an HTTP endpoint.

   ○ **C.** Create one TCP endpoint and one HTTP endpoint.

   ○ **D.** Create an HTTPS endpoint.

4. You would like to use HTTP naming conventions to create services locally and to allow them to be registered from remote systems. How would you accomplish this task? (Select the best answer.)

   ○ **A.** Create services using standard SQL names and establish aliases.

   ○ **B.** Create the service queue with an activation process.

   ○ **C.** Use `sp_reserve_http_namespace` and use this namespace for services, endpoints, and other objects.

   ○ **D.** Establish an `http` namespace in the `BEGIN DIALOG` operation.

5. You have a data file with its associated format file. You need to perform an import operation that allows for the use of both files. How can you accomplish this task? (Select all that apply.)

   ○ **A.** Use the same process that created the file.

   ○ **B.** Use BCP to perform the import.

   ○ **C.** Use `BULK INSERT` to perform the import.

   ○ **D.** Use OPENROWSET to perform the import.

   ○ **E.** Use SSIS to perform the import.

   ○ **F.** Use the `RESTORE` statement to perform the import.

6. You have created multiple queues for use by Service Broker. You have assigned each service to its own queue. You initiate a message from `BefService` targeting `AftService`. No queues have automation enabled. In which queue or queues would you find the initial message sent by `BefService`? (Select the best answer.)

   ○ **A.** In the queue assigned to `BefService`

   ○ **B.** In the queue assigned to `AftService`

   ○ **C.** In both the `BefService` queue and the `AftService` queue

   ○ **D.** In neither queue because the operation requires a shared queue

7. A message is defined using the `VALIDATION` clause with `VALID_XML`. What checks are performed against the message before it is delivered? (Select the best answer.)

   ○ **A.** The message must contain well-formed XML.

   ○ **B.** The message must contain a full XML document.

   ○ **C.** The message must contain an XML segment.

   ○ **D.** The XML must conform to the schema provided.

Answers to Exam Prep Questions

1. **D.** To achieve the best performance, you need to make sure that the file is in order when it is created. The order hint does not reorder data. Ordering the data at the time of import using any mechanism would be sluggish. Because you cannot create a file by using BULK INSERT, the only possibility is BCP file creation with a query to create the file in order. For more information see the "Using the Bulk Copy Program (BCP)" section.

2. **C.** SSIS is ideal for this situation. Depending on the details of the process, this can be performed directly by using replication. Given the complexity of the scenario, it is more likely that SSIS would be used because of its great flexibility. For more information, see the "Using SQL Server Integration Services (SSIS)" section.

3. **C.** Web services utilize HTTP or HTTPS endpoints and SOAP processing, whereas Service Broker requires a TCP endpoint. For more information, see the "Implementing Service Broker" section.

4. **C.** HTTP naming can either be done explicitly using sp_reserve_http_namespace or implicitly through creation of endpoints that apply and add to the namespace. For more information, see the "Implementing Service Broker" section.

5. **B, C, D, E.** It doesn't matter how the files were created. You can perform the import operation by using BCP, BULK INSERT, OPENROWSET, or SSIS . RESTORE can only work with files that were created with the BACKUP operation.

6. **B.** Service Broker automatically delivers any messages sent to the queue assigned to the service receiving the message. This makes it easier to control queues and operations against the queues. No service can gain access to messages that are not intended for the service. For more information, see the "Implementing Service Broker" section.

7. **D.** When VALID_XML is defined, the XML is checked against the schema that was assigned to the message type at the point of creation. For more information, see the "Designing a Service" section.

CHAPTER SIX

Database Maintenance

Terms you'll need to understand:

✓ SQL Server Agent

✓ Job

✓ BACKUP command

✓ RESTORE command

✓ Database snapshot

✓ Recovery model

✓ The INIT and NOINIT commands

✓ The SKIP and NOSKIP commands

✓ The FORMAT and NOFORMAT commands

✓ Scheduling

✓ The STOPAT option

✓ The HEADERONLY, VERIFYONLY, and LABELONLY options

Techniques you'll need to master:

✓ Viewing job details and history

✓ Using queries against the msdb system database

✓ Backing up and restoring databases and logs

✓ Utilizing database snapshots

✓ Implementing recovery modes and recovery options

✓ Scheduling maintenance

Database and server maintenance are ongoing in a production environment. As a database administrator or other IT manager, you must perform numerous maintenance activities to get the best performance out of the system and to be prepared for any outage that might occur.

Realistically, you cannot go through life working with computers without dealing with data recovery at some point. If you have not personally seen data corruption or hardware malfunctions, it is only a matter of time until you do.

Most SQL Server implementations provide mission-critical data services to corporations. Often, if not always, a system going down or data being lost has a direct financial impact on the company. This chapter looks into recovery operations you can undertake when the inevitable occurs. Chapter 9, "Implementing High Availability," takes this concept a step further by examining how to keep the server and its data available all the time.

SQL Server 2005 Database Maintenance

EXAM ALERT

The topics related to database maintenance represent a significant portion of the material on the 70-431 exam. You can expect to see several questions about the topics of backups, restoration, jobs, schedules, snapshots, and other related maintenance activities.

Database maintenance involves backing up and restoring data. You also need to consider automating maintenance procedures and how to use the information and tools available to ensure that maintenance processes are actually being performed as designed.

What's New in SQL Server Maintenance?

Although many of the concepts of database maintenance in a SQL Server 2005 environment remain the same as with previous SQL Server releases, you will find several new features. Like most other Microsoft exams, the 70-431 exam tests knowledge of the new features. In the data backup and recovery realm, several new features give administrators mechanisms for handling activities in a more efficient and reliable fashion.

There is significant overlap in topics between the 70-431 exam and other related exams. Many of the newer features are approached in the other exams if you continue with SQL Server 2005 certification. New features seem to be 70 to 80 percent of the actual exam material. The following are the new features you are likely to see on the 70-431 exam:

▶ **Database snapshots**—Snapshots provide a way to revert to a point of consistency. A database snapshot records the current state of the data at the point when the snapshot is created. Any later active transactions are not included. You can later revert the database to the state it was in at the time of the snapshot.

▶ **Partial database restores**—Users can access databases when a partial restore is performed. Partial restores can occur against the database at the file or page level, while allowing users access to any unaffected files and pages. Users cannot access the part of the database being restored until it is recovered.

▶ **The `CONTINUE_AFTER_ERROR` option**—In SQL Server 2005, you can now continue the backup and restore operations after a failure. This option allows the process to continue even if it receives an error. If multiple problems exist, the administrator can assess the scope and then resolve the problem.

▶ **Fast recovery**—SQL Server 2005 Enterprise Edition allows fast recovery during crash recovery and mirroring failover. The data becomes available during the undo phase, with partial availability during restore operations, database page checksums, and backup media mirroring. The other editions of SQL Server 2005 do not let users access the database until recovery completes.

▶ **The `RESTORE VERIFYONLY` and `BACKUP VERIFYONLY` options**—If the `TORN_PAGE_DETECTION` or `CHECKSUM` database options are set, the `VERIFYONLY` option allows the integrity of data pages to be validated during backup and restore operations.

▶ **Mirrored backup sets**—You can perform backups to mirrored sets to reduce the impact of the possible loss or corruption of one of the backups. If a backup device fails, a backup mirror can be used to restore the database.

EXAM ALERT

Maintenance is a central focus of the 70-431 exam, and you will therefore find numerous questions about the various maintenance features. Of course you will be tested on the newer features, and you will also be tested on features present in previous versions of the product.

Performing Database Backups

Backups are an important part of any maintenance strategy. In a SQL Server 2005 environment, you can perform backups through the SQL Server Management Studio interface, by using T-SQL code, by using a customized application, or via third-party tools.

> **EXAM ALERT**
>
> On the exam, you will see questions related to backup theories and the specifics of the options used for the BACKUP T-SQL command and Management Studio interface. Questions will likely pertain to recovery models and the VERIFYONLY, INIT, FORMAT, and SKIP options for performing backups, particularly to tape.

You can perform the SQL Server backup process while users are online and connected to the server. Although it is possible to perform backups any time, it is recommended that the procedure be scheduled for a time when there is little or no database activity. As discussed in the following sections, the type of backups you do and how you implement it depends on the recovery model in which the database is configured.

Recovery Models and Backups

The recovery model setting of each database determines how the database engine interacts with the data and log files. It also controls the backup and restore processes and their abilities. As changes are made to the data in the database, the information is first stored in the log. The committed changes in the log are then periodically pushed into the actual data files.

You have three choices when dealing with the recovery models:

- **Simple**—When you select this option, SQL Server does minimal logging to allow for recovery after a system crash.

- **Bulk-logged**—When you select this option, SQL Server fully logs most transactions and minimally logs bulk operations.

- **Full**—When you select this option, SQL Server fully logs all transactions.

You can set the model through the use of the sp_dboption stored procedure or through the Options page of the Database Properties dialog, as shown in Figure 6.1.

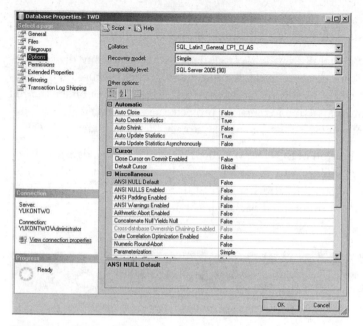

FIGURE 6.1   You use the Options page of the Database Properties dialog to set the recovery model.

With the simple model, after each backup, the transaction log is truncated. Transaction log backups are neither required nor permitted. An important aspect of this model is that it does not allow for point-in-time recovery. Without transaction log backups occurring, it is not possible to recover to the point of failure. You can restore the data only to the point provided by the last backup.

The simple recovery model is usually not an appropriate model for most production systems because there is definitive work-loss exposure. When a crash occurs, any operations performed between that time and the previous backup would have to be repeated. In some events, this would mean permanent loss of many changes that could not be repeated.

The bulk-logged recovery model provides only minimal logging of bulk operations. Although protecting against media failure and providing the best performance for bulk operations, this model increases the risk of data loss for bulk operations. Because only minimal logging occurs, a point-in-time restore may not be possible when the log backup contains any bulk-logged operations. In this situation, you can recover the database only to the end of the log backup, not to a point in the middle of the log.

A transaction log backup must capture both the log and the results of every bulk-logged operation (as occurs in the full model). Backing up a log that contains bulk-logged operations requires access to the data files containing the bulk-logged transactions, making a log backup potentially quite large.

The full recovery model prevents almost all data loss in almost any disaster scenario. It includes both database backups and transaction log backups, and it protects against media failure. To protect against loss of transactions under the full recovery model, the transaction log must be protected against damage. It is strongly recommend that you use fault-tolerant disk storage for the transaction log.

In the Enterprise Edition of SQL Server 2005, you can restore a database without taking all of it offline. You must set your recovery mode to full or bulk-logged for this to be possible. In Microsoft SQL Server 2005, you can back up the log while a data or differential backup is running.

EXAM ALERT

Remember that you must get the database out of the simple model to allow for point-in-time restore operations to occur.

Recovery Models Using T-SQL

In previous versions of SQL Server, you could set recovery models by changing the properties of the database options via the `sp_dboption` stored procedure. SQL Server still supports that option, but using the new SET RECOVERY option of the ALTER DATABASE statement is the preferred technique for setting the recovery model through code.

Using `sp_dboption` and setting the database option `trunc. log on chkpt.` (which means truncate log on checkpoint) to `true` sets the recovery model of the database to simple. Setting the `trunc. log on chkpt.` option to `false` sets the recovery model to full. If you set the `select into/bulkcopy` database option to `true`, you set the recovery model to bulk logged.

NOTE

Using the `select into/bulkcopy` database option is required to create a permanent table with SELECT INTO. In SQL Server 2005, however, this option is not required, and you should avoid it, using ALTER DATABASE with the SET RECOVERY option instead. The `sp_dboption` stored procedure will be removed in a future version of Microsoft SQL Server.

If you are making changes to the database options through a query, using ALTER DATABASE is the preferred technique for implementing any of these database changes, including setting the recovery model. The following example sets the Northwind database to the full recovery model:

```
ALTER DATABASE Northwind SET RECOVERY FULL
```

As well as setting the recovery model for a database, the ALTER DATABASE statement is used to modify a database or the files and filegroups associated with the database. You use this statement to add or remove files and filegroups from a database. You can use the ALTER DATABASE statement to change any of the database attributes, change the collation sequence, and set any of the other database options.

Backup Types and Scenarios

Making backups is an important part of a maintenance plan, and the 70-431 exam tests numerous options related to the backup process. The SQL Server backup process can make a backup of an entire database, a transaction log, or one or more files or filegroups. When you perform a backup, you must indicate whether it is to be a full, differential or transaction log backup. You can perform the backup to disk or tape, on one or multiple devices. You can set several options to perform a backup in the manner required by the maintenance plan and configuration.

You can select many of the options available in the backup process through the SQL Server Management Studio interface. The BACKUP T-SQL command, on the other hand, provides more functionality and a considerable number of additional options as discussed in the following sections.

EXAM ALERT

You can expect the 70-431 exam to include questions on many of the options of the BACKUP and RESTORE T-SQL commands. Although it is possible to perform the operations through Server Management Studio, the exam expects you to know the options for performing backups through use of the T-SQL statements. Pay close attention to the options described throughout the sections to follow.

The Microsoft SQL Server Management Studio provides most of the functionality you would ever need to perform and maintain backups in any production environment. Figure 6.2 shows the options available in Server Management Studio.

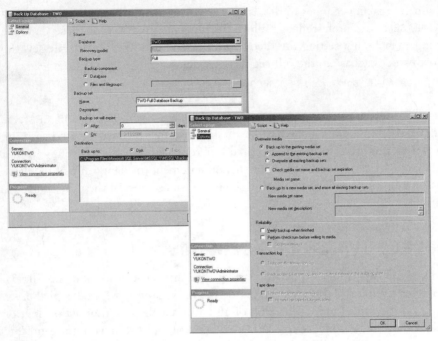

FIGURE 6.2   The Back Up dialog's options.

On the General page of the dialog, you first select the backup type. The back-up type has two elements: the type itself and the component to be backed up. It is important to note that the recovery model in Figure 6.2 is full, which allows for all possible backup types. The drop-down list in this dialog allows you to select the following options:

▶ **Full**—If you select the Full option, SQL Server will back up the entire database, including, at the end of the process, the transaction log. The log is needed so that the database can be recovered in its entirety in the event that a restore is needed. Because this backup includes the log, a full backup represents the database at the time the backup was made, including any operations that were completed while the backup was being created. This process of including the log allows a restore to be performed, using the point-in-time options to bring the database to its most recent form just before the point of failure.

▶ **Differential**—A differential database backup records only the data that has changed because the last full database backup is also referred to as the differential base. Differential backups are often used to supplement a full database backup because they are smaller and faster than full database backups.

▶ **Transaction Log**—A transaction log backup backs up only entries that have been recorded to the logs. Log backups generally use fewer resources than database backups because the only thing being backed up is the content of the log files. As a result, you can create them more frequently than database backups to reduce your risk of losing data.

A production environment generally combines all three backup types in a maintenance plan. A typical scenario may be to perform a full backup every Sunday, with daily differential backups and transaction log backups every few hours.

The second element of the backup type is the component. You can either select to back up the entire database or to back up a portion of the database by selecting files and filegroups and then choosing which files or filegroups to include in the backup.

Setting the Options of a Backup

The T-SQL BACKUP statement offers a full array of options for performing a backup. Many of these options are available through Server Management Studio, but there are a considerable number of options available only through the use of the T-SQL BACKUP command.

You need to have a good understanding of many of the options available. However, you don't want to go overboard. This chapter describes the level of detail you need to succeed on the 70-431 exam. Let us first look at the Options page of the Backup dialog and continue through the relevant options of the T-SQL BACKUP command.

You use the first set of elements on the Options page to specify to use existing media or create new media. You can append (that is, apply to the end) to an existing set or overwrite the content. If you are creating a new media set, you need to specify a media set name and description.

When you overwrite media, the current backup overwrites the existing contents. Overwriting always overwrites all backup sets in a media set. The tape headers are left in place. When you overwrite backups, any existing media header is preserved, and the new backup is created as the first backup. If there is no existing media header, a valid media header with an associated media name and media description is written automatically.

The second set of elements relate to ensuring the integrity and reliability of the backup. Backups should always be verified after being created to make certain that the content is valid. In SQL Server 2005, you can also perform a checksum operation to further ensure the validity of a backup. If a checksum fails and produces errors, you can select the Continue on Error check box to continue or abort the operation.

The third set of elements on the Options page is often grayed out because these elements apply only to transaction log backups. In a default transaction log backup, the log is truncated when the backup is complete. The alternative is to only back up the tail end of the file (by making a tail-log backup) that represents entries not previously backed up and to not remove any of the contents.

> **NOTE**
>
> If logs were never truncated, the log would grow until it filled all available space. The truncation process marks for reuse the space that was used by the old log records. This is why the log file does not reduce in size when truncation occurs. If you need to reduce the size of a log file, you must run a shrink procedure against the file.

A tail-log backup captures the portion of the log that has not been previously backed up. This also represents the last backup of interest in a recovery plan. A tail-log backup is often performed before a point-in-time restore is used. If you were to restore a database without first performing a tail-log backup, you would receive errors. If the tail portion of the log is not needed in a restore operation, you can avoid these errors by using the RESTORE statement and the WITH REPLACE or WITH STOPAT clause. Typically, you make a tail-log backup by using the BACKUP statement's NORECOVERY or NO_TRUNCATE option.

> **EXAM ALERT**
>
> If you need to get the database back to a specific point in time, you can do so by using a snapshot. Alternatively, assuming that you are in full recovery mode, you can perform a final tail-log backup and use the RESTORE statement WITH STOPAT to utilize a point-in-time recovery.

You use the final section of elements on the Options page of the dialog to indicate what happens to the tape that is used when the backup has completed. You can select to have a tape unloaded after backup and, if unloaded, optionally rewind the tape.

Options of the T-SQL BACKUP Statement

Many options are available with the T-SQL BACKUP statement. For the purpose of the exam, you need to concentrate on the subset of those that you are most likely to use. For more information on other options and more complete syntax examples, consult SQL Server Books Online. The following are some of the most commonly used features of the BACKUP statement:

- ▶ INIT, NOINIT, SKIP, and NOSKIP

- ▶ FORMAT and NOFORMAT

- ▶ UNLOAD, NOUNLOAD, REWIND, and NOREWIND

- ▶ STOP_ON_ERROR, CONTINUE_AFTER_ERROR, CHECKSUM, and NO_CHECKSUM

   - ▶ NO_LOG and TRUNCATE_ONLY

   - ▶ NORECOVERY and STANDBY

- ▶ COPY_ONLY

Many of these options apply to specific implementations of the backup process and are not available for all types of backups. There are many common scenarios to look at in performing backups. Most operations perform a series of checks against the media before applying the backup. If you specify the SKIP option, you disable the checking of backup set expiration and name. You could also choose to initialize the backup set with INIT.

Overwriting Existing Backups and Preserving the Header (INIT)

SQL Server identifies backup storage media through the use of identification of the backup media as specific objects identified as media family. media family is a set of one or more backups created on a single named device. Each device is supplied with media header to identify the contents of the device. When you use the INIT option, all backup sets are overwritten, but the media header is preserved. You need to ensure that you truly do not want to keep the existing content because any existing backup set on that device is overwritten.

By default, BACKUP does not overwrite the media if any backup set has not yet expired. Also, if the backup set name given does not match the name on the media, no content is removed. INIT overrides this default process.

If SKIP is specified with the INIT option and the volume contains a valid media header, the media password is verified before any backup sets are overwritten on the media, and only the media header is preserved. If the media is empty, a new media header is generated.

When NOSKIP is set with the INIT option and the volume contains a valid media header, the media password is verified, and the media name, if supplied, is verified. The expiration of any set is verified, and the backup does not continue if any of the verifications fail. If there is no valid media header, one is generated.

Appending to Existing Backups (NOINIT)

With many operations, you simply want to add the current backup operation to the media, without destroying the previously saved content. The NOINIT option allows a backup to be appended to the specified set, preserving any existing backup sets. This is the default if no other options are specified.

If SKIP is specified with the NOINIT option and the volume contains a valid media header, the media password is verified before the data is appended to the existing media.

When NOSKIP is set with the NOINIT option and the volume contains a valid media header, the media password is verified, and the media name, if supplied, is verified before the data is appended to the existing media. If there is no valid media header, an error occurs.

Creating a New Media Set and Preparing a New Header (FORMAT)

At some point, you will want to completely reformat a media set and initialize a new header. As with any other format operation, you will lose any content that was previously stored on the media. FORMAT writes a new media header on all volumes used for the operation, overwriting any existing header and backup on the media. When you specify the FORMAT option, it also includes SKIP, so you do not need to specify the SKIP option. The default behavior is NOFORMAT, and the media header is not written.

Rewinding and Unloading the Tape When Finished (REWIND and UNLOAD)

You can use the REWIND option to release and rewind a tape after it fills. This is the default setting. You use NOREWIND to improve performance when performing multiple operations. When you supply this option, SQL Server keeps the tape open after the backup operation. NOREWIND includes NOUNLOAD, which means a tape is not unloaded automatically from the drive. You can use UNLOAD to specify that the tape is to be rewound and unloaded when the backup is finished. UNLOAD is the default setting.

Validating the Data as the Backup Occurs (CHECKSUM)

You should always verify a backup after it has completed, but in some situations, you might want to validate the data as the backup progresses. You can use the CHECKSUM option to specify that prior to writing a page to the backup media, the page should be verified. BACKUP verifies the page against a checksum or torn page, if that information is present on the page.

Regardless of whether page checksums are present, when you specify the use of a checksum the BACKUP operation generates a checksum of its own. A restore operation can use this generated value to validate the backup and ensure that it is not corrupt. The backup checksum is stored on the backup media, not on the database pages. BACKUP will never alter the data pages themselves. Because this is a processor-intensive operation, you can expect its use to affect workload and backup throughput. The default setting is NO_CHECKSUM, which explicitly disables the generation and validation of checksums.

You can use the STOP_ON_ERROR option in conjunction with CHECKSUM to stop further backup processing if a checksum does not verify. This is the default behavior. If a backup contains errors, it is usually best to repeat the backup operation anyway. CONTINUE_AFTER_ERROR instructs the SQL Server BACKUP command to continue despite encountering errors such as invalid checksums. You can use this option in place of NO_TRUNCATE to attempt a log backup on a damaged database.

Removing Inactive Log Entries and Truncating the Log (NO_LOG and TRUNCATE_ONLY)

You can use either the NO_LOG option or the TRUNCATE_ONLY option to perform a checkpoint against a database. A checkpoint removes the inactive part of the log without making a backup copy of it and truncates the log by discarding all but the active log. This frees up space in the log, but it risks possible data loss and does not affect the log file size. For recovery purposes, after using either of these options, you must immediately execute BACKUP DATABASE to make a full or differential database backup. (The NO_LOG and TRUNCATE_ONLY options will be removed in a future release.) You do not need to specify a backup device when using these options because the log backup is not saved. You should use manual log truncation in this manner in only special circumstances, and you should create backups of the data immediately following the operation.

Setting Up a Warm Backup Secondary Database (NORECOVERY)

You use the NORECOVERY option when you perform a log backup to back up the tail of the log. NORECOVERY leaves the database in the RESTORING state so that future log backups can be applied. NORECOVERY is useful when failing over to a secondary database or when saving the tail of the log before performing a RESTORE operation. You can use this option in conjunction with NO_TRUNCATE to perform a best-effort log backup that skips truncation and takes the database into the RESTORING state atomically.

Setting Up a Read-Only Secondary Server (STANDBY)

You use the STANDBY option with the name of a file to hold the rolled back changes during a transaction log backup. STANDBY performs a backup of the tail of the log and leaves the database in a read-only and STANDBY state. The STANDBY clause performs a rollback of uncompleted transactions but with the option of further restores. Using the STANDBY option is equivalent to using BACKUP LOG WITH NORECOVERY followed by RESTORE WITH STANDBY.

The standby file becomes part of the database. When you perform the backup operation, the file is overwritten if it exists. If the file does not exist, it is created during the process. Rolled-back changes must be reversed if RESTORE LOG operations are subsequently performed.

Performing an Extra Backup (COPY_ONLY)

You might want to perform a backup operation that does not interfere with the maintenance plans you have in place. When you use the COPY_ONLY option, the backup has no effect on the normal sequence of backups and does not affect the overall backup and restore procedures for the database. Any differential backups taken later behave as if the copy-only backup does not exist.

Using a Backup for a System Database

You might want to periodically back up the master, model, and msdb system databases. There is really no purpose in backing up the tempdb system database because its contents are used only for temporary purposes and constantly change. System database backups are subject to a variety of restrictions, depending on which database is being backed up:

▶ The master database can only be backed up in full. You cannot perform differential or log backups of any sort.

▶ You can back up the model and msdb databases as you would other databases. When installation occurs, these databases are set to a simple recovery mode. To perform log backups on model or msdb, you must change the recovery mode to full or bulk-logged.

Restoring Data from a Backup

When disasters occur and you need to get the data back to a known state, you need to perform a restore operation. At other times, you might want to restore data, such as when preparing for log shipping or copying data from one server to another. You can also use the RESTORE command to validate backups or read the catalog information from an existing media set.

Restore operations, just like backups, can be performed from the SQL Server Management Studio interface. For the 70-431 exam, as well as for the greatest flexibility, you must also know the command options for the RESTORE statement and how to apply them. Figure 6.3 shows the options available with the restore process in Server Management Studio.

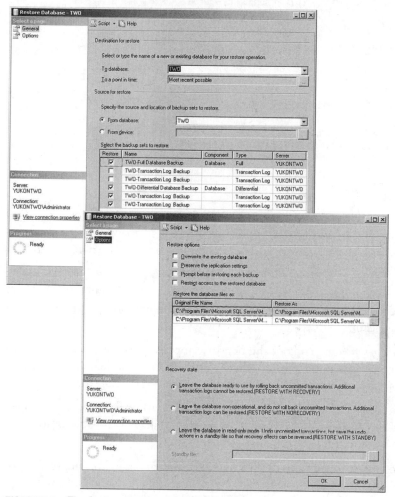

FIGURE 6.3 The Restore Database dialog's options.

On the General page, you essentially select what you intend to restore. If you leave the default settings, the interface automatically selects the options that provide you with the most recent data possible. The backups selected at the bottom of the interface indicate what is going to be restored. You can alternatively select a specific point in time (equivalent to using the RESTORE statement with the STOP_AT option); in this case, the appropriate selections are made at the bottom of the interface, as shown in Figure 6.4.

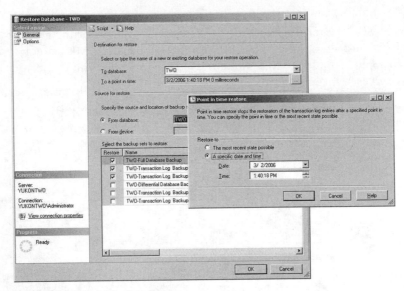

FIGURE 6.4 A point-in-time restore.

If you make a selection yourself from the bottom of the dialog, as shown in Figure 6.4, you end up restoring the database to the end of what is in the last backup selected.

If you have created an extra backup or you want to restore data backed up from another server, you can use the From Device option and browse to the location where the backup is stored.

If you want to create a copy of the database for test purposes, you can restore the data into a different database than the one originally backed up by selecting the appropriate receiving database from the To Database drop-down list.

The Options page of the Restore dialog allows you to fine-tune a restore operation as desired. Most of the options in Server Management Studio are fairly straightforward and self-explanatory.

You can choose to overwrite data in any existing database. You might need to select this option when restoring data that was originally in another database or on another server. You have to change the file locations if the original paths are different from the destination file paths.

You can preserve the replication settings when restoring is available only by selecting the option Leave the Database Ready for Use by Rolling Back the Uncommitted Transactions, which is equivalent to restoring a backup with the RECOVERY option. If you select this option, SQL Server prevents replication settings from being removed when a database backup or log backup is restored on a warm standby server and the database is recovered.

When you select Prompt Before Restoring Each Backup, you must confirm each backup set before you restore it. This option is useful when you must swap tapes for different media sets when the server has only one tape device.

Restrict Access to the Restored Database makes the restored database available only to the members of db_owner, dbcreator, or sysadmin. This helps prevent users from accessing the data and gives administrators the ability to perform further operations.

On the bottom of the restore dialog, you can select the recovery options desired. The default, RESTORE WITH RECOVERY, places the database in a standard usable state. If you want to apply further backups, as in the case of a warm secondary database, you can choose to leave the database non-operational by selecting RESTORE WITH NORECOVERY. When creating a read-only secondary server, you can select RESTORE WITH STANDBY and provide the path to the undo file.

EXAM ALERT

Be prepared for exam questions pertaining to point-in-time recovery and the setup of secondary databases. Both topics are common on Microsoft exams.

As you can see from the restore dialog, Server Management Studio provides similar options to those available when you use the T-SQL RESTORE statement.

Using the T-SQL RESTORE Statement

You can use the T-SQL RESTORE statement to recover a database and restore backups. This command enables you to perform a variety of recovery procedures and restore an entire database, a portion of a database, a specific file or files, a specific filegroup or filegroups, a specific page or pages, or a log. You can also use options of this command to verify a backup or read information from existing backup media.

Many options are available for use with the T-SQL RESTORE statement. In addition, there are several options with BACKUP, but many of them are the same and perform in a similar manner. This chapter concentrates on the ones you are most likely to use that have not been discussed yet in this chapter. For more information on other options and more complete syntax examples, consult SQL Server Books Online.

The following are the most commonly used features of the RESTORE statement that we have yet to discuss:

▶ **FILELISTONLY**—RESTORE FILELISTONLY returns a result set that contains a list of the database and log files contained within the backup.

▶ **HEADERONLY**—RESTORE HEADERONLY returns a result set that contains all the backup header information for all backup sets on a particular device.

▶ **LABELONLY**—RESTORE LABELONLY returns a result set that contains information about the backup media identified by the given device.

▶ **VERIFYONLY**—You use RESTORE VERIFYONLY to verify a backup. This option tells SQL Server to ensure that the backup set is complete and the entire backup is readable, but it does not attempt to verify the structure of the data contained in the backup volumes. In Microsoft SQL Server 2005, RESTORE VERIFYONLY has been enhanced to do additional checking on the data to increase the probability of detecting errors. The goal is to be as close to an actual restore operation as practical.

This shortened list of options is used to gain information from backup devices without actually performing a restore. These options are often used for obtaining information about the contents of the media created from other databases and/or servers.

EXAM ALERT

For the 70-431 exam, you need to be able to differentiate between the functionality of the FILELISTONLY, HEADERONLY, and LABELONLY options.

You can set up backup and restore operations as scheduled jobs, as discussed later in this chapter.

Using Database Snapshots

Database snapshots, which are new in SQL Server 2005, are available only in the Enterprise Edition. All recovery models previously discussed support the use of database snapshots. A database snapshot is a read-only, static view of a database captured at a specific time. It is important to be able to create multiple snapshots for use in reporting or other implementations where capturing the historical data as it sits at a specific point in time. Each snapshot is transactionally consistent with the database as of the moment of its creation.

While snapshots are useful for reporting purposes, they can also be used as a recovery mechanism. You can implement recovery by using a snapshot to revert a database to the state it was in when the snapshot was created. When working with snapshots, the database is subject to several limitations:

- The database cannot be dropped, detached, or restored.

- Performance is reduced due to increased I/O on the database from a copy-on-write operation to the snapshot for every page update.

- Files cannot be dropped from the database or from any snapshots.

- The source database must be online unless the database is a mirror.

Although snapshots are quite useful in many instances, you should not confuse a database snapshot with the ability to use a restore operation to get the database state to a specific moment in time. The STOP_AT restore option to perform a point-in-time restore has no associated overhead, a snapshot has considerable overhead. Reverting a database by using a snapshot is the same thing as restoring from a snapshot. One of the limitations of working with snapshots is that you cannot back up or restore a snapshot. After you make a snapshot of a database, you can back up the database as you normally would; the database is unaffected by snapshots. A snapshot is subject to a number of limitations:

- A snapshot must be created and remain on the same server as the database.

- A database snapshot always works on an entire database; you cannot base a snapshot on a portion of the data.

- If a snapshot runs out of disk space or encounters some other error, the snapshot becomes suspect and must be deleted.

- Snapshots are read-only.

- Snapshots of the model, master, and tempdb databases are prohibited.

- You cannot change any specifications of a snapshot file.

- You cannot drop files from a snapshot.

- You cannot back up or restore a snapshot directly, although you can revert a database to a point that a snapshot was taken by using the RESTORE command.

- You cannot attach or detach snapshots.

- You cannot create snapshots on FAT32 file system or RAW partitions.

- Full-text indexing is not supported on snapshots. Full-text catalogs are not propagated from the database.

▶ A database snapshot inherits the security constraints of its source database at the time of snapshot creation. Inherited permissions cannot be changed, and permission changes made to the source are not reflected.

▶ A snapshot always reflects the state of filegroups at the time of snapshot creation: Online filegroups remain online, and offline filegroups remain offline.

▶ If a database enters the state RECOVERY_PENDING, its snapshots may become inaccessible. After the issue on the database is resolved, however, its snapshots should become available again.

▶ Reverting is unsupported for read-only filegroups as well as for compressed filegroups.

▶ In log shipping, snapshots can be created only on the primary database, not on the secondary database. If you switch roles, you must drop all the snapshots before you can set up the primary database as a secondary.

You can create a series of snapshots to capture database activity through time. However, each snapshot continues to operate until it is explicitly dropped. Over time, the snapshot itself continues to grow. A regular maintenance plan of deleting older snapshots is recommended.

Creating and Deleting Database Snapshots

Any user who has permission to create a database can create a snapshot, although the only way to create snapshots is by using the T-SQL CREATE DATABASE statement. The following code creates a snapshot called TWOSnapshot01 on the TWO database:

```
CREATE DATABASE TWO_TWOSnapshot01 ON
( NAME = TWO_Data,
FILENAME = 'E:\Data\TWO_data_01.ss' )
AS SNAPSHOT OF TWO
```

Because creating snapshots requires SQL knowledge, the ability to create a database on the server should be strictly controlled, especially in a production environment.

To delete a snapshot, you must also use T-SQL. You use the DROP DATABASE statement with the name of the snapshot to delete a snapshot. To delete the TWOSnapshot01 snapshot you just created, for example, you would use the following command:

```
DROP DATABASE TWOSnapshot01
```

When the snapshot is dropped, any user session connected to the snapshot is terminated. Any files associated with the snapshot are deleted.

Using snapshots in SQL Server is in its infancy. Although snapshots are potentially useful, their associated overhead, limited capabilities, and numerous limitations make them rather cumbersome to use, particularly for novice administrators. These limitations, however, do no preclude the use of the material on the exam. The opposite is true; being a new feature in the product, you can expect to have exam questions centering on the appropriate use of database snapshots.

To use a database snapshot, clients and their applications need to know where to find it and how to utilize it. Users can read from one snapshot while another is being created or deleted. Users can manually connect to a database snapshot by using SQL Server Management Studio. To support snapshots in a production environment, you need a programmatic solution that transparently handles snapshots and their use in reporting and other implementations. You can schedule snapshot creation and deletion as you do most other tasks. Producing a snapshot on schedule can be useful in minimizing the administrative load associated with the feature.

Automating Maintenance with Job Scheduling

Many of the maintenance features discussed so far in this chapter are important, but they can be time-consuming. However, that doesn't necessarily have to be the case. Essentially any task that can be performed from SQL Server Management Studio or through the use of a T-SQL query can be automated through the creation of a job or a schedule.

Wouldn't it be nice to have an agent working on your behalf to get the regular database maintenance activities done on a scheduled basis? Of course, the agent would have to provide feedback when things didn't quite go as expected. It would also be essential for summaries to be received from time to time, perhaps by email, providing documentation of exactly what had happened, when it was performed, and what activities failed. Fortunately, SQL Server framework has just such functionality: the SQL Server Agent.

The SQL Server Agent runs as a Microsoft Windows service. When running, the agent executes scheduled tasks. Each task is defined within SQL Server as a job. The agent performs the steps defined in the job and stores the job information and history within the `msdb` database. SQL Server Agent can run a job on a schedule, in response to a specific event, or on demand.

EXAM ALERT

For the 70-431 exam, you will not be expected to perform the coding necessary to create individual job steps. The focus of the exam in this area is more on ensuring that jobs are executed on schedule. You need to know how to query msdb, when and why you would perform the query, and what information you can obtain. In particular, you need to know what processes are available to obtain similar information without executing queries directly against msdb.

Most jobs contain multiple steps, although it is possible for a job to be made up of a singular process. You define a workflow to instruct the agent on how to proceed between the individual tasks. The workflow allows for decision making in a job with a variety of outcomes, based on the results of completing or not completing steps within the job.

Viewing Job Details and History

Whereas most object information is stored in the master database in SQL Server, when you create a job, the information about the job is stored in several tables of the msdb database. You could query these tables, like any others, to find information about the jobs in the system. Among other tables used in msdb, the most useful are the following, which store the job, schedule, and history information. SELECT operations can be performed on the following objects to acquire information on jobs and schedules that have been created.

- ▶ **msdb..sysjobs**—Stores information for jobs created.

- ▶ **msdb..syschedules**—Contains information about schedules.

- ▶ **msdb..sysjobschedules**—Stores schedule associated job information.

- ▶ **msdb..sysjobhistory**—Contains the history of job executions.

Although you can query these tables directly or you can formulate a complex join query to obtain the information you want, it is far easier to use the existing system stored procedures that have already been formulated for that purpose. The following stored procedures can be used to provide information about jobs and related schedule objects.

- ▶ **sp_help_job**—Returns information about all jobs created.

- ▶ **sp_help_jobschedule**—Returns information about jobs and their associated schedules. (You provide a job ID or job name as an input parameter.)

- ▶ **sp_help_jobhistory**—Returns information about the historical execution of jobs. (You provide the job ID or job name as an input parameter.)

It is easiest to view the job information from within SQL Server Management Studio. You can view job history by right-clicking a job name and then selecting View History. You can even see step breakdown information in Server Management Studio if you expand the details of a step. To view schedule information for a specific job, you simply double-click the desired job and then select the Schedules page. A sample schedule is shown in Figure 6.5.

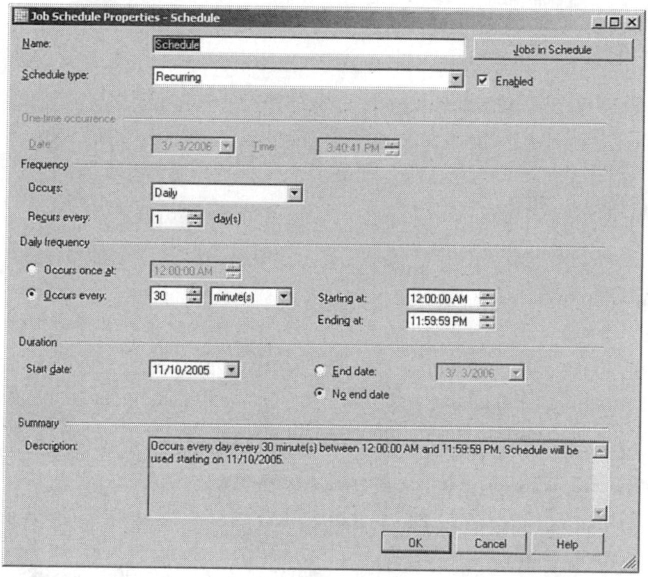

FIGURE 6.5 The Job Schedule Properties dialog.

Jobs are flexible mechanisms and can be quite complex. The scope of the 70-431 exam is not on the creation of jobs but on being able to maintain any jobs that are already on the server. For more information on SQL Server Agent, jobs, and the details of their use, consult SQL Server Books Online.

Exam Prep Questions

1. An error has occurred that has corrupted one of the databases on the server. The database is set to full recovery, the last full backup occurred last night, and log backups have been continuing on an hourly basis throughout the day. No differential backups are currently performed. What steps do you need to take to get the database up and running again with the least loss of data? (Choose all that apply.)

   ○ **A.** Restore the last full backup.

   ○ **B.** Restore the last differential backup.

   ○ **C.** Restore logs from the last full or differential backup.

   ○ **D.** Restore logs from the last full or differential backup by using STOPAT.

   ○ **E.** Perform a log backup.

   ○ **F.** Perform a differential backup.

   ○ **G.** Perform a full backup.

2. You are creating a database backup schedule for all system and user databases. You would like to perform nightly full backups and hourly log backups for all these databases. What must you do to accomplish this? (Choose all that apply.)

   ○ **A.** Ensure that no databases are set to simple recovery.

   ○ **B.** Ensure that all databases are set to simple recovery.

   ○ **C.** Exclude the master, model, and msdb databases from the log backups.

   ○ **D.** Exclude the master database from the log backups.

   ○ **E.** Exclude the model and msdb database from the log backups.

3. You have a tape that contains the copy of a backup. You want to verify that the data has not been corrupted. What do you do? (Choose the best answer.)

   ○ **A.** Use the RESTORE statement with the VERIFYONLY option.

   ○ **B.** Use the BACKUP statement with the VERIFYONLY option.

   ○ **C.** Use the RESTORE statement with the CHECKSUM option.

   ○ **D.** Use the BACKUP statement with the CHECKSUM option.

   ○ **E.** This cannot be done. Verification has to occur at the time of the backup.

4. You have found a backup tape that has been created on another server. The tape was not labeled, and you would like to determine its contents. You want to find out which backup sets are on the tape. How do you perform this task? (Choose the appropriate answer.)

○ **A.** Use RESTORE VERIFYONLY.

○ **B.** Use RESTORE HEADERONLY.

○ **C.** Use RESTORE LABELONLY.

○ **D.** You must access this information from the originating server.

5. You have just created and scheduled the maintenance plans for your company. You have created many jobs and schedules. You would like to back up these plans so that they can be recovered, if needed. What is the easiest method of performing this task? (Choose the appropriate answer.)

○ **A.** Back up the master database.

○ **B.** Back up all user databases.

○ **C.** Back up the msdb database.

○ **D.** Create scripts for all jobs and schedules.

6. You would like to confirm that one of your scheduled jobs was successful. You do not have access to a SQL Server Management Studio installation, but you can run queries and stored procedures against the server. What is the easiest technique for finding the information? (Choose the appropriate answer.)

○ **A.** Run a query against the master..sysobjects table.

○ **B.** Run a query to join the msdb..sysjobs and msdb..sysjobhistory tables.

○ **C.** Run a query against the msdb..sysschedules table.

○ **D.** Run a query by using sp_help_jobhistory.

7. You would like to use log shipping and want to start the process by using a full backup and the most recent log backup from the source database. How do you get these back-ups onto the destination and implement the configuration and query? (Select all that apply.)

○ **A.** Restore the full backup, using RECOVERY.

○ **B.** Restore the full backup, using NORECOVERY.

○ **C.** Restore the full backup, using STANDBY.

○ **D.** Restore the log backup, using RECOVERY.

○ **E.** Restore the log backup, using NORECOVERY.

○ **F.** Restore the log backup, using STANDBY.

Answers to Exam Prep Questions

1. **A, D, E.** To get the database back to as current a point as possible, you need to back up the log one final time to get any entries that have occurred from the last log backup to the point of the failure. You then need to restore the last full backup as a known point where the whole database was saved. To get the data as current as possible from that point, you need to restore all logs by specifying the STOPAT option to get a point-in-time restore to a moment just before the damage occurred. For more information, refer to the sections "Setting the Options of a Backup" and "Restoring Data from a Backup" in this chapter.

2. **A, D.** To perform log backups, you cannot have the databases set to a simple recovery mode. You need to select either the full model or the bulk-logged model for each database. You cannot perform log backups on the master database. Every other database can be included. For more information, consult the sections "Recovery Models Using T-SQL" and "Using a Backup for a System Database" in this chapter.

3. **A.** You can validate the backup media at any time by using the RESTORE VERIFYONLY statement. The CHECKSUM operation can be performed only at the time of the backup. For more information, refer to the section "Using the T-SQL RESTORE Statement" in this chapter.

4. **B.** The HEADERONLY option provides a list of the backup header information for every backup set on the media. LABELONLY returns a result set that contains information about the backup media identified by the given device but no details about the backup sets. You can validate the backup media at any time by using the RESTORE VERIFYONLY statement, but this doesn't solve the problem in question. Backups would be rather useless if they could only be used from the originating server. For more information, refer to the section "Using the T-SQL RESTORE Statement" in this chapter.

5. **C.** The information for all jobs and schedules is maintained in the msdb database. If you restore this database from a backup, you will recover anything of this nature that you have created. It is possible to create scripts for all these processes, but that would be a lengthy and arduous task. For more information, refer to the section "Automating Maintenance with Job Scheduling" in this chapter.

6. **D.** The master..sysobjects table contains information about a lot of objects stored on the server but not for jobs and schedules that are exclusively stored in msdb. You could execute a join query to resolve the problem, but it would take a significant amount of time to formulate one that would produce the desired results. The msdb..sysschedules table contains schedule information but no historical information about the job's execution. When in doubt, you should use stored procedures to solve a problem like this. For more information, refer to the section "Automating Maintenance with Job Scheduling" in this chapter.

7. **B, E.** Any time you intend to restore more backups onto a destination database, you use the NORECOVERY option. You use STANDBY only if the destination is to be a read-only server. RECOVERY makes the database active, and no further logs can be restored. For more information, refer to the "Setting the Options of a Backup" section in this chapter.

CHAPTER SEVEN

Monitoring SQL Server Performance

Terms you'll need to understand:

✓ System Monitor
✓ Database Engine Tuning Advisor (DTA)
✓ Profiler
✓ Activity Monitor
✓ Trace flag
✓ Database console command (DBCC)
✓ Statistics
✓ Workload
✓ Dynamic management view
✓ Baseline

Techniques you'll need to master:

✓ Using tools to monitor performance
✓ Generating workload for DTA
✓ Recording activity over time

This chapter investigates the tools that are provided with SQL Server to inspect and record activity in an installation. With the information gathered you can then attempt to provide for an optimal database and application environment. Several of these tools ship with SQL Server, and some are built in to the Windows operating system.

SQL Server Management Studio is the tool you use to access most of the other tools. The Activity Monitor is useful for gathering a basic level of information. The Log File Viewer provides access to every SQL Server–related log. Dynamic management functions and views provide a version-specific method for troubleshooting. Using the database console command (DBCC) has always been the preferred SQL Server troubleshooting and optimizing method. The Windows System Monitor provides access to quantitative analysis results. SQL Server Profiler provides the deepest and most granular level of information to aid in analysis. Many other individual tools are also presented in this chapter.

SQL Server Management Studio

Microsoft SQL Server Management Studio is the primary graphical interface used to interact with the database engine. With this interface, you can create databases as well as the objects they contain, such as views and tables.

Management Studio provides for administration over the SQL Server security environment, server and database configuration, and statistical analysis and management, and it provides a complete set of administrative tools. Essentially, it is the only tool you need for almost all day-to-day operations in a SQL Server environment.

When you go beyond the day-to-day tasks and require more in-depth analysis, you must reach beyond Management Studio and use the other tools supplied for the purpose of investigation and problem determination. From within the Management Studio, you can access information on the current activity within the server, but often you need other tools to observe the database performance in an ongoing manner. Activity Monitor offers the first level of database-specific information.

Over time, the size of a database needs to be adjusted to accommodate new data or data removal. The configuration of the server in any given installation may vary greatly. The applications that a server is intended to handle direct the configuration. In troubleshooting and tweaking the performance of any installation, you need to know how the server is being used. Before you can make any alterations to improve performance, you need to gather statistical information on how the server is performing within the production environment.

Troubleshooting, performance tuning, and resource optimization require in-depth knowledge of how SQL Server operates, as well as knowledge of the applications to which the database server is being applied. As described in the earlier chapters in this book, you can use numerous tools and options to assist in this process.

One problem you will face on the 70-431 exam is knowing which tool to use, given a set of circumstances. Second, you need to present a course of action for monitoring and troubleshooting. Third, you need to read and diagnose the output and then select an appropriate solution. A person who implements databases needs to be comfortable in all these areas, and you will find a few of each type of question on the exam.

This chapter focuses on gathering information and the types of information each of the tools provides. Chapter 8, "Troubleshooting and Optimizing SQL Server," takes this information further, showing you how to improve the server and provide the best of all possible operating environments.

The tools discussed in this chapter help gather information that will aid in determining whether your SQL Server system is performing optimally. You need to take data at regular intervals. You should even be collecting data when there are no particular problems or issues. Regularly collecting information will help you establish a server performance baseline. A baseline allows you to compare results of measurements with results taken earlier, and it helps you determine peak and off-peak hours of operation for scheduling of maintenance, provide production-query or batch-command response times, and determine the database backup and restore completion times.

Monitoring and Recording Performance

To gather statistical information on how a server is performing requires, you need to use operating system tools to gather a broad scope of information. System Monitor and Event Viewer are two operating system tools you can use to gather hardware information and information pertaining to the interaction between SQL Server and the operating system.

At the database engine and database level, you use the SQL Profiler by itself and in combination with other SQL Server–specific tools. As you begin to do a more granular inspection, you need to use the Database EngineTuning Advisor (DTA).

You can use a number of specialized techniques for gathering more specific information about the server and its processes. To better understand this information and provide an organized technique for gathering the information, we will begin with current information—information about what is happening on the server now—and progress through the monitoring tools for more granular data.

Using Activity Monitor for the Here and Now

Activity Monitor enables you to determine, at a glance, the volume and general types of activity on the system that are related to current blocked and blocking transactions in the system, connected users, the last statement executed, and locks that are currently in effect. This tool should be familiar to those who have used the Current Activity tool in previous versions of SQL Server. Activity Monitor provides a display of process information; locks, broken down by process identification; and locks, broken down by object.

The process information in Activity Monitor provides information on all activity currently executing against the system. It also lists current connections that may not be active but are still using resources. Activity Monitor has the following process information columns:

▶ **Process ID**—This is the SQL Server process identifier (SPID).

▶ **System Process**—This column identifies whether a process belongs to the system.

▶ **User**—This column identifies the user who executed the command.

▶ **Database**—This column identifies the database currently being used by the process.

▶ **Status**—This is the status of the process.

▶ **Open Transactions**—This is the number of open transactions.

▶ **Command**—This column identifies the command currently being executed.

▶ **Application**—This column identifies the name of the application program being used.

▶ **Wait Time**—This is the current wait time, in milliseconds. When the process is not waiting, the wait time is zero.

▶ **Wait Type**—This is the name of the last or current wait type.

▶ **Wait Resources**—This is a textual representation of a locked resource.

▶ **CPU**—This column identifies the cumulative CPU time for the process.

▶ **Physical IO**—This column identifies the cumulative disk reads and writes.

▶ **Memory Usage**—This is the number of pages in the procedure cache that are currently allocated. A negative number indicates that the process is freeing memory allocated by another process.

▶ **Login Time**—This column identifies the time at which a client process logged in to the server.

▶ **Last Batch**—This column identifies the last time a client process executed a remote stored procedure call or an EXECUTE statement.

▶ **Host**—This is the name of the workstation.

▶ **Network Library**—This is the column in which the client's network library is stored. Every client process comes in on a network connection. Each network connection has a network library associated with it that enables it to make the connection.

▶ **Network Address**—This is the assigned unique identifier for the network interface card on each user's workstation.

▶ **Blocked By**—This is the SPID of a blocking process.

▶ **Blocking**—This is an indicator as to whether a process is blocking others.

▶ **Execution Context**—The execution context identifier is used to uniquely identify the subthreads operating on behalf of a process.

Activity Monitor is a good source for determining the current situations in the server. Filter settings are available to focus the display on a particular area of processing. With the filters set, you can view a specific application, database, user, or other element by simply providing the details to the filter. A limitation of the Activity Monitor is that it provides a current snapshot of the activity on the server and does not record information for future analysis.

Activity Monitor allows you to apply filters to the information shown. By using filters, you can isolate a single application, user, database, or type of process desired. Using filters can make problems easier to find and can identify processes that are being affected by locks and blocking. You can user filters to show processes that are being blocked, doing the blocking, or a combination.

EXAM ALERT

You use the `BlockedAndBlocking` filter from the Blocking Type drop-down to assist in finding deadlocks showing processes that are blocking others as well as being blocked themselves. You use the `BlockedOrBlocking` setting to assist in finding all processes being affected by a lock or set of locks showing any process on either side of the blocking equation.

One of the best uses for the information you obtain from Activity Monitor is to provide a quick determination of the status of locking within the system. This can help isolate problems with processes that interfere with updates, such as locking, blocking, and deadlocks. For ongoing and historical problem analysis, however, this information provides little value, and you need to perform a deeper analysis by using the SQL Server Profiler.

Management Studio: Log File Viewer

SQL Server stores a significant amount of information for future reference. You can find historical events occurring within the database engine and other events that affect the performance of the engine. One set of logs is maintained by the operating system for all applications, and the second is specific to SQL Server. In addition, SQL Server stores a lot of metadata-style information in its own system tables.

In SQL Server 2005, log information is centrally accessible from within Management Studio. The Log File Viewer is a tool that allows you to view the contents of SQL and Windows logs within a single interface. You can even select multiple logs to provide a view that overlays the information from more than one source, as illustrated in Figure 7.1.

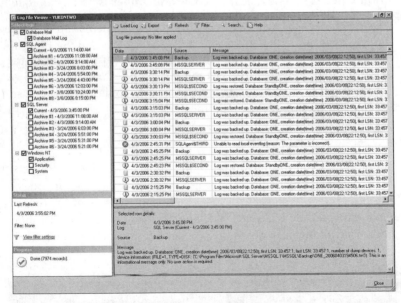

FIGURE 7.1 Overlaying information from multiple logs.

You can find data from Windows Event Viewer in the SQL Server Log Viewer, under the Windows NT tree. There are three primary logs within the viewer: the Application log, Security log, and System log. The Application log maintains the information that is most pertinent to SQL Server. Events recorded in these logs, with the sources MSSQLSERVER, MSSQL$*InstanceName*, SQLSERVERAGENT, and SQLAgent$*InstanceName*.

Windows NT Logs

The information you see in the Log File Viewer is limited to what SQL Server shows for the view and does not provide all the information sometimes needed to resolve the problem. There is usually sufficient information in the error message itself. In some cases, you will find more information about a particular error on the Microsoft website. In that case, it is helpful to open the Application Log from the Windows menu instead of from within Management Studio.

To access further information about the error message online, you open the Application log from the Event Viewer within the Administrative Tools from the Control Panel. To view information for any particular event, you simply double-click the event or right-click the event and select properties from the context menu that appears. You can select the hyperlink to navigate to the Microsoft website, where you find the applicable error information. This link is not provided from within the SQL Server Log File Viewer.

From the Windows NT event logs, you can quickly spot problems and diagnose the steps that led up to any given situation. The Event Viewer and the Log File Viewer both have options available for you to filter events to specific categories and severity. You can also select other computers to view to find additional information about an event.

SQL Server Logs

SQL Server maintains other logs that contain information about the database engine, SQL Server Agent, and Database Mail. The server maintains a set of logs. The Current log contains the events that have occurred since the service was started. Every time you reboot the server or restart the service associated with the log, the logs are advanced.

A considerable amount of information is maintained in the logs. When the logs are cycled, the oldest log is removed, and each archive moves down a position, with the Current log becoming the first archive. In many environments, the log information is periodically exported and permanently stored so that no entries are permanently lost.

These log files are physically stored within the file system. By default, the error log is located at Program Files\Microsoft SQL Server\MSSQL.n\MSSQL\ LOG\ERRORLOG and ERRORLOG.*n* files, where *n* is a sequential number. You can use the sp_cycle_errorlog stored procedure to force the error logs to cycle. This may be desired if the server has been running for a long time without a restart. The procedure cycles the error log files without having to restart the instance of SQL Server.

> **EXAM ALERT**
>
> By default, SQL Server retains the previous six logs in the C:\Program Files\Microsoft SQL Server\MSSQL.n\MSSQL\LOG\ folder. The most recent log has the extension .1, the second .2, and so on. The current error log has no extension. The SQL Server Agent log is stored in C:\Program Files\Microsoft SQL Server\90\mssql90\Log\ as Sqlagent.out.

Both SQL Server logs and the Windows NT application log are useful in helping to identify problems and their causes. Of course, the information in these logs is historical in nature but can help isolate errors.

Server-Maintained Information

SQL Server stores in its many system tables metadata pertaining to objects maintained by the server. *Metadata* is information about the properties of data, such as the type of data in a column (numeric, text, and so on) or the length of a column. It can also be information about the structure of data or information that specifies the design of objects, such as cubes or dimensions.

You can view metadata via direct query from the system tables or through a number of views, functions, and stored procedures. It is recommended that you not query system tables directly but instead use associated views and procedures to gain the necessary information from these tables.

Dynamic Management Functions and Views

Dynamic management views and functions return server state information. You can use this information to monitor the server. These views and functions can assist in diagnosing problems and can provide information that may assist in performance tuning. They also return implementation-specific state information. The structure the views use to return data may change in future releases of SQL Server. Therefore, dynamic management views and functions may not be compatible with future versions of SQL Server and are not recommended for system process design use.

EXAM ALERT

Dynamic management functions and views can be quite useful but are limited for the SQL Server version in which they are associated. You cannot use these functions and views for any process that must remain compatible from version to version.

All dynamic management views and functions exist in the sys schema. All of these objects follow the naming convention dm_*. When you use a dynamic management view or function, you must prefix the name of the view or function by using sys. All view and function names should therefore be similar to sys.dm_*.

Database Console Command (DBCC)

One of the most useful diagnostic/tuning tools available to SQL Server database developers and administrators is the DBCC command. Today, DBCC stands for database console command. In previous versions of SQL Server, it stood for Database Consistency Checker.

DBCC allows you to diagnose and repair some common situations on a server. You can use DBCC statements to check performance statistics and the logical and physical consistency of a database system. Many DBCC statements can fix detected problems. For this reason, DBCC is revisited in Chapter 8.

Some DBCC operations provide useful information about the processes that have been performed most recently on the server. This type of information can be useful in pinpointing the source of SQL activities. Each of the options provides a small piece of a large puzzle, but collectively they can provide a useful picture of the current server activity. The following are some of the most commonly used DBCC options:

▶ **DBCC INPUTBUFFER**—Provides the last statement sent from a client to the server.

▶ **DBCC OPENTRAN**—Provides transaction information for the oldest active transaction, distributed transaction, and nondistributed replicated transaction.

▶ **DBCC OUTPUTBUFFER**—Returns the current output buffer in hexadecimal and ASCII format for the specified SPID.

▶ **DBCC PROCCACHE**—Displays information about the procedure cache.

▶ **DBCC SHOWCONTIG**—Displays fragmentation information for the data and indexes. This is one of the most frequently used DBCC status operations. Because it can display information specific to data and index fragmentation, it is useful in determining when to carry out maintenance operations.

Many other DBCC options are available. To gain a complete understanding of everything DBCC can do, you need to work with it on a regular basis.

> **EXAM ALERT**
>
> Expect to see DBCC options as potential answers for many of the 70-431 exam question scenarios. Useful in gathering information as well as troubleshooting, repairing, and optimizing, DBCC is a commonly used tool for database administrators.

Although DBCC represents one of the most frequently used Microsoft tools available to SQL Server administrators, there are other alternatives for troubleshooting. For example, trace flags have long been used as debugging tools. However, with other graphic tools now available that are easier to use and decipher, the use of trace flags is decreasing. Microsoft has stated that behaviors available with these flags may not be supported in future releases of SQL Server. However, because trace flags are still used today and may appear on the 70-431 exam, the following section discusses them.

Trace Flags

Trace flags display information about specific activities within a server and are used to diagnose problems or performance issues. They are particularly useful in deadlock analysis. Trace flags temporarily set specific server characteristics or switch off particular behaviors. Trace flags are often used to diagnose and debug stored procedures and analyze complex system elements. Four trace flags are commonly used for troubleshooting different elements of SQL Server:

▶ **260**—Determines dynamic link library (DLL) version information. (To determine dynamic link library version information, see the support for GetXPVersion() in SQL Server Books Online, without the use of a flag.)

▶ **1204**—Finds the command affected by deadlock and finds the type of lock.

▶ **2528**—Disables or enables parallel checking of objects during DBCC use. (Parallel DBCC checking should not usually be disabled.)

▶ **3205**—Disables or enables tape drive compression support. (Tape dumps and backups should usually be compressed.)

SQL Server provides many flags to aid in server troubleshooting. The administrator is responsible for specific aspects of the use of the flags and should not put them in place without understanding the repercussions.

Simple Network Management Protocol (SNMP)

SNMP is an industry-standard protocol for monitoring computer systems and other related hardware. An SNMP Manager can query devices throughout the environment. It is possible to query a SQL server that has SNMP installed and enabled to obtain statistical and state information about the server.

By using SNMP, you can monitor SQL Server across different platforms (for example, UNIX and different versions of Microsoft Windows). You can use SNMP applications available from a number of vendors to monitor the status and performance of instances of SQL Server, explore defined databases, and view server and database configuration parameters.

Using Windows System Monitor

Microsoft Windows server operating systems offer the System Monitor graphical tool (formerly known as Performance Monitor [PerfMon]) to measure the performance of all aspects of the server. You can use System Monitor to view SQL Server and other applications from a coarse perspective, looking at events from a high level. You can view SQL Server objects and performance counters by using the System Monitor tool. You can also use it to gather information pertaining to the behavior of processors, memory, cache, and other object resources on the server.

Each object you monitor by using System Monitor has an associated set of counters. These counters are put in place when software is installed in the Windows environment. You can use them to measure aspects of an object, such as device usage, queue lengths, delays, and other factors. In general, when looking at information on how the server as a whole is operating and how application are performing in respect to the server's performance, the System Monitor provides you with optimum benefits.

When you install SQL Server and its related components, several sets of counters are placed in the environment and made available for monitoring. The general list of objects available to be monitored depends on which SQL components have been installed. The following prefixes identify the objects you can monitor in SQL Server:

- ▶ **.NET CLR**—Use this prefix to access the common language runtime.
- ▶ **MSAS 2005**—Use this prefix to access Microsoft Analysis Services.
- ▶ **MSFTESQL**—Use this prefix to access the Microsoft Full-Text engine.
- ▶ **MSRS 2005**—Use this prefix to access Microsoft Reporting Services.

▶ **MSSQL$*InstanceName***—Use this prefix to access a named instance of the database engine.

▶ **SQLAgent$*InstanceName***—Use this prefix to access a named instance of the SQL Server Agent.

▶ **SQLAgent**—Use this prefix to access the default instance of the SQL Server Agent.

▶ **SQLServer**—Use this prefix to access the default instance of the database engine.

Each of the software categories has several related objects, and within each object is a set of one or more counters. Depending on the information you want to gather, you need to select the objects in the software prefix you are looking for and then select one or more counters from that object's list. Each of the software categories has some counters that may be of interest.

Although we could easily spend several chapters going over this one utility, there is no need for that level of coverage on System Monitor for the 70-431 exam. You need to be familiar with a few of the counters; Table 7.1 lists the most important of them.

TABLE 7.1   Common System Monitor Counters

Counter	What It Monitors	Most Commonly Accessed Counts
.NET CLR:Data	Specifics about data connections	Current connections, pooled connections, failed connections
.NET CLR Exceptions	Specifics about exception instances	Exceptions thrown
.NET CLR:Networking	Specifics about data flow through the network	Bytes sent, bytes received
MSAS 2005:Cache	Particulars about the Analysis Services cache	Lookups, hits, misses
MSAS 2005:Memory	Particulars about the memory utilization of Analysis Services	Memory usage
MSAS 2005: Proactive Caching	Particulars about Analysis Services proactive caching use	Notifications
MSFTESQL:Catalogs	Facts about text index catalogs	State

TABLE 7.1 *Continued*

Counter	What It Monitors	Most Commonly Accessed Counts
SQLAgent:Jobs	Data about jobs executed under agent control	Active jobs, failed jobs, queued jobs
SQLAgent:JobSteps	Data about individual job steps	Active steps, queued steps
SQLAgent:Alerts	Data about alerts fired	Activated alerts
SQLServer:Locks	Information about lock requests made	Lock time-outs, deadlocks per second
SQLServer: Plan Cache	Information about the SQL Server cache	Hit ratio, objects in use
SQLServer: Buffer Manager	Information about memory buffers and their use	Buffer cache hit, lazy writes, read-aheads
SQLServer:SQL Statistics	Information about aspects of T-SQL queries	Batch requests
SQLServer:General Statistics	Information about general serverwide activity	Users connected, active temporary tables, logins
SQLServer: Databases	Information about a SQL Server database	Free log space, number of transactions, transactions per second

EXAM ALERT

On Microsoft exams, always be on the lookout for misleading answers. You will find it easiest to answer some of the performance-related questions if you first eliminate the obviously incorrect responses. For example, you should not select any counters that don't deal with the product being monitored. The 70-431 exam is not an operating system exam, so you don't need to know about every counter available.

As you begin any of these processes, you need to begin with the hardware and operating system and then proceed into the application server. As you get further into data gathering and analysis, you should look into each database and the interactions between the data and the user applications. To view SQL Server tasks in detail, after the initial data-gathering processes, you use the SQL Server Profiler to develop a more complete picture.

Using SQL Server Profiler

The SQL Profiler tool is a graphical mechanism that enables you to monitor SQL Server events. This tool enables you to capture and save data about every event on a server. The data can be stored to a file or SQL Server table. You can later analyze stored data replay events. This allows for the scheduling of the Profiler or other execution for deferred analysis, when time permits.

You should use SQL Profiler to monitor only the events of interest. Monitoring all events on the server produces so much data that it can become overwhelming. You can filter large traces so that you view only the information you want to see, such as a single database or single user. You can use filters to view a subset of the event data captured. Monitoring too many events also adds excessive overhead to the server. This overhead can slow the monitoring process and cause the large amounts of output from the trace to create a file or table that is large. This is particularly important when you are performing monitoring over long periods.

It is a good idea not to run the SQL Server Profiler on the same server you are monitoring. Running the Profiler uses considerable resources, and that can noticeably affect the server's performance. Instead, you should run Profiler on another server or workstation that can act as a monitoring machine and have all data collected there.

SQL Profiler is a useful tool that you can use to do the following:

▶ Monitor the performance of SQL Server.

▶ Debug T-SQL statements and stored procedures.

▶ Identify long-running queries.

▶ Step through procedures to ensure that they are working as expected.

▶ Capture events on a production system and replay them on a test system.

▶ Diagnose problem situations by capturing event data.

▶ Audit and review events.

In troubleshooting the SQL Server environment, you typically use SQL Profiler. You can best use this tool to find queries that are not performing well or ones that are executing for long periods. Profiler is also useful in identifying causes of data blocking and deadlock situations. In monitoring a healthy server, you generally use SQL Profiler to monitor performance and to audit application, user, database, and job activity.

> ### CAUTION
>
> Caution! Profiler can affect overall database performance, sometimes significantly, so you should use it sparingly and remember to turn it off as soon as it has captured the necessary information.

Before you start using Profiler, you should become familiar with profile templates. A *template* defines the criteria for each event you want to monitor with SQL Profiler. You can use predefined templates for individual circumstances, and you can create your own templates as well, specifying the events, data columns, and filters to use. You can save a template, and at any time, you can load a trace and then start it with the template settings. To help identify long-running queries, you use Profiler's Create Trace Wizard to run the TSQL_Duration template. You can specify the length of the long-running queries you are trying to identify and then have them recorded in a log.

SQL Profiler captures data by using a trace based on the selected events, data columns, and filters. The trace is the basis for all data collected; you can define a trace on an ad hoc basis, draw a trace from a template, or a combination of the two. Even after you have defined the data collected, you can apply filters to the data after it is captured to focus on the type of information you want. You might therefore want to save traces even after you are finished with the current activity. You can possibly apply a past trace to various circumstances.

At times, when monitoring with Profiler, you may find the amount of data provided to be considerable and possibly overwhelming. It can be difficult to find what you are looking for in a trace that covers a broad range of events. A useful technique that can ease this process is to write a trace to a SQL Server table and then query the table from within the Query Analyzer. If you know what you are looking for, this method can greatly speed up finding the data in the trace you need.

Profiler can store captured data in a text file or in a table. If you decide to store the data in a SQL Server table, you should not store it in a database you are profiling, and, if possible, not even on the same server because it could affect the performance of the server you are profiling. Instead, you should store the trace data in a database on another server. After data is captured (which is the easy part of the process), you must sift through the data collected to draw some meaning from the results.

Profiler can use many existing templates to gather information for various types of circumstances. You might want to select some of them to see what information is being gathered. After a trace is created, it is permanently stored until it is deleted. You can start a trace again by name through the Profiler interface or via a stored procedure.

To use the output generated by a trace, you must first determine what type of data you are most interested in from the trace. The next section describes how to get the most valuable information from the trace results.

Defining a Profiler Trace

When using SQL Profiler to define a trace, you use event categories to select the events to monitor. Event categories are grouped into classes of events, and you can select the following classes:

- **Broker**—Finds events produced by the Service Broker.

- **CLR**—Finds events produced through the loading of assemblies.

- **Cursors**—Finds events produced by the use of cursors.

- **Database**—Finds events produced when files grow or shrink automatically.

- **Deprecation**—Finds events produced by elements of SQL Server that are to be removed in a future release.

- **Errors and Warnings**—Finds events produced when an error or warning occurs.

- **Full Text**—Finds events produced by use of full-text indexing and full-text queries.

- **Locks**—Find events produced when a lock is acquired or other lock activity occurs.

- **OLEDB**—Finds events produced through calls from an OLE DB interface.

- **Objects**—Finds events that occur as objects are created, opened, closed, or deleted.

- **Performance**—Finds events produced when SQL data manipulations execute.

- ▶ **Progress Report**—Finds events produced through online index operations.

- ▶ **Scans**—Finds events produced when tables and indexes are scanned.

- ▶ **Server**—Finds general server events produced.

- ▶ **Security Audit**—Finds events used to audit server activity.

- ▶ **Sessions**—Finds events produced by clients connecting and disconnecting.

- ▶ **Stored Procedures**—Finds events produced by the execution of procedures.

- ▶ **Transactions**—Finds events produced by the execution of Microsoft Distributed Transaction Coordinator transactions or through writing to the transaction log.

- ▶ **TSQL**—Finds events produced by the execution of T-SQL statements.

- ▶ **User Configurable**—Finds user-configurable events.

Each event class can monitor various objects. To select any of the objects when defining a trace, you use the Events tab of the Trace Properties dialog box. You add and remove objects, not whole classes, although you can trace a whole class of objects, if desired.

Using Profiler Traces to Diagnose Locking

SQL Profiler provides the Locks event classes to monitor locking behavior during trace operations. Several of these classes are useful in monitoring locking, blocking, and deadlocking situations on a server:

- ▶ **Lock:Acquired**—This event fires to show the acquisition of a resource lock.

- ▶ **Lock:Cancel**—With this class, an event is fired when a lock on a resource has been cancelled. SQL Server can cancel a lock because of a deadlock or through a programmatic process cancellation.

- ▶ **Lock:Deadlock**—With this class, a deadlock occurs if two concurrent transactions have deadlocked each other by trying to obtain locks on resources that the other owns.

- ▶ **Lock:Deadlock Chain**—With this class, you can see the chain of events produced for each of the processes leading up to a deadlock situation.

- ▶ **Lock:Escalation**—With this class, an event fires when the server determines that a lock should be converted to a larger scope.

- ▶ **Lock:Released**—With this class, an event fires when a resource lock is released.

- ▶ **Lock:Timeout**—This event fires when a lock request has timed out because another process is blocking a resource with its own lock.

You use `Lock:Acquired` and `Lock:Released` to monitor the timing of lock behavior. These events indicate the type of lock and the length of time the lock was held. Often, a redesign of the application that is setting the locks in place can lessen the lock duration considerably.

You use `Lock:Deadlock`, `Lock:Deadlock Chain`, and `Lock:Timeout` to monitor deadlock and timeout situations. This information is useful in determining whether deadlocks and timeouts are affecting the user or application.

EXAM ALERT

Locking is one of the most common aspects queried on the 70-431 exam. You need to remember to first check the current activity to get a snapshot perspective on locking. You use Profiler when you want to analyze locking over time.

The SQL Profiler Results window is segmented into two view panes. If you have included `TextData` as one of the columns in your definition, the bottom pane shows SQL statement information. The top pane illustrates the current trace data view where event information is displayed, based on current filter settings.

After you have collected trace event data, you can save the trace to replay it later. The SQL Profiler Playback feature is powerful but carries a little overhead. It is well worth considering having a test machine available to act as a playback and troubleshooting server.

Playback of events is accomplished through the SQL Server multithreaded playback engine. This engine can simulate user connections and SQL Server authentication. The event data can be played back to reproduce the activity captured in the trace. Replay can be useful in troubleshooting an application or another process problem.

Trace Playback and Diagnosis

After you have identified a problem and implemented corrections, you should run the trace that was originally collected against the corrected application or process to see whether the proposed solution accomplishes the desired effect.

Replaying the original trace can be useful in designing solutions. The trace replay feature has advanced debugging support, enabling you to make use of break points and run-to-cursor features.

When the target computer is going to be a computer other than the computer originally traced, you must ensure that the database IDs on the target are the same as those on the source. You can accomplish this by creating (from the source) a backup of the `master` database as well as any user databases referenced in the trace and restoring them on the target. In this manner, you can use a test server as a debugging server for any multiple-application environment.

The default database for each login contained in a trace must be set on the target. The default database of the trace activity login must be set to the database that matches that login name, even in cases in which the database name might be different. To set the default database of the login, you use the `sp_defaultdb` system stored procedure.

You have the option of replaying the events in the order in which they were traced. This option enables debugging, which means you can implement debugging techniques such as stepping through the trace. You can replay the events using multiple threads to optimize performance; however, this disables debugging. The default option is to display the results of the replay. If the trace you want to replay is a large capture, you might want to disable this option to save disk space.

Using Profiler to Gather a Workload

One of the most common uses of Profiler is to collect an event's workload sampling for tuning the physical database. You can analyze the database design from a workload file by using the DTA. SQL Server Profiler provides a predefined Tuning template that gathers the appropriate T-SQL events in the trace output so it can be used as a workload for the DTA.

The DTA can use a workload file generated by Profiler to analyze performance effects. After analyzing the effects of a workload on a databases, DTA provides recommendations to add, remove, or modify physical design structures. These physical performance structures include clustered indexes, nonclustered indexes, indexed views, and partitioning. Chapter 8 discusses the DTA in more detail.

Exam Prep Questions

1. You need a sample of database query activity to discover whether you can speed up transactions. You would like to replay the sample on another SQL Server computer. You need to capture the sample, but you want to minimize any increase to the workload of the server. What should you do?

   ○ **A.** Run Profiler on a client computer. Configure SQL Profiler to monitor database activity and log data to a `.trc` file.

   ○ **B.** Run Profiler on the server. Configure SQL Profiler to monitor database activity and log data to a database table.

   ○ **C.** Run System Monitor on a client computer. Configure System Monitor to monitor database activity and log data to a `.blg` file.

   ○ **D.** Start SQL Server from a command prompt. Specify trace flag `1204` to enable verbose logging.

2. The company website has grown in popularity, and database utilization has increased. You need to collect data about the utilization of server resources so that you can provide capacity planning. You want to automate the collection process so that information is gathered as quickly as possible. What should you do?

   ○ **A.** Configure System Monitor to collect data and store it in a SQL Server table.

   ○ **B.** Create a job that executes the `sp_statistics` stored procedure daily.

   ○ **C.** Use SQL Profiler to trace server activity and store the results in tables.

   ○ **D.** Configure alerts to store information in the Windows application event log.

3. You have a mission-critical application that runs in the context of the company's server. Database activity is high during the day because sales transactions are entered through network point-of-sale terminals. Sales clerks are reporting that transactions are taking too much time and customers are annoyed with the waiting period for updates to information. What would you do to diagnose the situation?

   ○ **A.** Increase the amount of memory on the server.

   ○ **B.** Upgrade the processor on the server or move to a multiple-processor machine.

   ○ **C.** Use `sp_configure` to increase the number of locks available to the server.

   ○ **D.** Run SQL Profiler in the day and use the output for the DTA.

   ○ **E.** Run SQL Profiler in off-peak times and use the output for the Tuning Wizard.

4. A user is reporting that a message that says "unable to perform update, batch is in use" is coming from his application. You suspect that another user's data updates are causing locks within the system. What should you do?

- ○ **A.** Restart the SQL Server service to clear all current locks.

- ○ **B.** Run SQL Server Profiler and trace activity to find where the locks are coming from.

- ○ **C.** Use Activity Monitor to locate the user who is performing updates and have the user complete his or her activity.

- ○ **D.** Use System Monitor to observe the `SQLServer:Locks` counters.

5. You are trying to locate information about an error that occurred in the database engine several days ago. You know that the server has been rebooted three times since the problem occurred. Where could you look to find the error details? (Select all that apply.)

- ○ **A.** The Windows system log

- ○ **B.** The Windows application log

- ○ **C.** The `Errorlog.3` file

- ○ **D.** The `Errorlog` file

- ○ **E.** `SQLAgent.out`

- ○ **F.** SQL Server Archive #3 of the Log File Viewer

- ○ **G.** SQL Agent Archive #3 of the Log File Viewer

6. You are trying to document detailed activity on the server utilization and at the same time use the information gathered to view information about specific tables. What should you do?

- ○ **A.** Configure System Monitor to collect data and store it in a SQL Server table.

- ○ **B.** Create a job that executes the `sp_statistics` stored procedure daily.

- ○ **C.** Use SQL Profiler to trace server activity and store the results in tables.

- ○ **D.** Configure alerts to store information in the Windows application event log.

Answers to Exam Prep Questions

1. **A.** Although it would be most desirable to run the query on another server, it is always best to select a machine other than the production machine to absorb the overhead of running Profiler. For more information, see the section "Using SQL Server Profiler."

2. **C.** To monitor detailed activity of SQL Server, you should use the SQL Server Profiler and configure a trace to take in the necessary data and filter for the desired objects. For more information, see the section "Using SQL Server Profiler."

3. **D.** You need to perform some diagnosis during the period in which the issues exist. There is no sense in changing the physical configuration of the server until some diagnosis has been performed. Although adding memory and/or upgrading the processor may improve the situation, it is impossible to know whether that is even an issue before you perform some tests. SQL Profiler tests should be performed during activity; to get an accurate reading of the database usage, a Profiler trace should be performed during the day when the system is being used. For more information, see the section "Using SQL Server Profiler."

4. **C.** To find information about what is currently occurring, you use Activity Monitor. Of course, the problem could be resolved by restarting the service, but that is extremely hazardous in a production environment and could corrupt data. SQL Server Profiler can only track down locking that is going to occur or that regularly occurs; starting a trace does not identify anything that is currently in place. System Monitor could provide only quantitative information about locks; it cannot isolate how a lock was put in place. For more information, see the section "Using Activity Monitor for the Here and Now."

5. **B, C, F.** Because the error occurred in the database engine, you could find it logged to the Windows application and SQL Server logs. Because the server has been rebooted three times, it would be within the third archive, and this archive would have the extension .3. For more information, see the section "Management Studio: Log File Viewer."

6. **C.** To monitor detailed activity in SQL Server, you should use SQL Server Profiler and configure a trace to take in the necessary data, and should also filter for the desired objects. For more information, see the section "Using SQL Server Profiler."

CHAPTER EIGHT

Troubleshooting and Optimizing SQL Server

Terms you'll need to understand:

- ✓ Statistics
- ✓ Execution plan
- ✓ Query Optimizer
- ✓ Database Engine Tuning Advisor (DTA)
- ✓ Lock
- ✓ Block
- ✓ Deadlock
- ✓ Fill factor
- ✓ Clustered and nonclustered indexes
- ✓ Covering indexes
- ✓ Database console command (DBCC)
- ✓ Alerts

Techniques you'll need to master:

- ✓ Creating, updating, and maintaining statistics
- ✓ Using the DTA
- ✓ Finding and resolving locking issues
- ✓ Creating and configuring indexing for performance
- ✓ Using partitioning to improve performance
- ✓ Utilizing DBCC to troubleshoot and repair databases

The topics of troubleshooting and optimization are closely related. Often, the problem you have to troubleshoot is directly associated with performance and resource utilization. Your ability to adjust the configuration to achieve the optimal environment depends on the quality of information the changes are based on. For that reason, both troubleshooting and optimization rely heavily on server monitoring, which is covered in Chapter 7, "Monitoring SQL Server Performance." This chapter attempts to take information gathered, troubleshoot bottlenecks and other problems, and make recommendations that will help improve the performance and stability of the system.

Data Analysis and Problem Diagnosis

It is a given that in any computerized environment, things will not be perfect. Machines break down. Programs have bugs. Users make mistakes. Most systems are not optimized from the outset. Imperfections should be expected as part of automation. It is a good thing that in this day and age, tools are available to troubleshoot problems, analyze performance, and implement changes to improve systems. In particular, SQL Server and the Windows operating system provide the mechanisms needed to perform standard database management troubleshooting. Let us begin by looking at the diagnosis and resolution of some common problems.

Tuning the Operating System and Hardware

Much of the performance of any database system relies on the application and database designers. The use of the network, processor, memory, and disk storage can all be dictated by the type of database design and the use of the applications operating against the database server. For this reason, the operating system usually acts as only a starting point in any performance analysis testing. If the hardware configuration is not adequate and the operating system is not properly configured, the database engine will not be able to respond optimally.

The first task that the hardware and operating system serve in any database system is to provide a means to store and operate the database software and objects. The operating system is also responsible for reporting hardware and software problems, as well as making it possible for you to monitor everything executing on the machine.

The minimum hardware for a SQL Server installation in production is somewhat laughable. To review recommended hardware configurations, reread the section "Preparations for Installation" in Chapter 1, "Installing and Configuring SQL Server 2005." Hardware discussions and operating system tweaks over and above what we have already discussed are beyond the scope of this book because the 70-431 exam does not tend to test on them.

EXAM ALERT

The 70-431 exam may include a question concerning RAID configurations. Ensure that you are comfortable with the definitions for RAID 0, RAID 1, and RAID 5, as well as where they would be used in a database installation. RAID 0 is good for data files because it provides good performance. RAID 1 is good for logs because it provides for 100% recovery. RAID 5 is poor performing and should not be used in production.

Creating and Maintaining Statistics

The SQL Server Query Optimizer is the database engine component of SQL Server 2005. As the database engine, it oversees all data-related interaction. It is responsible for generating the execution plans for any SQL operation. In diagnosing a query, the Optimizer must decide on the most efficient means of executing the query and interacting with the database objects.

SQL Server has a cost-based optimizer that can be extremely sensitive to the information provided by statistics. Without accurate and up-to-date statistical information, SQL Server has a great deal of difficulty determining the best execution plan for a particular query.

Often, non-updated statistics cause a system to slow and become unresponsive over time. Periodically checking and using UPDATE STATISTICS on most production systems is warranted.

EXAM ALERT

You should know all the settings that affect the creation and updating of statistics. Database properties should be set to Auto Create Statistics and Auto Update Statistics. You can use the Create Statistics statement to add to the default set of statistics and the Update Statistics command to ensure that statistics are up-to-date.

SQL Server goes through a considerable process when it chooses one execution plan out of several possible methods of executing a given operation. This optimization is one of the most important components of a SQL Server database system. Although the Optimizer's analysis process incurs some overhead, that overhead is saved in execution.

The Optimizer uses a cost-based analysis procedure. Each possible method of execution has an associated cost, which is determined in terms of the approximate amount of computing resources used in execution. The Query Optimizer must analyze the possible plans and choose the one that has the lowest estimated cost.

It is not uncommon for some complex SELECT statements to have thousands of possible plans. Of course, in such a case, the Optimizer does not analyze every possible combination. It uses a complex series of processes to find a plan that has a cost that is reasonably close to the minimum—a minimum that is only theoretical and unlikely to be achieved.

The SQL Server Optimizer generally makes the best choice for any given execution. It is possible to override the Optimizer's choices by using code and forcing the execution with hints; however, this is not recommended without significant testing. When a query using hints performs better, you usually implement additional indexing instead of using the hint in production.

Locks, Blocks, and Deadlocks

One of the hallmarks of a true database management system (DBMS) is whether it has the capability to handle more than one user performing simultaneous data modifications. The problem is that when several users in a database make changes, it is likely that they will eventually want to update the same record(s) at the same time. To avoid the problems this would cause, SQL Server and most other DBMSs provide a locking mechanism.

A locking mechanism provides a way to check out a particular row or set of rows from the database so that they cannot be changed by another user until the connection is finished and the changes are made. For connections that are reading data, locking provides a mechanism to prevent other connections from changing the data for the duration of the read or longer. There are two basic types of locks:

- ▶ **Shared locks**—A shared lock occurs when a user is trying to read a row of data; for some duration, depending on the transaction isolation level (which is covered later in this chapter in the "Levels of Locks" section), the user owns a shared lock on the table. Because the user is just trying to read the record, there can be several shared locks on the row, so many people can read the same record at the same time.

- ▶ **Exclusive locks**—A user obtains an exclusive lock when he or she needs to change the row. Exclusive locks are not shared; there can be only one user with an exclusive lock on a row at any given time. If a user needs to acquire an exclusive lock to a row that is already locked by another user, lock contention occurs. Some level of contention is normal in a database that is frequently updated. Typically, an application waits for some arbitrary amount of time for the locks to clear and the transaction to complete. This results in an apparent slowdown of the application and the server, and excessive amounts of contention lead to performance degradation and possibly user complaints.

Reducing Lock Contention

There are a few things you can do to reduce lock contention. First, you can make transactions as simple as possible and keep extraneous logic out of transactions. The best case is when you do all the gathering of data and validation of that data outside the transaction, and the transaction is used only to update and insert rows. Second, you should make sure that the application does not have any transactions that wait for user input because users tend to do such things as go to lunch while they have windows open, waiting for them to enter data to complete their transactions.

In general, you should try to collect all the data at once, and then you should start the transaction, make the changes, and commit the changes. You should design applications and databases with concurrency in mind. You should keep tables that are frequently updated small by moving columns that don't belong in the table or that aren't changed very often into another table. If a table is going to be updated frequently, you should make sure that it isn't indexed more than necessary. Data modification statements, such as INSERT, UPDATE, and DELETE, have to change the indexes as they go, so having too many indexes on a table requires them to modify several indexes.

> **EXAM ALERT**
>
> You can view blocked access through Activity Monitor. You can see which process is being blocked and the process that is doing the blocking. For counts on the numbers of locks in place and statistical information related to locking, you use System Monitor. For more specific troubleshooting of locking behaviors and deadlock activity, you can use SQL Server Profiler.

With contention also comes a circumstance known as a *deadlock*. A deadlock occurs when two processes are locking resources and each one wants the resource that the other has locked. Deadlocks occur when two or more transactions cannot complete because of mutual locks. SQL Server detects a deadlock and rather randomly kills one of the user processes.

Levels of Locks

In addition to using shared and exclusive locks, SQL Server also locks objects at different levels. SQL Server can lock a single row of a table, a single data page, or an entire table.

Typically, SQL Server operates in the page lock mode, in which it locks the data pages being requested. After a certain amount of blocking is noticed, SQL Server slips into a row locking mode, in which single rows are locked.

On the other end of the scale, when a connection attempts to update a certain percentage of a table, SQL Server automatically escalates to a table lock, in which it automatically locks the entire table either exclusively (in the case of a full table update) or in a shared mode (in the case of a full table read). SQL Server also determines lock escalation based on the activity occurring in the table at the time of the lock request. If the activity level is low, SQL Server saves itself some time by escalating the lock sooner so that it has less effect on other users.

There are shared page locks, shared row locks, and shared table locks for reads, along with exclusive page locks, exclusive row locks, and exclusive table locks for writes. Locks and the control of locking behavior are important in DBMSs. To aid in management over a DBMS, you can also implement transactions that directly affect locking behavior. The following section explains how to do this.

Diagnosing Lock Problems

You can diagnose lock, block, and deadlock problems by using the System Monitor (How many are occurring?), Activity Monitor (What is currently occurring?), and SQL Server Profiler (What series of events causes the problem?). A number of stored procedures, dynamic management views or functions, and system tables can also provide information about locking.

Locking-Related Stored Procedures

The sp_lock stored procedure reports snapshot information about locks, including the object ID, index ID, type of lock, and type or resource to which the lock applies. The sp_lock procedure is also a Transact-SQL (T-SQL) alternative that you can use to view lock activity in the Activity Monitor in SQL Server Management Studio. The sp_lock procedure is provided only for backward compatibility and is considered a deprecated function. You may want to query locking information from dynamic management views as an alternative.

Locking-Related Dynamic Management Views

You can query the sys.dm_tran_locks dynamic management view to obtain information about the current state of locking. This is a preferred source of information in SQL Server 2005, although, as with all other dynamic views, it is supported only within the current version of SQL Server.

You can use the sys.dm_exec_sessions view to retrieve information about processes currently running on the server, and you can use sys.dm_exec_requests to get further information about procedures blocking an execution request.

SQL Server Profiler Lock Events

You can use SQL Server Profiler to trap several lock events:

- **Deadlock Graph Event Class**—Provides an XML description of a deadlock.

- **Lock:Acquired Event Class**—Indicates whether a lock has been acquired on a resource.

- **Lock:Cancel Event Class**—Tracks requests for locks that were canceled before the locks were acquired.

- **Lock:Deadlock Chain Event Class**—Is used to monitor when deadlock conditions occur and which objects are involved.

- **Lock:Deadlock Event Class**—Tracks when a transaction has requested a lock on a resource already locked by another transaction, resulting in a deadlock.

- **Lock:Escalation Event Class**—Indicates that a finer-grained lock has been converted to a coarser-grained lock.

- **Lock:Released Event Class**—Tracks when a lock is released.

- **Lock:Timeout (timeout > 0) Event Class**—Tracks when lock requests cannot be completed because another transaction has a blocking lock on the requested resource.

- **Lock:Timeout Event Class**—Tracks when lock requests cannot be completed because another transaction has a blocking lock on the requested resource.

It is a good idea to trap most of these events if you are using SQL Server Profiler as a means of diagnosing locking and deadlocks in applications.

System Monitor Lock Counters

The SQLServer:Locks object provides information on locking. Minimizing locks increases concurrency, which can improve performance. You can monitor multiple instances of the Locks object at the same time. The following are the available SQL Server Locks counters:

- **Average Wait Time (ms)**—Monitors the average time (in milliseconds) for each lock request.

- **Lock Requests/sec**—Monitors the number of new locks and lock conversions per second.

▶ **Lock Timeouts (timeout > 0)/sec**—Monitors the number of lock requests per second that timed out, excluding NOWAIT locks.

▶ **Lock Timeouts/sec**—Monitors the number of lock requests per second that timed out, including NOWAIT locks.

▶ **Lock Wait Time (ms)**—Monitors the total wait time (in milliseconds) for locks.

▶ **Lock Waits/sec**—Monitors the number of lock requests per second that required the caller to wait.

▶ **Number of Deadlocks/sec**—Monitors the number of lock requests per second that resulted in deadlock.

Obviously, you want the number of deadlocks per second to be non-existent, but this is the most common counter utilized when monitoring locking behavior.

Tuning the Database Structure

From the first stages of the database design, you make decisions that directly affect performance. Many tools are available to assist with the tuning of a database after you begin the implementation, but it is important to consider the design from the outset. Many performance gains can come out of the database design itself.

The table structures and relationships, indexing, and other physical objects contribute to performance gains. You need to consider controlling the environment right from the beginning of any project. The following sections describe some of these techniques.

Indexing Strategies

A lot of factors affect SQL Server and the applications that use its data resources. Improving performance and response time from a server are primary concerns of database developers and administrators. One key element in obtaining the utmost from a database is having an indexing strategy that helps to achieve the business needs of the enterprise, in part by returning data from queries in a responsive fashion.

You can use one clustered index per table, If a clustered index is implemented, it determines the physical order of the data. Nonclustered indexes act like those in the back of a book—pointing out the physical location of the data. You can create nonclustered covering indexes in cases in which the exact query content is known. This means the indexes include all columns referenced by the query.

Keys, ranges, and unique values are strong selections for index candidates. Seldom-used data, binary data, and repeating values are weaker index candidates. After you have selected index candidates, you need to monitor application usage. You can adjust the indexing strategy regularly to provide reliably high performance.

Until you understand the implications of indexes, you should not use a lot of them throughout your table structures. Although indexes provide good query performance, they can also take away from other processes. You can expect performance to degrade when performing updates against the data:

▶ Indexes consume hardware resources and processing cycles.

▶ Memory overhead is associated with index use.

▶ Regular maintenance is required to keep indexes at optimum levels.

▶ Many database processes have to work within the presence of the index.

EXAM ALERT

Any SQL Server indexing strategy should begin with the most basic element of providing a primary index, but there are more advanced tuning and design considerations, as well. The 70-431 exam covers indexing in many categories, including index selection, tuning, maintenance, and specialty implementations.

What to Index

Column selection is a major step in the process of indexing. In general, you should consider indexing on columns that are frequently accessed by WHERE, ORDER BY, and JOIN clauses. When you build indexes, you should try to narrow them down to the minimum number of columns needed. Multicolumn indexes have a negative impact on performance. Columns with unique values serving as primary keys are also good candidates.

The challenge for a database designer is to build a physical data model that provides efficient data access. This can be done by minimizing I/O processing time. The following columns are good ones to index:

▶ A column that acts as the table's primary or foreign key

▶ Columns that are regularly sorted by the ORDER BY clause

▶ Columns that are filtered on an exact condition, using the WHERE clause (for instance, WHERE state= 'Ca')

▶ Columns that are queried on joins

▶ Columns that hold integer values rather than character values

▶ Searches for rows with search key values in a range of values (for example, WHERE Royalty BETWEEN 1000 and 4000)

▶ Queries that use the like clause, but only if they start with character data (for example, WHERE au_fname LIKE 'sm%')

The true test of any indexing strategy occurs when queries are processed during day-to-day operations.

What Not to Index

Strong guidelines exist on what should not be indexed. You really can't and shouldn't index all the columns in a table. Doing so would significantly decrease performance on insertions and deletions, even though most queries would run fast. When determining whether to index a small table, you should determine whether more page reads are needed to scan the index than there are pages in the table. In such a case, an index would hurt performance, not help it. Therefore, a table with fewer than three pages is not helped by any index.

You should learn to use the SQL Server Query Analyzer tool as a guide for whether an index is useful. You need to recognize table scans; the process of reading all records from a table in sequence may take fewer cycles than accessing an index first—particularly on small tables.

The following are some conditions under which you should not index a column:

▶ If the index is never used by the Query Optimizer

▶ If the column values exhibit low selectivity, often greater than 95% for nonclustered indexes

▶ If the columns to be indexed are very wide

▶ If the table is rarely queried

▶ If the columns are not used in WHERE clauses, aggregated, or used in sorting or in JOIN operations

Using indexes involves many trade-offs. Although queries may show a performance improvement, INSERT, UPDATE, and DELETE operations could see a decline in performance. You might not know the power of indexes until you perform large searches on tables that have tens of thousands of rows. Implementing an indexing strategy would not be proper for a small database with a few tables containing no more than 50 rows.

Indexing has the following benefits:

- ► Indexes help increase efficiency on complex searches on large tables.

- ► Indexes are easy to implement.

- ► Indexes can be used to enforce uniqueness throughout rows in tables.

Indexed Views

Creating indexes against a view is new to SQL Server 2005. With this functionality, you can provide a few advanced implementations. You need to pay particular attention to restrictions and required settings because they are sure to be covered on the exam.

An indexed view is a materialized view, which means it has been computed and stored. You index a view by creating a unique clustered index. Indexed views dramatically improve the performance of queries that aggregate many rows. However, they are not well suited for underlying data sets that are frequently updated.

Revisiting Indexing Postimplementation

It is a rarity for any complex database system design to implement all the right indexes on the first attempt. You can use the DTA to analyze existing index structures against a workload to determine what changes need to be implemented.

You should also periodically perform maintenance on existing indexes through defragmentation and rebuilding of index structures. You can use the ALTER INDEX command with the REORGANIZE option to defragment an index, and using the REBUILD option drops the existing index and then re-creates it. The REBUILD statement is preferred over DBCC DBREINDEX, which you can still use now but will be removed in a future version.

Leaving Space for Inserts (Fill Factor)

Fill factor is the percentage at which SQL Server fills leaf-level pages upon creation of indexes. Provision for empty pages enables the server to insert additional rows without performing a page-split operation. (A page split occurs when a new row is inserted into a table that has no empty space for its placement.) As the storage pages fill, page splits occur, and this can hamper performance and increase fragmentation. The fill factor is a configuration option that you set through the Enterprise Manager or the sp_configure stored procedure.

You normally find that queries (which read of existing data) outweigh data updates by a substantial margin. Providing extra room slows down the query process as empty space must be transversed during the reading process. Therefore, you might not want to adjust the fill factor value at all in static systems, where there are smaller numbers of additions.

Setting the fill factor too low hampers read performance because the server must negotiate a series of empty pages to fetch the desired data. It is beneficial to specify a fill factor when you create an index on a table that already has data and will have a high volume of inserts. If you do not specify this setting when creating an index, the server default fill factor setting is chosen.

The percentage value for the fill factor is not maintained over time; it applies only at the time of creation. Therefore, if inserts into a table occur frequently, it is important to take maintenance measures for rebuilding the indexes to ensure that the empty space is put back in place. You can rebuild a specific index by using the CREATE INDEX T-SQL command with the DROP EXISTING option. In addition, you can defragment indexes by using the DBCC INDEXDEFRAG command, which also reapplies the fill factor.

The pad index setting, which is closely related to the setting for fill factor, allows space to be left in non-leaf levels. You cannot specify the pad index by itself, and you can use it only if you supply a fill factor. You do not provide a value for this setting; it matches the setting given for the fill factor.

Data Partitioning Across Servers

You may be able to improve query performance by partitioning a table or an index or creating a partitioned view. This depends on the types of queries that are most frequently run and on the hardware configuration.

Partitioned Views

A partitioned view joins horizontally partitioned data. The data is presented as a single rowset, although it may come from a set of member tables across one or more servers. The view can be created from a set of member tables on the same instance; creating a local partitioned view in this manner is included for backward compatibility. The preferred method for partitioning data locally is by using partitioned tables.

Partitioned views can be created from member tables across multiple servers, creating a distributed partitioned view and forming a federation of database servers. A *federation* is simply a group of servers administered independently but that cooperate to share the processing and data storage. Forming a federation of database servers by partitioning data lets you scale out a set of servers to support the processing requirements of large, multitiered websites.

Partitioned Tables and Indexes

If queries that involve equi-joins are frequently run, improved performance may result if the partitioning columns are the same as the columns on which the tables are joined.

In partitioning scenarios, the tables or their indexes should be collocated, which means they should either use the same named partition function or use different ones that are essentially performing the same division. Partition functions are considered equivalent when they have the same number of parameters of corresponding data types, define the same number of partitions, and define the same boundary values for partitions.

The Query Optimizer can process a join faster, because the partitions can be joined. If a query joins two tables that are not partitioned on the join field, the presence of partitions may actually slow query processing.

Partitioning generally improves performance because of the addition of hardware components that work together to retrieve data. However, you need to be careful when you configure partitions. If partitions are mapped to filegroups, each accessing a different physical disk drive, data is sorted first by partition. SQL Server accesses one drive at a time under this mapping, and that reduces performance. A better configuration of partitions is to stripe data files of the partitions across more than one disk by using RAID 0.

Using the DTA

The DTA is a tool that analyzes database performance. You run workloads created using SQL Server Profiler against one or more databases. The DTA provides recommendations to add, remove, or modify clustered indexes, nonclustered indexes, indexed views, and/or partitioning.

The DTA has two interfaces: a standalone graphical interface and a command-line utility program, dta.exe, for DTA functionality in software programs and scripts.

In versions of SQL Server prior to SQL Server 2005, some of the DTA functionality was available within the Index Tuning Wizard. The DTA evaluates more types of events and structures than the Index Tuning Wizard, and it provides higher-quality recommendations as well.

> **EXAM ALERT**
>
> You can expect to see questions about the DTA on the 70-431 exam. In particular, you need to know the variety of settings that are available to provide variations on the diagnosis process.

The DTA provides a variety of settings so that you can specify objects to analyze and structures to maintain, and it provides advanced settings for online index recommendations. You can use these settings to specify how the DTA is to perform its analysis. Figure 8.1 shows the DTA interface and its available options.

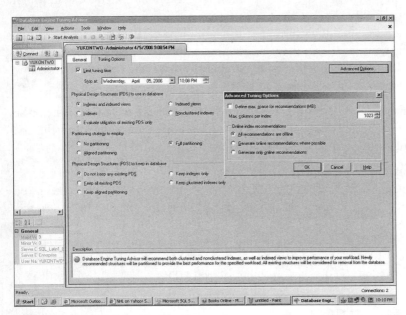

FIGURE 8.1 The DTA graphical interface.

The DTA has two groups of physical design structures (PDS) settings. The first, near the top of the interface, allows for the selection of potential new structures to analyze for inclusion in the database. The second, on the bottom of the interface, allows for the selection of existing PDS elements to keep in the database and not analyze for removal.

When analyzing existing structures by using the DTA, if you want no additional PDS structures implemented, you can select the Evaluate Utilization of Existing PDS Only option from the Physical Design Structures (PDS) to Use in the Database area of the DTA. Alternatively, you can select the Do Not Keep Any Existing PDS option from the Physical Design Structures (PDS) to Keep in the Database area of the dialog to evaluate all existing structures.

Within the Partitioning Strategy to Employ section of the DTA, you can identify the style of partitioning to analyze for implementation. You can select anything from no analysis to full analysis. The Aligned Partitioning option recommends only partitions that are aligned with existing partitions.

Within the Advanced Tuning Options section of the DTA, you can identify the online index recommendations. The selection All Recommendations Are Offline generates the best recommendations possible, but it does not recommend that any physical design structures be created online. The option Generate Online Recommendations Where Possible chooses methods that can be implemented with the server online. This analysis occurs even if the implementation can be performed faster offline. The Generate Only Online Recommendations selection makes only recommendations that allow the server to stay online.

Server Configuration Maintenance

Several maintenance activities should be performed regularly. Over time, a database becomes fragmented and is likely to become much larger than needed. You might want to shrink database files because setting them to automatically shrink causes a performance hit on the system.

You should configure maintenance plans for most of the databases on a server to ensure that they are operating optimally. You can use maintenance plans to create a workflow of the maintenance tasks required to make sure that your database performs well, is regularly backed up in case of system failure, and is checked for inconsistencies.

You can use the Maintenance Plan Wizard to create core maintenance plans and to initiate maintenance workflows. After you create plans by using this wizard, you can make modifications and additions to these plans manually, which gives you quite a bit of flexibility. In the SQL Server 2005 database engine, maintenance plans create a job that performs these maintenance tasks automatically at scheduled intervals.

Using the Database Console Command (DBCC)

A number of DBCC operations should be performed periodically. You can effectively use many of the DBCC options in troubleshooting. The following options can provide valuable data to help you determine how to improve performance:

- ▶ **DBCC SHOW_STATISTICS**—Displays the current distribution statistics for the specified target on the specified table.

- ▶ **DBCC SQLPERF**—Provides statistics about the use of transaction log space in all databases.

▶ **DBCC TRACESTATUS**—Displays the status of trace flags.

▶ **DBCC USEROPTIONS**—Returns the SET options that are active (that is, set) for the current connection.

EXAM ALERT

DBCC SHOW_STATISTICS displays the current statistic distribution, and DBCC SQLPERF provides information about available log space. All DBCC operations will be supported going forward, unlike the dynamic views sys.dm_db_index_ operationalstats and sys.dm_db_index_physicalstats, which provide the same information but may not be supported in the next version.

DBCC Validation Operations

After status information has been generated, the next task in information retrieval is obtaining validation data, which can also give you insight into a server. The validation options represent tools that can reveal database storage problems and also provide the mechanisms to modify and fine-tune the environment. To validate various objects on a server, you can use the following:

▶ **DBCC CHECKALLOC**—Checks the consistency of disk space.

▶ **DBCC CHECKCATALOG**—Checks for consistency in system tables.

▶ **DBCC CHECKCONSTRAINTS**—Checks the integrity of constraints.

▶ **DBCC CHECKDB**—Checks the allocation and structural integrity of all the objects in a database.

▶ **DBCC CHECKFILEGROUP**—Checks the allocation and structural integrity of tables in a filegroup.

▶ **DBCC CHECKIDENT**—Checks the current identity value for a table and, if needed, corrects the value.

▶ **DBCC CHECKTABLE**—Checks the integrity of the data, index, text, ntext, and image pages.

▶ **DBCC NEWALLOC**—Checks the allocation of data and index pages. It is equivalent to CHECKALLOC and is used for backward compatibility only.

NOTE

Use of CHECKALLOC is unnecessary if CHECKDB is used first. CHECKDB contains a superset of options that includes all the functionality provided by CHECKALLOC.

Some of these functions are CPU and disk intensive. You should exercise caution about the time of day you perform a DBCC CHECKDB operation. Other functions can also affect the server and temporarily increase system overhead.

EXAM ALERT

On the 70-431 exam, you might see a question that provides a series of the CHECK options and expects you to know the granularity of what is being checked by the operation. Therefore, be familiar with each of the options in the previous list.

NOTE

DBCC DBREPAIR was never used often, and has been removed from the product. It is recommended that you use DROP DATABASE to drop damaged databases. DBCC DBREPAIR is no longer supported.

DBCC Maintenance Operations

Regular maintenance is needed in all database environments. Data and index pages become fragmented. Data may become corrupt, and file sizes may need to be adjusted. Regular maintenance helps you optimize the server environment. The DBCC options that you use in maintenance processes are as follows:

- ▶ **DBCC DBREINDEX**—Rebuilds one or more indexes.

- ▶ **DBCC INDEXDEFRAG**—Defragments clustered and secondary indexes of the specified table or view.

- ▶ **DBCC SHRINKDATABASE**—Shrinks the size of the data files in the specified database.

- ▶ **DBCC SHRINKFILE**—Shrinks a specified data file or log file.

- ▶ **DBCC UPDATEUSAGE**—Reports and corrects inaccuracies in the sysindexes table, which may result in incorrect space use reported by sp_spaceused.

Miscellaneous DBCC Operations

Some DBCC options do not directly fit into any of the categories described so far in this chapter. Listed as miscellaneous options, these DBCC operations can provide assistance, help to free and better use resources, and provide some tracking mechanisms:

▶ **DBCC dllname (FREE)**—Unloads the specified extended stored procedure DLL from memory.

▶ **DBCC HELP**—Returns syntax information for the specified DBCC statement.

▶ **DBCC PINTABLE**—Marks a table to be pinned and does not flush the pages for the table from memory.

▶ **DBCC ROWLOCK**—Is used for Microsoft SQL Server 6.5, enabling insert row locking operations on tables.

▶ **DBCC TRACEOFF**—Disables trace flags. (Trace flags are discussed in the next section.)

▶ **DBCC TRACEON**—Enables trace flags. (Trace flags are discussed completely in the next section.)

▶ **DBCC UNPINTABLE**—Marks a table as unpinned. Table pages in the buffer cache can be flushed.

NOTE

The DBCC ROWLOCK option is somewhat antiquated. Row-level locking is enabled by default in SQL Server 2005, where the locking strategy is row locking with possible promotion to page or table locking. DBCC ROWLOCK is included in SQL Server 2005 for backward compatibility. In a future version of SQL Server, DBCC ROWLOCK may not be supported.

Setting Alerts to Automate Problem Identification

SQL Server Agent can monitor performance conditions and fire alerts when specific thresholds are met. This can help in notifying an administrator when disk space is running low or when applications are unresponsive. You can also set up alerts to fire based on criteria within the data. You are not likely to run into this on the 70-431 exam, but it is a useful feature of SQL Server.

Exam Prep Questions

1. You are working for a small manufacturing company that has been operating well for some time. Lately, the end users have been reporting that when performing queries against information on customers, the system is growing increasingly slow. After examining the system, you determine that the table definition has recently been altered. You want the response time to improve and be similar to what it was before the change. How would you fix the problem?

   - ○ **A.** Run DBCC DBREINDEX.

   - ○ **B.** Drop and re-create the table's clustered index.

   - ○ **C.** Drop and re-create all indexes.

   - ○ **D.** Update the index statistics.

   - ○ **E.** Stop and restart the server.

2. You are working on a database implementation in a production environment. You would like to perform analysis on the server hosting the database. You need to get detailed information on the types of queries being performed and the locking effects of all operations. Which tool should you use?

   - ○ **A.** Event Viewer

   - ○ **B.** SQL Server Profiler

   - ○ **C.** System Monitor

   - ○ **D.** Activity Monitor

   - ○ **E.** Database Engine Tuning Advisor

3. Tom needs to achieve optimum performance within his application. He is examining different view technologies as a way to improve data access performance. He is currently managing a database that is replicated between five servers (for load balancing) and contains customer information for six sales divisions. The Customer Purchase table currently contains a consolidated list of 100,000,000 customer records. What could Tom try to implement to improve server performance?

   - ○ **A.** Indexed views

   - ○ **B.** Partitioned views

   - ○ **C.** Complex views

   - ○ **D.** Full outer views

4. After a system crash, one of your production databases is experiencing problems. The problems center around a group of tables that have all been assigned to the same data file in a partitioned environment. None of the tables in other files seem to be affected. Which of the following will assist in troubleshooting the issue further?

   ○ **A.** DBCC CHECKFILEGROUP

   ○ **B.** DBCC CHECKCATALOG

   ○ **C.** DBCC CHECKDB

   ○ **D.** DBCC CHECKTABLE

5. You are using System Monitor to diagnose performance issues on a server. You would like to see if there are any locking issues within one of your production databases. The two applications that use the database both utilize transactions to perform their updates. From which counter category would you select?

   ○ **A.** MSAS 2005:Locks

   ○ **B.** SQLServer:Locks

   ○ **C.** Distributed Transaction Coordinator

   ○ **D.** SQLAgent:JobSteps

6. You are using the Database Engine Tuning Advisor to analyze a workload file. You would like to perform a test to determine the optimum settings for partitioning to achieve the best performance. Which option should you select?

   ○ **A.** No partitioning

   ○ **B.** Aligned partitioning

   ○ **C.** Full partitioning

   ○ **D.** Keep aligned partitioning

7. You have used the SQL Server Profiler with the Tuning template against all the activity on a server over a period when the server activity was at its highest. The activity is saved to a table. You would like to analyze the session, but you are interested in only a single database. How would you extract and analyze the appropriate events?

   ○ **A.** Re-create the session and set a filter for the desired database when running SQL Server Profiler.

   ○ **B.** Use the Database Engine Tuning Advisor and select only the desired database on the General tab.

   ○ **C.** Open the session in SQL Server Profiler, set a filter for the desired database, and export the T-SQL events.

   ○ **D.** Open the session in SQL Server Profiler, set a filter for the desired database, and save the file as a new trace table.

Answers to Exam Prep Questions

1. **D.** Because the table structure has recently been altered, there is a good possibility that this change has caused the indexing information to become unstable or that statistics affecting the index have not been updated. If you restart the service, SQL Server should then update the statistical information accordingly, but this may affect use of the server, so it may not be a possibility. After the restart, you might want to ensure that all statistics are intact. You should also consider index fragmentation as a possible source of the problem. For more information, see the section "Using the Database Console Command (DBCC)."

2. **B.** To perform analysis of this type, you use SQL Server Profiler to gather detailed serverwide information. Activity Monitor and System Monitor do not provide any details of commands being used. Event Viewer only reports on locking if it causes errors and is therefore not suitable in this situation. The Database Engine Tuning Advisor is for database structure analysis, not procedure execution.

3. **B.** Partitioned views, and specifically distributed partitioned views, may improve the data access for Tom's database. Because a large number of rows could be separated by sales division per server (with one server maintaining information for two divisions), Tom's database tables may be ideal candidates for distributed partitioned views. For more information, see the section "Data Partitioning Across Servers."

4. **A.** The CHECKCATALOG option checks for consistencies in system table storage and does not help much in a production database. CHECKDB checks the allocation and structural integrity of all the objects in the database, not just the tables affected. CHECKTABLE could be used, but only to check one table as a time. CHECKFILEGROUP checks the allocation and structural integrity of tables in a file or filegroup. For more information, see the section "Using the Database Console Command (DBCC)."

5. **B.** MSAS 2005:Locks and any MSAS counters deal only with analysis services and would not be appropriate for production databases. Distributed Transaction Coordinator counters would only provide information for two-phase commit-style processing across multiple databases. SQLAgent counters have nothing to do with database usage. SQLServer counters pertain to the database engine and the objects controlled by the engine. For more information, see the section "Locks, Blocks, and Deadlocks."

6. **C.** No Partitioning would not perform the desired analysis. Aligned Partitioning would limit partition analysis to what is currently set up. To analyze all partitioning options to achieve the best performance from partitioning, you should select Full Partitioning. For more information, see the section "Data Partitioning Across Servers."

7. **B.** The Database Engine Tuning Advisor can perform the analysis from one or more databases within a single workload file without the need for any other alterations. For more information see the section "Using the DTA."

CHAPTER NINE

Implementing High Availability

Terms you'll need to understand:

✓ Database mirroring
✓ Log shipping
✓ Witness
✓ Secondary database
✓ Replication
✓ Publisher
✓ Distributor
✓ Subscriber
✓ Latency
✓ Failover
✓ Clustering
✓ Data mart
✓ Data warehouse

Techniques you'll need to master:

✓ Utilizing database mirroring with and without a witness
✓ Setting up, initiating, and implementing log shipping
✓ Defining replication and designing the replication architecture
✓ Defining clustering, data mart, and data warehouse
✓ Understanding techniques for controlling latency

High availability is important in most database systems. Having data available 24 hours a day, 7 days a week, every day of the year is important in many environments. Every database administrator aims at achieving the elusive "five nines," which means the system is up, running, and available to users 99.999% of the time.

In addition to being available, a system must perform well. High availability also means that the server, its hardware, and the database configuration perform well within the system. Response times must be sufficient. Transaction speeds must be maintained.

A truly available environment must achieve five-nines reliability while receiving a passing mark in performance.

High-Availability Solutions

Database server failures can be costly in production environments. A high-availability solution is a solution that minimizes failures and downtime. In a good solution, the effects of hardware or software failures are minimal, if they exist at all. The idea is to maintain the availability of the server and its objects, allowing applications to interact without fail. Downtime needs to be minimized, eliminated, or scheduled for times when applications do not need access to the data.

You can do many things to minimize or eliminate downtime and to prepare a disaster recovery plan in the event that something does occur. You start with backups and scheduled maintenance. Throughout this book, you have looked at many of the aspects of SQL Server that can help in this area. There are, however, still many areas and a few exam topics left to cover.

In some cases, you can have a single, standalone server. Even with backup, if something goes wrong, you have to restore from a backup to get back up and running again. A solution in which every minute of downtime costs hundreds of dollars is not a good solution.

In other cases, you can implement one of the secondary server solutions, often called *warm backups*. Through log shipping or replication, you can achieve a better percentage of uptime, at a reasonable cost. In these scenarios, a secondary server is constantly being refreshed with the latest information. If something goes wrong with the primary server, it is simply a matter of switching processing over to the secondary server, which requires much less loss of processing and data access time than does restoring from backup.

You can also use more costly solutions, such as using redundant hardware and simultaneous update solutions (for example, database mirroring, failover clustering). With several solutions, you update data simultaneously within multiple database engines. If one system fails, the other can take over without missing a beat.

Generally, at the lowest end of the spectrum, you have low cost but high risk and essentially no high-availability solution in place. As you move up to the high-availability solutions, you have a low cost with some risk (loss due to failure) and a degree of latency (the amount of time before data agrees in two locations). At the higher end, you achieve lower risk and minimal latency, but at higher cost.

Implementing Log Shipping

Log shipping is a reasonably low-cost solution for increasing availability. Log shipping operates at the database level, and it provides for redundant storage of data in a multiple-server environment. With log shipping, one or more standby databases operate as warm backups. These secondary databases are referred to as *warm copies* of the primary database. The primary database is the only copy that can be updated, and the secondary database can be set up as a read-only database to offload query-related processing from the primary server. The secondary database can also be set up solely as a standby, offline copy of the primary database.

You initiate a secondary database by restoring a full backup of the primary database without recovery. You can do this ahead of time or as part of the log shipping setup. (The no-recovery and standby restore techniques are discussed and illustrated in Chapter 6, "Database Maintenance.") After you restore the full backup with no recovery, the secondary database reflects the standby status in Management Studio. In Figure 9.1, the ONE database on the default instance of YUKONTWO has been fully backed up, and that backup has been restored onto the StandbyONE database on the YUKONTWO\SECOND instance of the server.

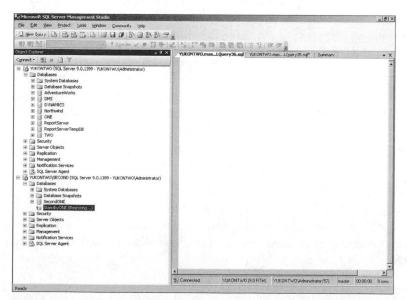

FIGURE 9.1 Standby status is indicated by (Restoring…) in Management Studio.

A log shipping configuration includes two or more instances of SQL Server. One instance holds the primary database, and one or more instances hold copies of the database as secondary databases. You also can optionally configure a monitor server. You control the process by creating and executing jobs at the appropriate servers.

The primary server performs log backups at regular intervals. A single job is created on the server to perform these backups on schedule and stores the backups on a network share that is accessible to both the primary and secondary machines. The default is to perform the operation every 15 minutes, but you can alter this timing if you want more or less frequency. The timing here and the timing of the associated jobs on the secondary server determine the actual latency.

Each secondary server utilizes two jobs to perform regular updates of its secondary database from log backups created on the primary server. The first job performs a copy of the log backup to a destination folder (usually located on the secondary server). The second job controls the restore operations. You can have the restore use no recovery to keep the database offline or use the standby option to cause the server to become read-only, for reporting purposes.

The monitoring instance executes one job on a regular basis to identify and alert an operator if the log shipping is not operating as it is designed to operate. Log shipping has no automated failover to the secondary instance. This brings with it the risk of downtime in the event of failure. There is also an associated risk of data loss for the interval between log backups if there is a failure in the logging hardware. Before failover can occur, the secondary databases must be brought fully up-to-date manually. Secondary databases also have limited availability during restores, so they might be unavailable as reporting sources during restores.

You can perform the complete setup of log shipping, including the configuration of all tasks, by using Management Studio. To do so, you right-click the primary database and select Tasks and then Ship Transaction Logs. Figure 9.2 shows an example of this configuration. In this example, all three instances are running on the same physical machine, which is an unlikely scenario in a production environment and in fact would defeat the purpose of attempting to provide a high-availability solution.

You can use log shipping alone or as a supplement to database mirroring. When these solutions are used together, the current principal database of the database mirroring configuration is also the current primary database of the log shipping configuration.

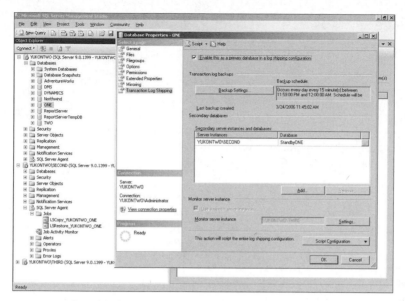

FIGURE 9.2 Log shipping configuration using three SQL Server instances.

Using Database Mirroring

SQL Server 2005 offers database mirroring for evaluation only, and you can find the following warning message throughout SQL Server Books Online:

Microsoft support policies do not apply to the database mirroring feature in SQL Server 2005. Database mirroring is currently disabled by default, but may be enabled for evaluation purposes only by using trace flag 1400 as a startup parameter. (For more information about trace flags, see Trace Flags (Transact-SQL).) Database mirroring should not be used in production environments, and Microsoft support services will not support databases or applications that use database mirroring. Database mirroring documentation is included in SQL Server 2005 for evaluation purposes only, and the Documentation Policy for SQL Server 2005 Support and Upgrade does not apply to the database mirroring documentation.

> **EXAM ALERT**
>
> Microsoft does not support database mirroring in a production environment! Therefore, any exam question that offers database mirroring as an answer for a production environment implementation should be completely discounted as not even being a possible valid answer. The only time database mirroring would be a correct answer would be for a question that clearly states that you are evaluating the feature.

Enabling Trace Flags in a Test Environment

You can enable trace flag 1400 to get a look into database mirroring; to do so, you have two choices:

▶ You can stop the service and run `sqlsrvr.exe` from the command prompt by using the following:

```
sqlservr
   -d"C:\Program Files\Microsoft SQL Server\MSSQL.1\MSSQL\Data\
   ➥master.mdf"
   -T1400
```

▶ You can add the `-T1400` flag as a startup option in SQL Server Configuration Manager. You must separate each startup option from the previous option with a semicolon, as shown in Figure 9.3.

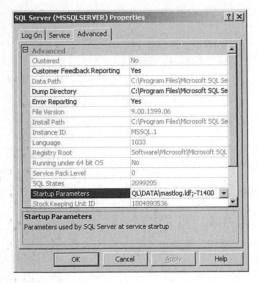

FIGURE 9.3 Adding trace flags to the SQL Server startup.

SQL Server database mirroring is implemented on a per-database basis to increase availability. You must have the database set to the full recovery model, and you cannot mirror the `master`, `msdb`, `tempdb`, or `model` databases.

Mirroring maintains two copies of a database. Each copy is held on a separate instance of SQL Server. Optionally, a third instance can act as a mirroring witness to observe activity and to alert and/or fail over if problems occur. In database mirroring, the witness server is an instance of SQL Server that monitors the status of the principal and mirror servers. The witness, by default, can initiate automatic failover if the principal server fails. Typically, each instance resides on a separate machine, but it is possible to configure all three instances on the same computer.

The principal database is the updatable version of the database, and the mirror copy duplicates the activity of the principal. The two instances communicate over database mirroring endpoints that control the mirroring sessions. If a witness is used, a third endpoint is created on that instance for communication purposes.

You begin mirroring similar to the way you begin log shipping: You perform a full backup of the principal database and restore the backup onto the mirror instance with the no recovery option. You then proceed to perform log backups of the principal database, having them restored onto the mirror copy. The applications can be performed synchronously or asynchronously. If you are configuring as synchronous with automatic failover, a witness instance is mandatory. If the configuration is synchronous without failover or asynchronous, the witness is optional.

> **EXAM ALERT**
>
> You might see the three possible mirroring configurations as a topic of the 70-431 exam: synchronous with automatic failover (high availability), asynchronous (high performance with some latency), and synchronous (high protection).

A synchronous configuration commits changes to both servers simultaneously. The asynchronous configuration first commits the changes on the principal database and then transfers the changes to the mirror copy. If automatic failover is configured, the witness controls the failover to the mirror if the principal server becomes unavailable.

Because these configurations are not currently supported in a production environment, the only true failover configuration available in a SQL Server environment is failover clustering.

Using Failover Clustering

Failover clustering provides high-availability support for SQL Server. In the event of a failure, SQL Server can maintain business operations through the use of multiple instances of the database engine. You can configure the environment such that one node of a cluster can fail over to another node in the cluster during any failure.

A failover cluster is set up as a series of one or more nodes. Each node is a server in its own right. The nodes operate with two or more shared disks. The shared disks maintain the resources that the node set accesses. This disk configuration is known as the *resource group* or *grouping*. Collectively, the entire configuration makes up a single virtual server. Applications communicate with a singular machine over a single IP address.

A SQL Server virtual server appears as if it were a single computer. This allows applications to perform their database access without the need for reconfiguration if something happens to one of the nodes in the cluster. A failover cluster is a hardware configuration that requires special computer hardware. Of course, this special hardware comes at a cost, making a failover cluster implementation much more costly than other forms of high availability. If you lack the budget or hardware to implement this strategy, replication may be a better solution.

Using Replication

Replication is the process by which data and database objects are distributed from SQL Server to other database engines that reside across an enterprise; this data can be distributed to other SQL Server databases or even non–SQL Server databases such as Oracle and others. Replication can be explained by using a publisher/subscriber/distributor metaphor. To understand replication, you must understand and become familiar with the basic concept of the publisher/distributor/subscriber metaphor. This metaphor defines the different roles SQL Server can play in the replication process. Each role provides functionality that aids in the replication process:

▶ **Publisher**—In replication terminology, the publisher is the server that produces the original data for the use of the replication process. The publisher can produce many publications or sets of data to be distributed to other subscribing machines. One publisher can produce data to be replicated to many subscribers. Also, many publishers can produce data to be distributed to just a single, central subscriber. The former is implemented as a standard central publisher/distributor/subscriber replication model, and the latter is referred to as *central subscriber replication*.

▶ **Distributor**—The distributor is the server that contains the distribution database, data history, and transactions; as its name implies, it sends data to subscribers. The distributor can be implemented on the same physical server as the publisher or subscriber, although it doesn't need to be. It can reside on a separate server somewhere else in the world and be connected via a network. The placement of the distributor and its characteristics depend on the type of replication used.

▶ **Subscriber**—A subscriber, in SQL Server terms, is the server that receives replicated data through the distributor. Subscribers can choose from the publications available at the publisher and don't necessarily need to subscribe to them all.

Other replication terminologies are also important to the process and fall in line with the subscription metaphor. When a subscription is set up, a publication made up of one or more articles is configured. Simply put, articles are data structures made up of selected columns and/or rows from a table. An article could also be an entire table, although it is recommended that the content of an article be kept to just the minimum amount of data needed for a particular implementation. One or more articles are bundled into a publication to be used for replication. Articles must be grouped into a publication before they can be replicated. In short, a publication is a collection of one or more articles and is capable of being replicated.

Replication Strategies

Replication, with its many benefits, serves as a backbone for many businesses. Placing the same data on multiple servers, with each server closer to the user's location, can reduce the use of bandwidth and provide the user with faster update operations and retrieval of data. Without replication, businesses would be incapable of carrying out robust branch operations around the globe. Database administrators favor replication for the following reasons:

- In using replication, businesses are capable of having data copied from server to server in a multisite enterprise. It provides flexibility and more efficient use of networking resources.

- Replication allows for greater concurrent use of data; that is, it allows more people to work with the data at the same time.

- Copies of the database can be distributed, bringing data closer to the end user and providing a form of load balancing.

- Replication is perfect for traveling salespeople and roaming disconnected users. It enables mobile users who work on laptops to be updated with current database information when they connect and to upload data to a central server.

Replication techniques can be applied to three replication models, as well as several different physical models. The physical aspects and models have no direct correlation. A replication model supplies the functionality, whereas the physical model shows the placement and roles of individual servers.

Merge, snapshot, and transactional replication all involve essentially the same basic elements to begin with. However, each model has idiosyncrasies of its own that require some thought during implementation design.

You can compress or save to a CD the initial snapshot that begins the replication process in order to offload some of the necessary communications. Doing so makes more efficient use of network bandwidth, especially in slow-link or dial-up environments.

You can set up a subscription as either a push subscription or a pull subscription:

▶ **Push subscription**—A publisher initiates a push subscription and provides the basis for scheduling the replication process.

▶ **Pull subscription**—The subscriber initiates a pull subscription and provides the basis and timing on which data is to be obtained.

In either case, whoever initiates a subscription selects the appropriate articles to be transmitted.

Replication can be set up in various ways. The different scenarios in which replication is set up each provide specific benefits and have unique characteristics. SQL Server can serve as the publisher, subscriber, or distributor. The individual roles can all be set up on a single machine, although in most implementations, there is at least a separation between a publisher/distributor and the subscribing machine(s). In some other scenarios, the subscriber of the data from one machine may republish the data to still other subscribers. The possibilities are endless. You can choose to implement any of the following common scenarios, which cover the basics of a physical replication model. In real-world scenarios, however, the actual physical model used could have any combination of these elements, based on a business's individual needs:

▶ Central publisher and multiple subscribers

▶ Multiple publishers and multiple subscribers

▶ Multiple publishers and a single subscriber

▶ Single publisher and a remote distributor

Using a Central Publisher and Multiple Subscribers

In replication using a central publisher and multiple subscribers, the data originates at the publishing server, and that original data is sent to multiple subscribers via the distributor. Depending on the form of replication used, changes to the data at the destination servers can enable updates to be propagated back to the publisher and other subscribers, or it can be treated as read-only data, in which updates occur only at the publisher. This type of scenario is typically used when a company has a master catalog at the headquarters and has many different subscribers located elsewhere.

An advantage of this configuration is that multiple copies of the data from a central server are available for user processing on multiple machines. Data can be distributed to the locations where it is needed. With this form of replication, data can be brought closer to the user, and this can reduce the load on a single server. Expensive bandwidth can also be utilized in an improved manner.

Using Multiple Publishers and Multiple Subscribers

In replication using multiple publishers and multiple subscribers, every server publishes a particular set of rows that relate to it and subscribes to the publications that all the other servers are publishing so that each of them can receive data and send data. This form of replication is typically used in a distributed warehouse environment with inventory spread out among different locations, and it can also be used in any other situation in which the data being held at each location-specific server needs to be delivered to the other servers, so that each location has a complete set of data.

For replication using multiple publishers and multiple subscribers, the correct database design is crucial to having each server publish and subscribe to the correct information. The table structure for the data involved in the publication is usually implemented with a compound primary key or unique index, although it is possible to use an identity or another algorithm that enables each location to be uniquely identified within the entire table. One portion of the key is an identifier for the location, and the second element is the data identifier.

Using Multiple Publishers and a Single Subscriber

In replication using multiple publishers and a single subscriber, a server subscribes to publications on some or all of a number of other publishing servers. This is needed when all data from all locations is required to be sent to only one site, possibly the headquarters. Data can be collected from widely dispersed areas, and the central location, the subscriber, would end up with a master database from all the publishers combined.

Using a Single Publisher and a Remote Distributor

Replication does not require a distributor residing on the same server or even within close proximity to the publisher. Instead, the machine handling the distribution can be implemented as a totally separate segment. This is practical when you need to free the publishing server from having to perform the distribution task and minimize costs that can be incurred over long-distance or overseas network connections. Data can also be replicated faster and delivered to many subscribers at a much lower cost, while minimizing the load on the publisher. In situations in which the connection between the publisher and the subscriber is over a slow link or over high-cost connections, a remote distributor should be used to lower the cost and increase data transfer rates.

The individual roles of each server are implemented in all types of replication scenarios; the physical configuration does not dictate the type of replication used. The next section examines the types of replication and their implementation.

Types of Replication

Each replication model provides different capabilities for distributing data and database objects. There are many considerations for selecting a replication type and determining whether replication is a suitable technique for data distribution. The many considerations to determine the suitability of each of the models include transactional consistency, the subscriber's capability or lack of capability to update data, latency, administration, site autonomy, performance, security, the update schedule, and the available data sources. Each of these is defined by the replication configuration, and they are discussed through the next several sections.

Other data distribution techniques that don't involve replication can offer a different set of features but may not provide the flexibility that replication offers. To determine which replication type is best suited to your needs, you need to consider three primary factors: site autonomy, transactional consistency, and latency. These three considerations are illustrated in Figure 9.4, which also compares and contrasts data distribution techniques.

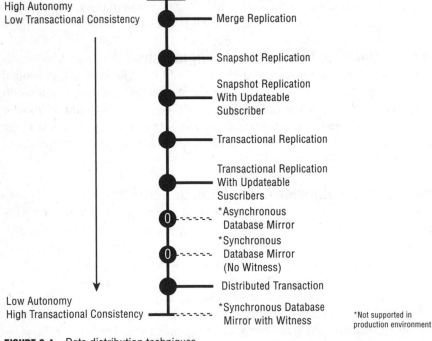

FIGURE 9.4   Data distribution techniques.

When you are in the position of selecting a data distribution technique, you need to answer three questions: How much site independence is required in processing changes to the data (autonomy)? How consistent does data need to remain after changes are made (consistency)? How soon does data need to agree at all replication locations (latency)? The answers to these questions, as described in the following sections, determine the approach you should use.

Site Autonomy in Replication

Site autonomy measures the effect of a site's operation on another site. A site that has full autonomy is completely independent of all other sites, which means it can function without even being connected to any other site. High site autonomy can be achieved in SQL Server replication where it would not be possible using other data distribution techniques. Not all replication configurations achieve autonomy; such high site autonomy can be seen best with merge replication.

Site autonomy directly affects transactional consistency. To achieve an environment that is autonomous and has a high degree of transactional consistency, the data definition must provide a mechanism to differentiate one site from the other. A compound primary key, for example, in a "central subscriber" or "multiple publisher, multiple subscriber" scenario, allows autonomy while achieving transactional consistency. If an implementation enables each site to update the same data, it will always have some degree of transaction inconsistency or at least a delay before consistency is achieved.

Transactional Consistency in Replication

Transactional consistency is a measure of changes made to data, specifically changes that remain in place without being rolled back. Changes can get rolled back due to conflicts, and this affects user changes and other user activities. In replication, you have multiple distinct copies of your data, and if you allow updates to each copy, it is possible for different copies of a piece of data to be changed differently. If this situation is allowed, as is the case in some forms of replication, you have imperfect (low) transactional consistency. If you prevent two copies from changing independently, as is the case with a distributed transaction, you have the highest level of transactional consistency.

In a distributed transaction, the application and the controlling server work together to control updates to multiple sites. Two-phase commits implemented in some forms of replication also help. The two phases used are preparation and committal. Each server is prepared for the update to take place, and when all sites are ready, the change is committed at the same time on all servers. When all sites have implemented the change, transactional consistency is restored.

Latency in Replication

Latency can be thought of as how long data in the subscriber has to wait before being updated from the copy of the data on the publisher. Several factors contribute to latency, but it is essentially the length of time it takes changes to travel from the publisher to the distributor and then from the distributor to the publisher. If there is no need for the data to be identical, at the same time, in all publishers and subscribers, the latency resident in a replication strategy will not negatively affect an application.

In SQL Server 2005, you can use the Tracer Tokens tab of the Replication Monitor to monitor latency. Tracer tokens, which are new to SQL Server, allow you to validate connections and to measure latency. A token is a small amount of data that is written to the transaction log of the publication database as though it were a typical transaction. It is then sent through the system for measurement.

EXAM ALERT

You can control tracer tokens by using the Replication Monitor and the interface or via stored procedures that are allocated to the tracer token information in the system.

The two-phase commit that SQL Server implements through the use of immediate updating can minimize latency on updates coming from the subscriber, but it has no effect on updates sent from the publisher. A number of factors can affect latency, including the workload on the publisher and distributor, the speed and congestion of the network, and the size of the updates being transported.

Elements of Replication

Each type of replication offers advantages and disadvantages. You must select the type based on the requirements of the business application. Three types of replication—snapshot, transactional, and merge—move data by using different principles.

Using Snapshot Replication

Snapshot replication distributes data and database objects by copying the entire contents of the published items via the distributor and passing them on to the subscriber exactly as they appear at a specific moment in time, without monitoring updates. A snapshot is stored on the distributor, which encapsulates data of published tables and database objects; this snapshot is then taken to the subscriber database via the distribution agent.

Snapshot replication is advantageous when replicated data is infrequently updated and modified. A snapshot strategy is preferable over others when data is to be updated in a batch. This does not mean that only a small amount of data is updated, but rather that data is updated in large quantities at distant intervals. Because data is replicated at a specific point in time and not replicated frequently, this type of replication is good for online catalogs, price lists, and the like, in which the decision to implement replication is independent of how recent data is.

Snapshot replication offers a high level of site autonomy. It also offers a great degree of transactional consistency because transactions are enforced at the publisher. Transactional consistency also depends on whether you are allowing updating subscribers and what type (immediate or queued) you are allowing.

Using Transactional Replication

Transactional replication involves moving transactions captured from the transaction log of the publishing server database and applying them to the subscriber's database. The transactional replication process monitors data changes made on the publisher.

Transactional replication captures incremental modifications that were made to data in the published table. The committed transactions do not directly change the data on the subscriber but are instead stored on the distributor. These transactions held in distribution tables on the distributor are sent to the subscriber. Because the transactions on the distributor are stored in an orderly fashion, each subscriber acquires data in the same order as is in the publisher.

When replicating a publication by using transactional replication, you can choose to replicate an entire table or just part of a table, using a method referred to as *filtering*. You can also select all stored procedures on the database or just certain ones that are to be replicated as articles within the publication. Replication of stored procedures ensures that the definitions they provide are in each setting where the data is to be found. Processes that are defined by the stored procedures can then be run at the subscriber. Because the procedures are being replicated, any changes to these procedures are also replicated. Replication of a stored procedure makes the procedure available for execution on the local server.

Using Merge Replication

Merge replication is the process of transferring data from the publisher to the subscriber, which enables the publisher and subscriber to update data while they are connected or disconnected and then merge the updates after they are both connected; this provides virtual independence. Merge replication therefore allows the most flexibility and adds the most autonomy to the replication process. Merge replication is also the most complex replication because it enables the publisher and subscriber to work independently. The publisher and subscriber can combine their results at any certain time, and they can also combine or merge their updated results.

The Snapshot Agent and the Merge Agent help in carrying out the process of merge replication. The Snapshot Agent is used for the initial synchronization of the databases. The Merge Agent then applies the snapshot; after that, the job of the Merge Agent is to increment the data changes and resolve any conflicts according to the rules configured.

Conflicts are likely to occur with merge replication. Conflicts occur when more than one site updates the same record. This happens when two users concurrently update or modify the same record with different values. When a conflict occurs, SQL Server has to choose a single value to use. It resolves the conflict based on either the site priority on the database site or a custom conflict resolver, which can be CLR based in any language, in SQL Server 2005.

> **NOTE**
>
> This chapter outlines the basics of replication, and although it discusses many of the principles and strategies, the actual configurations can be quite involved. As you have seen, there are many design considerations, and the administration over the replication sites is significant.
>
> To successfully implement replication, you must get much further into the depths of the agents and implementations. These techniques fall under the scope of administration processes and are thus beyond the scope of this book. For additional assistance or information, you can find a considerable amount of data in SQL Server Books Online, as well as the Microsoft Web resources.

Microsoft Analysis Services

To round off the discussion of high availability coverage on the 70-431 exam, let's quickly discuss a topic that is not within Microsoft's own preparatory documentation for the exam but falls into the realm of elements that may still be covered on the exam, Microsoft Analysis Services.

SQL Server, in particular the Enterprise Edition, ships with many associated features that, when installed on the server, require administration. Anyone responsible for the administration of the server should minimally familiarize himself or herself with the additional objects and processes that are functioning on the server. These, of course, affect the overall performance of the system.

Microsoft SQL Server 2005 Analysis Services (SSAS) provides online analytical processing (OLAP) and data mining functionality for business intelligence solutions. End users perform queries from OLAP, reporting, and custom business intelligence applications to access the data. These queries provide a business view over the relational data. By using Analysis Services, users can mine their data to look for specific patterns and trends.

When you install a Microsoft SQL Server analysis server, you will add a number of databases, assemblies, processes, and control objects to the server. The additional databases need to have physical resources allocated to their storage. The processing of reports against the data and the routine processes of loading and configuring the data utilize resources that also need to be managed.

Addressing the elements that are associated with Analysis Services can become quite confusing because of the inconsistent naming convention. Within the support tools are additional control objects whose naming depends on where you look. Some of the Analysis Services objects use the prefix SSAS (for SQL Server Analysis Services), and others use MSAS (for Microsoft Analysis Services). This naming confusion is carried further, through the terminology that Microsoft uses for its data analysis/mart/warehouse/mining tools, services, and server.

The 70-431 exam has little to do with how the system functions under Analysis Services. It is beyond the scope of this book to explain the use of Analysis Services. However, you do need to know a few definitions, and you need to be able to recognize that an object is associated with Analysis Services and not with the core functionality of the database engine itself. Analysis Services has its own processing and is controlled by its own operating system service.

EXAM ALERT

Anytime you see MSAS or SSAS, a reference is being made to Analysis Services. You need to understand the terminology used within this product, and you should not confuse it with the SQL Server database engine processes and objects. On the exam you will often see the acronyms for these services.

When you create a database within the Analysis Services framework, that database is controlled by a different service than the standard user databases. The database itself is really quite different from those that are controlled by the database engine. In addition, the objects in the database are also dissimilar. A database within Analysis Services is usually and more appropriately called a data warehouse. A subset of the information maintained within the *data warehouse* is referred to as a *data mart*. This information is often organized by department or other business division.

The processing that occurs in the realm of Analysis Services is generally divided into two categories: data loading/building and data querying/reporting. Data loading and other configuration activities can be processor intensive and are usually scheduled for overnight operation or at some other time when the effect on the end users would be minimized. Data querying and reporting are usually ongoing, although the activity increases near the end of a fiscal period and at other times when budgets and inventory are being analyzed.

Exam Prep Questions

1. You would like to set up log shipping. Currently, no backups exist. The recovery mode is set to full on both the primary and secondary databases. The secondary database will be used as a read-only machine once it is set up. You make a full backup of the primary database. What else do you need to do?

   ○ **A.** Restore the full backup on the secondary database by using `Recovery`.

   ○ **B.** Restore the full backup on the secondary database by using NO RECOVERY.

   ○ **C.** Restore the full backup on the secondary database by using STAND BY.

   ○ **D.** Restore the full backup on the secondary database by using STOPAT.

2. Transactional replication offers low site autonomy, and merge replication offers high site autonomy. What is meant by *site autonomy*?

   ○ **A.** The measuring of the consistency of transactions

   ○ **B.** How long data in the subscriber can stay without being renewed

   ○ **C.** The independence of one site in relationship to others

   ○ **D.** How many subscribers and publishers are involved in a replication process

3. You work in a finance company where changes to the values in the `Finance` table are made quickly, and you want these incremental changes to be propagated to subscribers as they occur. The subscribers are always connected to the publisher with a reliable connection. Which type of replication do you use when you want updated changes at the server in almost real-time?

   ○ **A.** Snapshot replication

   ○ **B.** Snapshot replication with updating subscribers

   ○ **C.** Transactional replication

   ○ **D.** Merge replication

4. You and Josh are replicating data to multiple subscribers who need to update data at various times and propagate those changes to the publisher and to other subscribers. These subscribers need to be able to make changes offline and later synchronize data. They therefore need a replication strategy that offers high autonomy. Which type of replication offers almost complete site autonomy?

   ○ **A.** Snapshot replication

   ○ **B.** Snapshot replication and transactional replication

   ○ **C.** Merge replication

    ○ **D.** Transactional replication

    ○ **E.** Transactional replication with updating subscribers

5. Your company has just purchased an accounting application from a vendor. The application stores its data in a database named `Accounting`. The tables in this database contain columns that function as primary keys, but `PRIMARY KEY` and `FOREIGN KEY` constraints are not used. You need to replicate data from this database to another SQL Server computer. That server will use the replicated data to generate reports. Most reports will run each month, but the accounting department needs to have the ability to run reports at any time. Reports should be accurate through the last full working day.

   You cannot make any changes to the database, but you need to implement replication. Which two actions should you take? (Select two answers, with each correct answer representing part of the solution.)

    ○ **A.** Implement merge replication.

    ○ **B.** Implement snapshot replication.

    ○ **C.** Implement transactional replication.

    ○ **D.** Schedule replication to run continuously.

    ○ **E.** Schedule replication to run during off-peak hours.

6. You want to implement a high-availability solution on your support database. You need to do so as inexpensively as possible, but you also need the server to continue automatically upon failure. Which of the following is the best solution?

    ○ **A.** Use log shipping to configure a monitor to implement failover.

    ○ **B.** Use database mirroring with a witness configured to implement failover.

    ○ **C.** Use merge replication.

    ○ **D.** Use failover clustering.

7. You would like to test database mirroring. You configure an endpoint on each machine and assign the endpoint to its partner. You make a full backup and you restore it to the mirror database. You would like to synchronize the databases to begin processing. What must you do?

    ○ **A.** Configure a witness to synchronize the machines.

    ○ **B.** Perform a log backup on the principal and restore it to the mirror.

    ○ **C.** Configure failover on the principal database.

    ○ **D.** Configure security on both databases.

Answers to Exam Prep Questions

1. **C.** You use the `Stand By` option of the `restore` command to place the database in read-only mode and allow it to be used for query- and reporting-based activity. `Recovery` is used to bring a database fully online and ready for use; no further log restores can be done. `No Recovery` allows for further log restores to occur but doesn't allow the database to be accessed as a read-only secondary. STOPAT is only used to attain a point-in-time recovery and is not applicable in this situation. For more information, see the section "Implementing Log Shipping" and Chapter 6.

2. **C.** Site autonomy refers to one site's independence from all other sites for processing modifications. Autonomy measures the effect of a site's operation on another site. A site that has full autonomy is completely independent of all other sites, meaning that it can function without even being connected to another site. See the section "Types of Replication" for more information on autonomy and other considerations.

3. **C.** Transactional replication is a good solution when you want updated changes at the server in almost real-time. Because of the frequency of the changes, snapshot replication is not a good solution. Merge replication can be set up in a single direction but is generally used only when the publisher and subscribers make updates while connected or disconnected. See the section "Using Transactional Replication" for more details.

4. **C.** Merge replication allows the most flexibility and adds the most autonomy to the replication process, enabling the publisher and subscriber to work virtually independently. The publisher and subscriber can combine their results and updates at any time. See the section "Using Merge Replication" for more details.

5. **B, E.** Because there is no primary key and because no other changes to the database can be performed, the only alternative you can use is snapshot replication. Because the data does not need to be up-to-the-minute, a scheduled data refresh occurring overnight or during other nonpeak times is most appropriate. See the section "Using Snapshot Replication" for more details.

6. **D.** Currently, in a production environment, only one supported configuration provides automatic failover. Log shipping with a monitor is not automated failover and requires manual intervention to implement the switch. Database mirroring, though offering an automated failover solution, is not supported by Microsoft within a production environment. Merge replication has no failover mechanism at all; although one server could continue to support its own clients if one server went down, it would not handle the missing server's clients. Failover clustering is the only supported configuration. For more information, see the section "Using Failover Clustering."

7. **B.** You have to synchronize the process by using a log backup of the principal restored to the mirror database. A witness is not required to initially synchronize the databases. By setting up the endpoints, you have already configured the security as long as you have used the same service ID. Failover needs to be performed only if something goes wrong after the principal and mirror are operational. For more information see the "Using Database Mirroring" section.

10
CHAPTER TEN
Practice Exam 1

The actual certification exam has 40 questions. To best simulate the exam circumstances, you should try to complete the 40 questions in this practice exam in 90 minutes.

Chapter 11, "Answers to Practice Exam 1," provides the answers to this practice exam. Each answer is accompanied by references to the applicable materials in SQL Server 2005 Books Online and on the Microsoft official websites.

Exam Questions

1. You are creating a database that will store sales order information. Orders will be entered in a client/server application and over the Internet via an ASP.NET application. Each time a new order is placed in the system, a unique order number must be assigned, and the order numbers must be in ascending sequence. It is expected that the system will generate in excess of 100,000 orders weekly. You create a new table named Orders and a related table named Order Details. How should you create the order number to provide the required functionality in the simplest manner?

   ○ **A.** Use a UniqueIdentifier data type.

   ○ **B.** Use an Integer data type and set the IDENTITY property for the column.

   ○ **C.** Use a TimeStamp data type and create a user-defined function that sets the order number.

   ○ **D.** Create a table to hold key values and assign order numbers from this table.

   ○ **E.** Have the front-end application assign sequential integer order numbers.

2. You are designing a query that must return related data from two tables. You must return only data that matches between the tables. One column of data allows null entries, and you are not to return data from either table in this case. Which of the following SQL items is needed? (Select two answers.)

   ○ **A.** JOIN

   ○ **B.** UNION

   ○ **C.** IN

   ○ **D.** BETWEEN

   ○ **E.** ISNULL

3. You are preparing a table design for a complex business database application. After data entry, it is a requirement of one of these fields that a series of complex business logic procedures must be performed to obtain the value for the field. Which of the following would you implement?

   ○ **A.** A user-defined type

   ○ **B.** A field-level constraint

   ○ **C.** A table-level constraint

   ○ **D.** A trigger

   ○ **E.** A computed column

4. A database that has been used in production is in need of analysis to attempt to make performance improvements. Which of the following is likely to improve performance, if correctly implemented? (Choose all that apply.)

   - ○ **A.** Table partitioning
   - ○ **B.** Covering indexes
   - ○ **C.** Triggers
   - ○ **D.** RAID 5
   - ○ **E.** C2 security

5. You have implemented a database for an international research organization and are performing test queries against the tables within the database. You have some date fields in the database that store only date information. No time information is maintained within these columns. You would like to have a listing of the data from only the year 2005. Which of the following queries represents the best solution to the problem?

   - ○ **A.**
```
SELECT * FROM RTab
    WHERE RDate BETWEEN '01/01/2005' AND '01/01/2006'
```

   - ○ **B.**
```
SELECT * FROM RTab
    WHERE RDate BETWEEN '12/31/2004' AND '12/31/2004'
```

   - ○ **C.**
```
SELECT * FROM RTab
    WHERE RDate BETWEEN '12/31/2004' AND '01/01/2005'
```

   - ○ **D.**
```
SELECT * FROM RTab
    WHERE RDate BETWEEN '01/01/2005' AND '12/31/2005'
```

   - ○ **E.**
```
SELECT * FROM RTab
    WHERE RDate BETWEEN '12/31/2005' AND '01/01/2005'
```

6. You have entered a query using a TOP function to limit the number of records being viewed to five. When you see the results of the query, the dates being viewed are not the first five in the data. What is the most likely source of the problem?

   - ○ **A.** The result set has not been grouped.
   - ○ **B.** The data contains NULL values.

   ○ **C.** There is an incorrect ORDER BY.

   ○ **D.** Table aliases were used.

   ○ **E.** Schema binding has been applied.

7. Your accounting system works with string variables that are aligned to the left in some cases and to the right in others. Space filling is used on all fields in the interface. You need to remove excess spaces from the strings prior to accepting the value into a table. What functions would you use? (Choose all that apply.)

   ○ **A.** TRIM

   ○ **B.** LTRIM

   ○ **C.** RTRIM

   ○ **D.** REPLACE

   ○ **E.** STR

8. You are working on a view that was created when the database was first implemented several years ago. You believe that indexing the view would improve its performance. When you try to implement the index, you are unsuccessful because an ANSI_NULLS error occurs. What must you do to implement the index?

   ○ **A.** Create the index with ANSI_WARNINGS set to OFF.

   ○ **B.** Create the index with ANSI_WARNINGS set to ON.

   ○ **C.** Re-create the view without SCHEMABINDING.

   ○ **D.** Re-create the view with ANSI_NULLS set to OFF.

   ○ **E.** Re-create the view with ANSI_NULLS set to ON.

9. A production database is accepting sales orders from an online catalog order business. Inserts to the sales table occur frequently. When it was created, the table had a FillFactor setting of 75%. You want to inspect size and fragmentation of the indexes in the table. What do you need to do? (Choose two answers.)

   ○ **A.** Check the Extended Properties page of the table from within SQL Server Management Studio.

   ○ **B.** Query sys.dm_fts_indexpopulation.

   ○ **C.** Query sys.dm_exec_query_stats.

   ○ **D.** Query sys.dm_db_index_physical_stats.

   ○ **E.** Check the Fragmentation page of the index from within SQL Server Management Studio.

10. You need to import a large amount of data into an existing table. To speed up the process, you would like to disable all indexing and enable it once again when the process is complete. How would you implement the process?

- ○ **A.** Use ALTER INDEX DISABLE and ALTER INDEX ENABLE.
- ○ **B.** Use DISABLE INDEX and ENABLE INDEX.
- ○ **C.** Use DROP INDEX and CREATE INDEX.
- ○ **D.** Use ALTER INDEX DISABLE and ALTER INDEX REBUILD.

11. You are diagnosing performance problems with one particular table in a major production database. A large amount of data has just been imported. You would like to repair any fragmentation and integrity issues and provide query response based on the newly imported data. Which statements would you use? (Choose three answers.)

- ○ **A.** DBCC CHECKTABLE
- ○ **B.** ALTER INDEX REORGANIZE
- ○ **C.** UPDATE STATISTICS
- ○ **D.** CREATE STATISTICS
- ○ **E.** DBCC SHOWSTATISTICS
- ○ **F.** DBCC UPDATEUSAGE

12. You need to map a local server login to a remote server login. Which process should you use?

- ○ **A.** sp_helplogins
- ○ **B.** sp_addlogin
- ○ **C.** sp_adduser
- ○ **D.** sp_addlinkedsrvlogin
- ○ **E.** sp_grantlogin
- ○ **F.** SSIS transfer logins

13. A special process developed for periodic maintenance needs to run under a system administrator's account. The process will be run by individuals who lack the permissions to perform the tasks contained in the process. What would you do?

- ○ **A.** Have a system administrator run the task when needed.
- ○ **B.** Use sp_change_users_login Auto_Fix.
- ○ **C.** Use sp_change_users_login Update_One.
- ○ **D.** Have the process run using EXECUTE AS.
- ○ **E.** As a system administrator, schedule the task to run and set the process to run.

14. You have upgraded a database from SQL Server 2000 and are now accessing the tables and other objects within the database. You need to supply the appropriate schema to be used for procedures within the upgraded system. Which schema would you use?

○ **A.** sys

○ **B.** db

○ **C.** dbo

○ **D.** sa

○ **E.** There is no schema for upgraded databases.

15. As deletions are made from one table within the system, you would like to automatically delete detail records within another table. How would you implement this functionality?

○ **A.** Use a DDL trigger.

○ **B.** Use a DML trigger.

○ **C.** Use a stored procedure.

○ **D.** Use a user-defined function.

○ **E.** Alter options within the table definition.

16. Someone in the IT department has been creating, deleting, and modifying tables in a production database without first having them tested in the lab environment. You would like to find out who is making changes to the databases. How would you implement this process?

○ **A.** Use a DDL trigger.

○ **B.** Use a DML trigger.

○ **C.** Schedule a stored procedure.

○ **D.** Change the permissions to only allow one ID to change the production system and implement password policies.

○ **E.** Alter the permissions of the schema.

17. You are implementing a partitioning plan to improve the performance and scalability of a production database. Which command do you execute first?

○ **A.** CREATE PARTITION

○ **B.** CREATE PARTITION SCHEMA

○ **C.** CREATE PARTITION FUNCTION

○ **D.** CREATE TABLE

○ **E.** CREATE INDEX

18. You are inspecting the transaction handling for an application that updates a number of tables from the SALES database. You would like to know how many transactions are currently open and not committed. What is the easiest way to solve this?

 ❍ **A.** Run DBCC OPENTRAN ('master').

 ❍ **B.** Run DBCC OPENTRAN ('SALES').

 ❍ **C.** Open the Activity Monitor and view open transactions in Process Info.

 ❍ **D.** Execute a query against sys.sysprocesses.

 ❍ **E.** Use sp_helptransaction.

19. You are creating a backup job and want to ensure that a new header is placed on the tape you are using. What option do you use to perform this task?

 ❍ **A.** INIT

 ❍ **B.** FORMAT

 ❍ **C.** INIT with SKIP

 ❍ **D.** INIT with NOSKIP

 ❍ **E.** NOINIT with NOSKIP

20. You would like to assign the same schedule to two separate jobs that perform unrelated activities. Sometimes each job will be run on a different schedule, as well. How do you implement this?

 ❍ **A.** Create one schedule and assign it to both jobs.

 ❍ **B.** Create two schedules, one for each job.

 ❍ **C.** Create a job that executes the other two jobs. Create one schedule for the newly created job.

 ❍ **D.** Create a job that executes the other two jobs. Create two schedules, one for each job.

21. Someone has created 60 jobs on the server to perform a variety of functions. You need to create a backup of the jobs so that they can be easily re-created in the event of a failure. What should you do?

 ❍ **A.** Back up the master database.

 ❍ **B.** Back up the model database.

 ❍ **C.** Back up all system databases.

 ❍ **D.** Create scripts for each of the jobs.

 ❍ **E.** Back up the entire server.

22. You have 50,000 records in a database file, and you know you want to add 25,000 records in the next month. Note that a new index is to be created, and you will change your FILLFACTOR; you also want fast input into the tables. What value should you specify for FILLFACTOR to maximize performance?

  ○   **A.** 0 (default setting)

  ○   **B.** 100

  ○   **C.** 70

  ○   **D.** 50

23. You are configuring log shipping on two servers. The source machine houses the internal accounting, human resources, and other related systems. The destination machine is in the human resources department. You want to set up the HR database at the destination so that it can be used for reporting purposes. How do you set up the procedure? (Select all that apply.)

  ○   **A.** Set the source to simple recovery.

  ○   **B.** Set the source to full recovery.

  ○   **C.** Perform a full backup and a log backup of the source.

  ○   **D.** Perform a full backup and a differential backup of the source.

  ○   **E.** Restore both backups at the destination. Restore the full backup with no recovery, and restore the second with recovery.

  ○   **F.** Restore both backups at the destination. Restore the full backup with no recovery, and restore the second with standby.

24. Last month, a database snapshot was created on the SALES database. You would now like to get a single table from the snapshot. You need to maintain the current copy of the database and not lose any data in the process. How do you access the table? (Select all that apply.)

  ○   **A.** Perform a full backup.

  ○   **B.** Create a new snapshot.

  ○   **C.** Restore from the backup.

  ○   **D.** Revert to the new snapshot.

  ○   **E.** Revert to the original snapshot.

  ○   **F.** Restore the snapshot to a different database.

25. What is true about the WITH SCHEMABINDING argument of the CREATE INDEX statement? (Choose all that apply.)

    ◯ **A.** It must be specified to create an indexed view.

    ◯ **B.** It allows a view's name and other properties to be changed dynamically.

    ◯ **C.** It prevents the dropping and altering of tables participating in the view.

    ◯ **D.** It has to be specified only when you are creating a unique clustered index on text data.

26. You would like to alter the content of a column in the SALES table that stores data in the XML type. Which method should you use?

    ◯ **A.** exist()

    ◯ **B.** modify()

    ◯ **C.** nodes()

    ◯ **D.** query()

    ◯ **E.** value()

27. You are a database developer for a computer manufacturing company. For a limited time, the company ships free software with the purchase of any desktop computer or notebook. The software titles, descriptions, values, and other information are located in the Software table. You configure full-text indexing on the Software_Description column that contains more than 2,000 rows and is located in the Software table. After executing a search by using FREETEXT for the word Windows, you notice an empty result set in the results pane. Why is this happening?

    ◯ **A.** The catalog is not populated.

    ◯ **B.** FREETEXT is not a valid keyword recognized by SQL Server 2005.

    ◯ **C.** FREETEXT is not allowed for columns that contain 2,000 or more rows.

    ◯ **D.** You didn't create a nonclustered index.

28. You are importing a large amount of data into the Customer table. The table has a trigger that sends emails to client representatives when new customers are added to the table. You would like to prevent the emails from being sent during the import. What should you use to accommodate the import?

    ◯ **A.** DISABLE TRIGGER and ENABLE TRIGGER

    ◯ **B.** ALTER TABLE DISABLE TRIGGER and ALTER TABLE ENABLE TRIGGER

    ◯ **C.** DROP TRIGGER and CREATE TRIGGER

○ **D.** ALTER TRIGGER NOT FOR REPLICATION

○ **E.** ALTER TRIGGER DISABLE and ALTER TRIGGER ENABLE

29. A database is about to be set up to be replicated to the human resources department. One of the tables contains a trigger that you do not want to fire when the data hits the destination database. How do you accommodate this?

○ **A.** Use DISABLE TRIGGER at the destination after replication setup has been completed.

○ **B.** Use DROP TRIGGER at the destination after replication setup has been completed.

○ **C.** Use sp_settriggerorder at the source before setting up replication.

○ **D.** Use sp_settriggerorder at the destination after setting up replication.

○ **E.** Use ALTER TRIGGER NOT FOR REPLICATION before setting up replication.

30. A small scientific laboratory needs a powerful database server to perform analysis of complex measures performed on scientists' regular experiments. The lab requires exact accuracy with all calculations because the results determine the fracture points of various metals. Which data type offers the most accurate results?

○ **A.** smallmoney

○ **B.** money

○ **C.** float

○ **D.** real

○ **E.** decimal

31. You want to import a large amount of data from text files. You would like to speed the operation by having the import be performed in primary key sequence. How can you do this?

○ **A.** Use an order hint with BCP.

○ **B.** Use an order element in the format file.

○ **C.** Use an order hint with BULK INSERT.

○ **D.** Use ORDER BY when creating the text files.

○ **E.** Use the SORT option with the bcp command.

32. You are designing a database that will serve as a back end for several large websites. The websites will communicate with each other and pass data back and forth by using XML. You would like to control the data displayed on the user's browser based on interactions with the user. In many cases, columns and rows need to be eliminated based on the criteria supplied. You would like to minimize round-trips to the server for data-exchange purposes. What technology should you apply?

- ○ **A.** Use a user-defined function with SCHEMABINDING set to the XML recordsets.

- ○ **B.** Create an indexed view of the XML recordset, specifying only the columns needed, and supply a WHERE condition based on the rows selected.

- ○ **C.** Create standard views of SQL Server data and export the requested data by using FOR XML.

- ○ **D.** Send data requests and updates directly from the client machine to the server by using the FOR XML and OPENXML options.

- ○ **E.** Use HTML and an XML schema to provide the necessary view of the data.

33. You are performing a BCP operation to import data from text files prepared on another system. The pipe (¦) character has been used as a field delimiter, and a colon (:) is the record delimiter. How do you accommodate this file?

- ○ **A.** Reformat the file as a tab-delimited text file.

- ○ **B.** Reformat the file as a comma-delimited text file.

- ○ **C.** Use the bcp command with all defaults.

- ○ **D.** Use BULK INSERT with all defaults.

- ○ **E.** Use a format file.

34. You are creating an application in which accuracy is important. Which data type will give the greatest possible precision?

- ○ **A.** int
- ○ **B.** bigint
- ○ **C.** decimal
- ○ **D.** real
- ○ **E.** float

35. Users inform you that recently, they have frequently been receiving error messages as query volume has steadily increased. One of the users captured the following message:

```
Transaction was deadlocked on resources with another
process and has been chosen as the deadlock victim.
Rerun the transaction.
```

What is your next step?

○ **A.** Use a different transaction isolation level.

○ **B.** Use SQL Profiler to capture deadlock events.

○ **C.** Use System Monitor to monitor locks.

○ **D.** Add more client access licenses to the server.

36. You are creating a remote service binding for use by the Service Broker in connecting to another machine. You would like the service to run in the context of a system administrator and require authentication to be performed within the connection. What command options should you use?

○ **A.** USER = SysAdmin, ANONYMOUS = ON

○ **B.** AUTHORIZATION = sa, ANONYMOUS = ON

○ **C.** AUTHORIZATION = sa, USER = SysAdmin

○ **D.** USER = SysAdmin, ANONYMOUS = OFF

○ **E.** AUTHORIZATION = sa, ANONYMOUS = OFF

37. You are creating an index for an existing table. There is already a nonclustered index on the primary key. You would like to put the data into address sequence, which is made up of several fields. The address is not the primary key. What should you do?

○ **A.** Change the primary key index to clustered and create a nonclustered index on the address.

○ **B.** Create a nonclustered index on the address.

○ **C.** Create a clustered index on the address.

○ **D.** Change the primary key to the address and make the index clustered.

○ **E.** Change the primary key to the address and make the index nonclustered.

38. You want to create an XML index on the `Customer` table of the `SALES` database. What do you do? (Select two answers.)

    ○ **A.** Create a standard primary clustered index.

    ○ **B.** Create a standard primary nonclustered index.

    ○ **C.** Create an XML primary index.

    ○ **D.** Create an XML secondary index.

    ○ **E.** Create a standard extended index.

39. You are testing the database mirroring functionality. You would like to try automatic failover. Which of the following are required? (Select all that apply.)

    ○ **A.** Synchronous operation

    ○ **B.** Asynchronous operation

    ○ **C.** High-performance mode

    ○ **D.** Witness

    ○ **E.** Monitor

40. You have a statistical database that has scheduled snapshots being created every night. To run a series of reports, you would like to get the database back to the point where it was two weeks ago. What do you do? (Select all that apply.)

    ○ **A.** Restore from the appropriate snapshot.

    ○ **B.** Restore from backup.

    ○ **C.** Create an additional snapshot.

    ○ **D.** Delete all snapshots.

    ○ **E.** Delete all snapshots except the one from two weeks ago.

11

Answers to Practice Exam 1

1. B	15. E	28. A
2. A, E	16. A	29. E
3. A	17. C	30. C
4. A, B	18. C	31. D
5. D	19. B	32. C
6. C	20. A	33. E
7. B, C	21. C	34. E
8. E	22. D	35. B
9. D, E	23. B, C, F	36. D
10. D	24. A, C, E	37. C
11. A, B, C	25. A, C	38. C, D
12. D	26. B	39. A, D
13. D	27. A	40. A, E
14. C		

Question 1

Answer B is correct. An `Integer` data type of one form or another would be the correct choice for the type for the order number. The size of integer used would be determined based on the total number of orders maintained in the table over time. By the looks of the volume being discussed, it may even be worth considering an `Alphanumeric` data type. `Small` and `Tiny` integers would be out of the question because they don't provide for a size large enough to even hold a week's worth of data. Using an `IDENTITY` column is the simplest way to implement sequential numbering. It can be automated at the data store and thus guarantee uniqueness. The front-end application solution could easily produce duplicates between two different entry points. Using a `UniqueIdentifier` data type is never a good choice for any field value that has the possibility of being placed within a key or an index. The space taken up by this type of field will hamper performance of data inserts and retrievals. Although a `TimeStamp` data type would produce the necessary uniqueness, it would be cumbersome to work with as an order number.

For more information, see the following sources:

▶ Chapter 1, "Installing and Configuring SQL Server 2005"

▶ SQL Server 2005 Books Online: "SQL Server Language Reference, Transact-SQL Reference, Data Types"

▶ SQL Server 2005 Books Online: "SQL Server Database Engine, Tables, Designing Tables, Enforcing Data Integrity, Primary Keys Constraints"

▶ "Database Designer Considerations for SQL Server Databases," http://msdn.microsoft.com/library/default.asp?url=/library/ en-us/vdbt7/html/dvcondatabasedesignerconsiderationssql.asp

▶ Within MSDN Library, go to MSDN Home, MSDN Library, Development Tools and Languages, Visual Studio.NET, Product Documentation, Developing with Visual Studio.NET, Designing Distributed Applications, Visual Database Tools, Reference, Database Server Considerations, SQL Server Databases.

Question 2

Answers A and E are correct. A `JOIN` operation is needed to return related items from two or more tables. To perform a comparison against `NULL` data, you use the `ISNULL` operation. A `UNION` could return results from two tables but does not relate the data. `BETWEEN` is used to test whether a value falls within a given range, and you use `IN` to see if a value falls within a set of values provided.

For more information, see the following sources:

- ▶ Chapter 3, "Implementing Database Objects"

- ▶ SQL Server 2005 Books Online: "SQL Server Database Engine, Accessing and Changing Database Data, Query Fundamentals, Join Fundamentals"

- ▶ SQL Server 2005 Books Online: "SQL Server Language Reference, Transact-SQL Reference, ISNULL"

- ▶ "Using Inner Joins," http://msdn2.microsoft.com/en-us/library/ ms190014(SQL.90).aspx

- ▶ Within MSDN Library, go to MSDN Home, MSDN Library, Enterprise Servers and Development, SQL Server, SQL Server 2005 Documentation, SQL Server 2005 Books Online, SQL Server Database Engine, Accessing and Changing Database Data, Query Fundamentals, Join Fundamentals, Using Joins, Using Inner Joins.

Question 3

Answer A is correct. The CLR now facilitates a user-defined type (UDT) that can include business logic and processing. Although you do not want to overuse this facet, it works well in this situation. A trigger will not work because the processing for a trigger occurs after the data enters the column, not before. Constraints are not applicable because they prevent values and restrict data, and they do no other processing. A computed column will work for simple calculations, but in more complex scenarios UDTs are better.

For more information, see the following sources:

- ▶ Chapter 2, "Creating Database Objects"

- ▶ SQL Server 2005 Books Online: "SQL Server Database Engine, Accessing and Changing Database Data, Elements of Transact-SQL, Data Types (Database Engine), Working with CLR User-defined Types, Using and Modifying Instances of User-defined Types"

- ▶ "CLR User-Defined Types," http://msdn2.microsoft.com/ en-us/library/ms131120.aspx

- ▶ Within MSDN Library, go to MSDN Home, MSDN Library, Enterprise Servers and Development, SQL Server, SQL Server 2005 Documentation, SQL Server 2005 Books Online, SQL Server Programming Reference, Database Engine .NET Framework Programming, Building Database Objects with Common Language Runtime (CLR) Integration, CLR User-Defined Types.

Question 4

Answers A and B are correct. Table partitioning should balance processing against multiple machines or align resources for more appropriate use. Covering indexes will make queries against index elements operate faster. By definition, covering indexes are those created by need, based on the queries being performed. Triggers generally slow performance due to additional processing during operations affecting the trigger. RAID 5 is a disk orientation in which data is written, a calculation is performed, and then a second write occurs. Two writes for every data operation would negatively affect performance. C2 security is complete auditing that could drastically slow performance.

For more information, see the following sources:

▶ Chapter 2, "Creating Database Objects"

▶ SQL Server 2005 Books Online: "SQL Server Database Engine, Designing and Creating Databases, Tables, Understanding Tables, Special Table Types"

▶ "Partitioned Tables and Indexes in SQL Server 2005," http://msdn.microsoft.com/library/default.asp?url=/library/en-us/dnsql90/html/sql2k5partition.asp

▶ "Chapter 14 - Improving SQL Server Performance," http://msdn.microsoft.com/library/default.asp?url=/library/en-us/dnpag/html/scalenetchapt14.asp

▶ Within MSDN Library, go to MSDN Home, MSDN Library, .NET Development, Improving .NET Application Performance and Scalability, Chapter 14 - Improving SQL Server Performance.

Question 5

Answer D is correct. Dates are inclusive with the BETWEEN function. Be careful when using comparisons that might rely on the time elements of the data because improperly formulating a condition could exclude some desired data.

For more information, see the following sources:

▶ Chapter 3, "Implementing Database Objects"

▶ SQL Server 2005 Books Online: "SQL Server Database Engine, Accessing and Changing Database Data, Query Fundamentals, Filtering Rows by Using Where and Having, Range Search Conditions"

▶ "Expressions in Queries," http://msdn.microsoft.com/library/default.asp?url=/library/en-us/vdtsql/dvovrusingexpressionsinqueries.asp

▶ Within MSDN Library, go to MSDN Home, MSDN Library, Servers and Enterprise Development, SQL Server, Writing SQL Queries: Let's Start with the Basics.

Question 6

Answer C is correct. You are probably not ordering the data to achieve the desired results. Grouping of the result set doesn't seem to be warranted because the question is asking for five rows. NULL values should not affect this query, although in some instances, NULL data can interfere with the results.

For more information, see the following sources:

▶ Chapter 3, "Implementing Database Objects"

▶ SQL Server 2005 Books Online: "SQL Server Database Engine, Accessing and Changing Database Data, Query Fundamentals, Grouping Rows, Sorting Rows with Order By"

▶ "Accessing and Changing Relational Data Overview," http://msdn.microsoft.com/library/default.asp?url=/library/en-us/ acdata/ac_oview_4pcx.asp

▶ Within MSDN Library, go to MSDN Home, MSDN Library, Servers and Enterprise Development, SQL Server, Writing SQL Queries: Let's Start with the Basics.

Question 7

Answers B and C are correct. Often, applications fill fields with spaces to the left and/or right to the size of the column. When printing reports and in other cases, these spaces are not desired. LTRIM is used to remove leading spaces, and RTRIM is used to remove training spaces. There is no function that combines them both. The REPLACE function replaces characters in a string. The STR function returns character data converted from numeric.

For more information, see the following sources:

▶ Chapter 3, "Implementing Database Objects"

▶ SQL Server 2005 Books Online: "SQL Server Language Reference, Transact-SQL Reference, Functions (Transact-SQL), String Functions (Transact-SQL)"

▶ "String Functions," http://msdn.microsoft.com/library/default.asp?url=/ library/en-us/tsqlref/ts_fa-fz_7oqb.asp

Question 8

Answer E is correct. It is quite possible, in particular when working with views previously created, that the view did not have the correct SET option in place when it was originally created. ANSI_NULLS must be set to ON for both the view creation and the application of the index to the view. If the view was not created in this manner, it needs to be dropped and re-created.

For more information, see the following sources:

▶ Chapter 3, "Implementing Database Objects"

▶ SQL Server 2005 Books Online: "SQL Server Database Engine, Designing and Creating Databases, Indexes, Designing Indexes, General Index Design Guidelines, SET options that effect results"

▶ "View Indexes," http://msdn.microsoft.com/library/default.asp?url=/library/en-us/architec/8_ar_da_490z.asp

▶ Within MSDN Library, go to MSDN Home, MSDN Library, Servers and Enterprise Development, SQL Server, SQL Server 2005, Database Architecture, Logical Database Components, SQL Indexes, SQL Server Architecture, View Indexes.

Question 9

Answers D and E are correct. Both performing a query against sys.dm_db_index_physical_stats and checking the fragmentation page of the index from within SQL Server Management Studio allow you to see fragmentation as well as many other physical characteristics. While querying sys.dm_fts_indexpopulation returns information about the full-text index populations currently in progress, sys.dm_exec_query_stats returns aggregate performance statistics for cached query plans.

For more information, see the following sources:

▶ Chapter 8, "Troubleshooting and Optimizing SQL Server"

▶ SQL Server 2005 Books Online: "SQL Server Language Reference, Transact-SQL Reference, System Views (Transact-SQL), Dynamic Management Views and Functions, Index Related Dynamic Management Views and Functions, sys.dm_db_index_physical_stats"

▶ "Fill Factor," http://msdn.microsoft.com/library/default.asp?url=/library/en-us/createdb/cm_8_des_05_9ak5.asp

Question 10

Answer D is correct. In many situations, it is a good idea to disable indexes while performing data imports. To do so, you use the ALTER INDEX command. The DISABLE option turns the index off to allow for more immediate data imports. To enable the index, you need to rebuild it. In particular, clustered indexes require data reordering when importing has been completed. To enable indexes, you use the REBUILD option. Dropping and creating indexes would work, although it is unnecessary because the disable functionality is available.

For more information, see the following sources:

- ▶ Chapter 3, "Implementing Database Objects"

- ▶ SQL Server 2005 Books Online: "SQL Server Database Engine, Designing and Creating Databases, Indexes, Implementing Indexes, Modifying Indexes, Disabling Indexes"

- ▶ "Chapter 14 - Improving SQL Server Performance," http://msdn.microsoft.com/library/default.asp?url=/library/ en-us/dnpag/html/scalenetchapt14.asp

- ▶ Within MSDN Library, go to MSDN Home, MSDN Library, .NET Development, Improving .NET Application Performance and Scalability, Improving SQL Server Performance.

Question 11

Answers A, B, and C are correct. DBCC CHECKTABLE can analyze and repair table issues. ALTER INDEX REORGANIZE can repair index fragmentation. UPDATE STATISTICS may provide for more appropriate query plans, particularly if it is used after mass alterations, additions, or deletions to data. CREATE STATISTICS provides the capabilities of creating additional statistics to be used by the Optimizer and does not apply in this instance. DBCC SHOWSTATISTICS displays distribution statistics for a table but does nothing to perform maintenance. DBCC UPDATEUSAGE reports and corrects pages and row count inaccuracies in the catalog views, providing for more accurate space usage readings.

For more information, see the following sources:

- ▶ Chapter 7, "Monitoring SQL Server Performance," and Chapter 8, "Troubleshooting and Optimizing SQL Server"

- ▶ SQL Server 2005 Books Online: "SQL Server Language Reference, Transact-SQL Reference, DBCC"

- ▶ SQL Server 2005 Books Online: "SQL Server Language Reference, Transact-SQL Reference, ALTER INDEX"

- ▶ SQL Server 2005 Books Online: "SQL Server Language Reference, Transact-SQL Reference, UPDATE STATISTICS"

- ▶ "Webcasts," http://msdn.microsoft.com/sql/community/webcasts/default.aspx

- ▶ Within MSDN Library, go to MSDN Home, SQL Server 2005 Webcasts: Many webcasts on fine tuning performance.

Question 12

Answer D is correct. You can programmatically map linked server logins by using the sp_addlinkedsrvlogin procedure. sp_helplogins provides information about logins and users but does nothing to create or map users. sp_addlogin can be used to add logins to the local instance. sp_adduser adds a login to a database. sp_grantlogin creates a SQL Server login on a local instance.

For more information, see the following sources:

- ▶ Chapter 1, "Installing and Configuring SQL Server 2005"

- ▶ SQL Server 2005 Books Online: "SQL Server Database Engine, Accessing and Changing Database Data, Distributed Queries, Accessing External Data"

- ▶ SQL Server 2005 Books Online: "SQL Server Language Reference, Transact-SQL Reference, System Stored Procedures (Transact-SQL), Distributed Queries Stored Procedures (Transact-SQL), sp_addlinkedsrvlogin"

- ▶ "Establishing Security for Linked Servers," http://msdn.microsoft.com/library/default.asp?url=/library/en-us/adminsql/ad_1_server_24tv.asp

- ▶ Within MSDN Library, go to MSDN Home, MSDN Library, Servers and Enterprise Development, SQL Server, SQL Server 2005, Managing Servers, Configuring Linked Servers.

Question 13

Answer D is correct. When an EXECUTE AS statement is run, the execution context of the session is switched to the specified login or username. sp_change_users_login maps an existing database user to a SQL Server login.

`Auto_Fix` links a user entry in the `sysusers` table in the current database to a SQL Server login of the same name. `Update_One` links the specified user in the current database to an existing SQL Server login. The username and login must be specified. The password must be `NULL` or not specified.

For more information, see the following sources:

- ▶ Chapter 3, "Implementing Database Objects"

- ▶ SQL Server 2005 Books Online: "SQL Server Database Engine, Security Considerations for Databases and Database Applications, Context Switching, Extending Database Impersonation by Using EXECUTE AS"

Question 14

Answer C is correct. An upgraded database with `default` or `dbo` ownership will fall into the `dbo` schema when upgraded to SQL Server 2005.

For more information, see the following sources:

- ▶ Chapter 2, "Creating Database Objects"

- ▶ SQL Server 2005 Books Online: "Installing SQL Server, Upgrading to SQL Server 2005"

- ▶ "An Overview of SQL Server 2005 for the Database Developer," http://msdn.microsoft.com/library/default.asp?url=/library/en-us/dnsql90/html/sql_ovyukondev.asp

- ▶ "SQL Server 2005 Upgrade Handbook," www.microsoft.com/technet/prodtechnol/sql/2005/sqlupgrd.mspx

- ▶ Within Microsoft Technet, go to TechNet Home, Products and Technologies, SQL TechCenter Home, SQL Server 2005, SQL Server 2005 Upgrade Handbook.

Question 15

Answer E is correct. In this situation, you want to implement cascading operations. To do so, you alter the table definitions and use the `CASCADE` clause within the implementation of foreign key constraints. DML triggers are not an efficient mechanism for preserving referential integrity, and DDL triggers lack the necessary functionality because they deal with a different set of objects.

For more information, see the following sources:

- ▶ Chapter 3, "Implementing Database Objects"

- ▶ SQL Server 2005 Books Online: "SQL Server Database Engine, Designing and Creating Databases, Designing Tables, Enforcing Data Integrity, FOREIGN KEY Constraints"

- ▶ "INF: Implementing Referential Integrity and Cascading Actions (White Paper)," http://support.microsoft.com/default.aspx?scid=kb;en-us;322323

Question 16

Answer A is correct. You can use DDL triggers to record information every time objects are created, deleted, or altered in a similar fashion to how you use DML triggers when inserting, deleting, and updating data. The question is not asking that the permissions be changed, and this should not be necessary in the given scenario.

For more information, see the following sources:

- ▶ Chapter 2, "Creating Database Objects," and Chapter 3, "Implementing Database Objects"

- ▶ SQL Server 2005 Books Online: "SQL Server Database Engine, Designing and Creating Database, DDL Triggers, Understanding DDL Triggers, Understanding DDL Triggers vs. DML Triggers"

- ▶ "Designing DDL Triggers," http://msdn2.microsoft.com/en-us/library/ms186406.aspx

- ▶ Within MSDN Library, go to MSDN Home, MSDN Library, Enterprise Servers and Development, SQL Server, SQL Server 2005 Documentation, SQL Server 2005 Books Online, SQL Server Database Engine, Designing and Creating Databases, DDL Triggers, Designing DDL Triggers.

Question 17

Answer C is correct. The correct order of commands is CREATE PARTITION FUNCTION, CREATE PARTITION SCHEMA, and then you can create an object on the partition.

For more information, see the following sources:

- ▶ Chapter 2, "Creating Database Objects," and Chapter 3, "Implementing Database Objects"

- ▶ SQL Server 2005 Books Online: "SQL Server Database Engine, Designing and Creating Databases, Partitioned Tables and Indexes, Implementing Partitioned Tables and Indexes, Creating Partitioned Tables and Indexes"

- ▶ "Creating Partitioned Tables and Indexes," http://msdn2.microsoft.com/ en-us/library/ms188730(SQL.90).aspx

- ▶ "Partitioned Tables and Indexes in SQL Server 2005," http://msdn.microsoft.com/library/default.asp?url=/library/ en-us/dnsql90/html/sql2k5partition.asp

- ▶ Within MSDN Library, go to MSDN Home, MSDN Library, Enterprise Servers and Development, SQL Server, SQL Server 2005 Documentation, SQL Server 2005 Books Online, SQL Server Database Engine, Designing and Creating Databases, Partitioned Tables and Indexes, Implementing Partitioned Tables and Indexes, Creating Partitioned Tables and Indexes.

- ▶ Within MSDN Library, go to MSDN Home, MSDN Library, Servers and Enterprise Development, SQL Server, Partitioned Tables and Indexes in SQL Server 2005.

Question 18

Answer C is correct. The DBCC OPENTRAN command will only give you the last open transaction for a particular database. There is no such command as sp_helptransaction, and executing a query against any system tables would be difficult to resolve the desired information, although it could be possible. By far the easiest technique, assuming access to the 2005 toolset, is to use the Activity Monitor.

For more information, see the following sources:

- ▶ Chapter 8, "Troubleshooting and Optimizing SQL Server"

- ▶ SQL Server 2005 Books Online: "Database Engine How-to Topics, Performance Monitoring and Tuning How-to Topics, Server Performance and Activity Monitoring How-to Topics, How to: Open the Activity Monitor (SQL Server Management Studio)"

- ▶ "sysprocesses," http://msdn.microsoft.com/library/default.asp?url=/ library/en-us/tsqlref/ts_sys-p_3kmr.asp

Question 19

Answer B is correct. The FORMAT clause of the BACKUP command initializes a tape and places a new header on the tape. The remaining options do not enforce these actions.

For more information, see the following sources:

▶ Chapter 6, "Database Maintenance"

▶ SQL Server 2005 Books Online: "SQL Server Database Engine, Administering the Database Engine, Backing Up and Restoring Databases, Managing Backups, Using Backup Media"

▶ "Initializing Backup Media," http://msdn.microsoft.com/library/ default.asp?url=/library/en-us/adminsql/ad_bkprst_22w5.asp

▶ Within MSDN Library, go to MSDN Home, MSDN Library, Servers and Enterprise Development, SQL Server, SQL Server 2005, Backing Up and Restoring Databases, Managing Backups, Using Backup Media, Initializing Backup Media.

Question 20

Answer A is correct. Schedules are objects in themselves and are independent of any procedures that use them. You can assign the same schedule to a number of procedures. The other answers are incorrect because they create too many schedules or unnecessary jobs.

For more information, see the following sources:

▶ Chapter 6, "Database Maintenance"

▶ SQL Server 2005 Books Online: "SQL Server Database Engine, Designing and Creating Databases, Databases, Maintaining Databases"

▶ SQL Server 2005 Books Online: "SQL Server Database Engine, Administering the Database Engine, Automating Administrative Tasks"

Question 21

Answer C is correct. To get a copy of all jobs, alerts, operators, and schedules, you back up the msdb database. SQL Server Agent maintains all this information within msdb. By backing up the system database, you also create emergency copies of other system metadata.

For more information, see the following sources:

- ▶ Chapter 6, "Database Maintenance"

- ▶ "Backing Up the `model`, `msdb`, and `distribution` Databases," http://msdn.microsoft.com/library/default.asp?url=/library/en-us/admin-sql/ad_bkprst_4rlf.asp

- ▶ Within MSDN Library, go to MSDN Home, MSDN Library, Servers and Enterprise Development, SQL Server, SQL Server 2005, Backing Up and Restoring Databases, Backing Up and Restoring System Databases, Backing Up the model, msdb, and distribution Databases.

Question 22

Answer D is correct. You know that 25,000 is 50% of 50,000, so filling the page by 50% and leaving 50% free space for the remaining 50,000 records seems logical. The default `FILLFACTOR` setting of 0 doesn't leave any room for additions, which would slow inserts. If you set the `FILLFACTOR` value too big, searches slow down because any query processed has to cycle through a lot of empty space.

For more information, see the following sources:

- ▶ Chapter 2, "Creating Database Objects"

- ▶ SQL Server 2005 Books Online: "Building SQL Server Applications, SQL-DMO, SQL-DMO Reference, Properties, F, FILLFACTOR"

- ▶ "Fill Factor," http://msdn.microsoft.com/library/default.asp?url=/library/en-us/createdb/cm_8_des_05_9ak5.asp

Question 23

Answers B, C, and F are correct. Log shipping is the process of sending regular backups of logs to be restored on a second instance. To be able to back up logs, you must get the database out of a simple recovery mode. The standby option is used to have the destination server be set up as a read-only server.

For more information, see the following sources:

- ▶ Chapter 9, "Implementing High Availability"

- ▶ SQL Server 2005 Books Online: "SQL Server Database Engine, Administering the Database Engine, Configuring High Availability, Log Shipping, Configuring Log Shipping:

▶ "How to Configure the Destination System for Log Shipping,"
http://msdn.microsoft.com/library/default.asp?url=/library/en-us/
bts06operations/html/7b4425f5-b105-4fb2-a503-94ca1e75ad55.asp

Question 24

Answers A, C, and E are correct. If you are intending to return the database to a known state, you have to start by performing a full backup. You can then revert the database, and when you are finished, you can restore from the backup you created.

For more information, see the following sources:

▶ Chapter 6, "Database Maintenance"

▶ SQL Server 2005 Books Online: "SQL Server Language Reference, Transact-SQL Reference, RESTORE Statements for Restoring, Recovering, and Managing Backups"

▶ "An Overview of SQL Server 2005 for the Database Developer,"
http://msdn.microsoft.com/library/default.asp?url=/library/
en-us/dnsql90/html/sql_ovyukondev.asp

Question 25

Answers A and C are correct. The WITH SCHEMABINDING argument of the CREATE INDEX statement is needed when creating an indexed view. When WITH SCHEMABINDING is specified, tables participating in the indexed view are prevented from being altered or deleted. Alteration of names for a dynamic view is irrelevant, and index type is of no consequence.

For more information, see the following sources:

▶ Chapter 2, "Creating Database Objects," and Chapter 3, "Implementing Database Objects"

▶ SQL Server 2005 Books Online: "Creating and Maintaining Databases, Views, Creating a View, Creating an Indexed View"

▶ "Improving Performance with SQL Server 2005 Indexed Views,"
http://msdn.microsoft.com/library/default.asp?url=/library/en-us/
dnsql2k/html/indexedviews1.asp

Question 26

Answer B is correct. modify() is used to specify XML DML statements to perform updates. query() is used to query over an XML instance, value() is used to retrieve a value of SQL type from an XML instance, exist() is used to determine whether a query returns a non-empty result, and nodes() is used to shred XML into multiple rows to propagate parts of XML documents into rowsets.

For more information, see the following sources:

- ► Chapter 4, "Supporting the XML Framework"

- ► SQL Server 2005 Books Online: "SQL Server Database Engine, Using XML in SQL Server, xml Data Type, xml Data Type Methods"

- ► "XML Options in Microsoft SQL Server 2005," http://msdn. microsoft.com/library/default.asp?url=/library/en-us/dnsql90/ html/sql2k5xmloptions.asp

- ► "XML Support in Microsoft SQL Server 2005," http://msdn. microsoft.com/library/default.asp?url=/library/en-us/dnsql90/ html/sql2k5xml.asp

- ► Within MSDN Library, go to MSDN Home, MSDN Library, Servers and Enterprise Development, SQL Server, XML Best Practices for Microsoft SQL Server 2005.

Question 27

Answer A is correct. Before executing full-text searches, you must create and populate a full-text catalog. Population usually occurs when the catalog is created. A full-text catalog is the basis of the storage used for indexes. These catalogs should periodically be repopulated to ensure usefulness. Repopulation can be done by schedule or by administrative task.

For more information, see the following sources:

- ► Chapter 2, "Creating Database Objects," and Chapter 3, "Implementing Database Objects"

- ► SQL Server 2005 Books Online: "Full-Text Search"

- ► "SQL Server 2005 full-text search includes improved and updated noise word files," http://support.microsoft.com/default.aspx?scid=kb; en-us;905617

- ► Within MSDN Library, go to MSDN Home, SQL Server Developer Center, Community, Webcasts, Full-Text Search Q and A.

Question 28

Answer A is correct. You use DISABLE TRIGGER to disable a trigger while performing other activities. This keeps the trigger intact, but the trigger will not fire when alterations to the data occur. You use ENABLE TRIGGER to put the trigger back in place. DROP and CREATE trigger would also work, but dropping the trigger is unnecessary in SQL Server 2005.

For more information, see the following sources:

- ▶ Chapter 3, "Implementing Database Objects"

- ▶ SQL Server 2005 Books Online: "SQL Server Language Reference, Transact-SQL Reference, DISABLE TRIGGER"

Question 29

Answer E is correct. Triggers usually perform their work when changes occur within the data. In a replication scenario, you usually don't want those procedures to be performed in both the source and destination locations. To prevent that from occurring, you can set the trigger as NOT FOR REPLICATION so that it will not fire in the destination. This option can also be applied to identity columns and constraints. Disabling or dropping the triggers is likely to remove required functionality at the source.

For more information, see the following sources:

- ▶ Chapter 3, "Implementing Database Objects"

- ▶ SQL Server 2005 Books Online: "SQL Server Replication, Configuring and Maintaining Replication, Implementing Replication, Implementation Considerations for Replication, Considerations for All Types of Replication, Controlling Constraints, Identities, and Triggers with NOT FOR REPLICATION"

- ▶ "ALTER TRIGGER," http://msdn.microsoft.com/library/ default.asp?url=/library/en-us/tsqlref/ts_aa-az_9036.asp

Question 30

Answer C is correct. Float gives accuracy up to 308 decimal places, which is almost 10 times better than can be achieved with any of the other types. The real and decimal data types provide only 38 decimal places of accuracy at most, and money and smallmoney have accuracy to only the ten-thousandths.

For more information, see the following sources:

- ▶ Chapter 1, "Installing and Configuring SQL Server 2005," and Chapter 2, "Creating Database Objects"

- ▶ SQL Server 2005 Books Online: "Transact-SQL Reference, Data Types"

Question 31

Answer D is correct. To import data using bulk tools the data must be prepared in sequence. You can do this by exporting the data using a SQL query with the ORDER BY clause. There is no mechanism available to alter the order by using the BCP or BULK INSERT commands.

For more information, see the following sources:

- ▶ Chapter 5, "Data Consumption and Throughput"

- ▶ SQL Server 2005 Books Online: "SQL Server Database Engine, Administering the Database Engine, Importing and Exporting Bulk Data"

Question 32

Answer C is correct. This is a perfect situation for sending a recordset to the client machine that can then be used by the front-end application to show only the data needed. XML provides a mechanism by which the data is shipped to the client, resides in the background of the client machine, and is presented by the front end in any manner desired. SCHEMABINDING refers only to SQL Server objects—specifically tables, views, and user-defined functions. An XML schema cannot be bound in this manner. XML resides in memory and is processed against its own internal set of rules, referred to as a schema. An XML schema interacts directly with the data to supply logic and display attributes on the user's browser. HTML does not have the required functionality.

For more information, see the following sources:

- ▶ Chapter 4, "Supporting the XML Framework"

- ▶ SQL Server 2005 Books Online: "SQL Server Database Engine, Using XML in SQL Server"

- ▶ "XML Options in Microsoft SQL Server 2005," http://msdn. microsoft.com/library/default.asp?url=/library/en-us/dnsql90/ html/sql2k5xmloptions.asp

▶ "XML Support in Microsoft SQL Server 2005," http://msdn.
microsoft.com/library/default.asp?url=/library/en-us/dnsql90/
html/sql2k5xml.asp

▶ Within MSDN Library, go to MSDN Home, MSDN Library, Servers
and Enterprise Development, SQL Server, XML Best Practices for
Microsoft SQL Server 2005.

Question 33

Answer E is correct. Anything other than the default delimiters requires the use
of a format file to identify the field and record orientation used for the data.

For more information, see the following sources:

▶ Chapter 5, "Data Consumption and Throughput"

▶ SQL Server 2005 Books Online: "SQL Server Database Engine,
Administering the Database Engine, Administering the Database Engine,
Importing and Exporting Bulk Data, Format Files for Importing or
Exporting Data"

▶ "Using Format Files," http://msdn.microsoft.com/library/
default.asp?url=/library/en-us/adminsql/ad_impt_bcp_9yat.asp

▶ Within MSDN Library, go to MSDN Home, MSDN Library, Servers
and Enterprise Development, SQL Server, SQL Server 2000, Importing
and Exporting Data, Using bcp and BULK INSERT, Using Format
Files.

Question 34

Answer E is correct. float gives accuracy up to 308 decimal places, which is
almost 10 times better than can be achieved with any of the other types. The real
and decimal data types provide only 38 decimal places of accuracy at most, and
int and bigint have no accuracy because they have no fractional component.

For more information, see the following sources:

▶ Chapter 1, "Installing and Configuring SQL Server 2005," and Chapter
2, "Creating Database Objects"

▶ SQL Server 2005 Books Online: "Transact-SQL Reference, Data Types"

Question 35

Answer B is correct. In most instances, deadlock scenarios are a result of poor application design. Numerous types of design flaws can cause deadlock scenarios, including accessing objects in an inconsistent order or setting unnecessary locks. To isolate the part of the application that is causing the problem, you need to test the program within its production environment. Although the System Monitor would be able to provide you with information on the numbers of deadlocks, it does not provide much specific information about where they are occurring. The SQL Profiler is specifically designed to closely monitor what is going on within the DBMS and provide detailed information.

For more information, see the following sources:

- ▶ Chapter 7, "Monitoring SQL Server Performance," and Chapter 8, "Troubleshooting and Optimizing SQL Server"

- ▶ SQL Server 2005 Books Online: "Accessing and Changing Relational Data, Locking"

- ▶ SQL Server 2005 Books Online: "Administering SQL Server, Monitoring Server Performance, Monitoring with SQL Profiler"

- ▶ "Understanding and Avoiding Blocking," http://msdn.microsoft.com/library/default.asp?url=/library/en-us/optimsql/odp_tun_1a_4uav.asp

- ▶ Within MSDN Library, go to MSDN Home, MSDN Library, Servers and Enterprise Development, SQL Server, SQL Server 2005, Application Design.

Question 36

Answer D is correct. USER specifies the database principal that owns the certificate associated with the connection. ANONYMOUS specifies whether anonymous authentication is used when communicating with the remote service. AUTHORIZATION sets the owner of the binding.

For more information, see the following sources:

- ▶ Chapter 5, "Data Consumption and Throughput"

- ▶ SQL Server 2005 Books Online: "SQL Server Language Reference, Transact-SQL Reference, CREATE REMOTE SERVICE BINDING"

- ▶ "Remote Data Binding with Remote Data Service," http://msdn.microsoft.com/library/default.asp?url=/library/en-us/iissdk/html/9afe4014-2e20-4c5b-8546-8cb4fdc496ac.asp

▶ Within MSDN Library, go to MSDN Home, MSDN Library, .NET Development, Web Services, Building XML Web Services Using Industry Standardized WSDLs.

Question 37

Answer C is correct. Sequencing the physical data requires the use of a clustered index. A primary key does not have to have a clustered index assigned to it.

For more information, see the following sources:

▶ Chapter 2, "Creating Database Objects"

▶ SQL Server 2005 Books Online: "SQL Server Database Engine, Designing and Creating Databases, Indexes, Understanding Indexes"

▶ "Index Tuning Recommendations," http://msdn.microsoft.com/library/default.asp?url=/library/en-us/optimsql/odp_tun_1_6583.asp

▶ Within MSDN Library, go to MSDN Home, MSDN Library, Servers and Enterprise Development, SQL Server, SQL Server 2000, Database Design, Physical Database Design, Index Tuning Recommendations.

Question 38

Answers C and D are correct. The creation of XML indexes requires a minimum of a primary XML index. In addition, if indexing is to use exacting XML XQueries, you need to create a secondary XML index based on the initial primary one. Creating other types of indexes is irrelevant to the question.

For more information, see the following sources:

▶ Chapter 4, "Supporting the XML Framework"

▶ SQL Server 2005 Books Online: "SQL Server Database Engine, Using XML in SQL Server, xml Data Type, Indexes on xml Data Type Columns"

▶ "XML Indexes in SQL Server 2005," http://msdn.microsoft.com/library/default.asp?url=/library/en-us/dnsql90/html/xmlindexes.asp

▶ Within MSDN Library, go to MSDN Home, MSDN Library, Servers and Enterprise Development, SQL Server, XML Indexes in SQL Server 2005.

Question 39

Answers A and D are correct. To achieve automatic failover of a mirrored database set, you must have the mirror configured for synchronous delivery, and you also need to have a witness configured. The witness actually identifies the state in which the failover is triggered.

For more information, see the following sources:

- ▸ Chapter 9, "Implementing High Availability"

- ▸ SQL Server 2005 Books Online: "SQL Server Database Engine, Administering the Database Engine, Database Mirroring, Database Mirroring Sessions, Role Switching During a Database Mirroring Session, Automatic Failover"

Question 40

Answers A and E are correct. To revert a database to the point at which a database snapshot was taken, you must first eliminate all the other database snapshots. You then use the RESTORE command to revert the database, using the remaining snapshot. You do not create an additional snapshot because you would be removing it when you removed all the others.

For more information, see the following sources:

- ▸ Chapter 6, "Database Maintenance"

- ▸ SQL Server 2005 Books Online: "SQL Server Language Reference, Transact-SQL Reference, RESTORE Statements for Restoring, Recovering, and Managing Backups"

- ▸ "An Overview of SQL Server 2005 for the Database Developer," http://msdn.microsoft.com/library/default.asp?url=/library/ en-us/dnsql90/html/sql_ovyukondev.asp

12

Practice Exam 2

The actual certification exam has 40 questions. To best simulate the exam circumstances, you should try to complete the 40 questions in this practice exam in 90 minutes.

Chapter 13, "Answers to Practice Exam 2," provides the answers to this practice exam. Each answer is accompanied by references to the applicable materials in SQL Server 2005 Books Online and on the Microsoft official websites.

Exam Questions

1. You are attempting to create an index on an existing view called SalesOverQuota, created in the SALES database. When the view was initially created, no preparation was done for indexing. You want to maintain the condition that was originally attached to the WHERE clause of the view. How do you implement the index?

   ○ **A.** Re-create the view by using WITH CHECK.

   ○ **B.** Re-create the view by using WITH SCHEMABINDING.

   ○ **C.** Use DROP EXISTING when creating the index.

   ○ **D.** Create the index as nonclustered.

   ○ **E.** Re-create the view, removing the WHERE clause.

2. You are still attempting to create an index on an existing view called SalesOverQuota, created in the SALES database. You would like to create a non-clustered index on the CustomerName column of the view. No other indexes have been created on the view. The underlying table has a clustered index on the primary key. What is the first step in implementing the index?

   ○ **A.** Create a suitable clustered index on the view.

   ○ **B.** Create a nonclustered index on the view.

   ○ **C.** Ensure that the primary key is included in the view.

   ○ **D.** Ensure that the primary key is unique.

   ○ **E.** Create a unique nonclustered index.

3. You are setting up the ODBC connection for a client computer. The server was installed using the default protocol and communications configuration. What TCP/IP port should be configured?

   ○ **A.** 433

   ○ **B.** 443

   ○ **C.** 1433

   ○ **D.** 1443

   ○ **E.** 4443

4. Within a test environment, you are configuring a connection to an instance of SQL Server that is on the same machine as the application. Protocols have been configured to not allow access to SQL from external machines and applications. What is the most secure way to connect to SQL Server?

   ○ **A.** TCP/IP

   ○ **B.** SSL

   ○ **C.** HTTP

   ○ **D.** HTTPS

   ○ **E.** Shared memory

5. You have started SQL Server from the command prompt by using `SQLSERVR.EXE -f` to get the server into single-use operations. You notice that users are still able to connect to the server. What is wrong?

   ○ **A.** The server has not been paused.

   ○ **B.** The server has not been stopped.

   ○ **C.** Minimal configuration allows multiple connections.

   ○ **D.** The service option was not used in startup.

6. You are about to install a new instance of SQL Server. What connection protocols are available for use? (Select all that apply.)

   ○ **A.** Named pipes

   ○ **B.** Multiprotocol

   ○ **C.** Shared memory

   ○ **D.** TCP/IP

   ○ **E.** Virtual Interface Adapter

7. An application needs to query different data, based on user-selected criteria. The interface is presented to the user via a Windows application interface. After the selection is made, the data is drawn from the server and returned to a grid layout on the user's computer. What technology would be used for the implementation?

   ○ **A.** Stored procedure using the common language runtime

   ○ **B.** Stored procedure using Transact-SQL

   ○ **C.** Stored procedure using parameters and the common language runtime

   ○ **D.** Stored procedure using parameters and Transact-SQL

   ○ **E.** Stored procedure implemented through Web Services

8. A procedure being called by an application needs to perform a series of complex calculations. The interface is presented to the user via a Windows application. After the user makes selections, the application calls the procedure. Results are returned to the user's computer. What technology would be used for the implementation?

- ○ **A.** Stored procedure using the common language runtime
- ○ **B.** Stored procedure using Transact-SQL
- ○ **C.** Stored procedure using parameters and the common language runtime
- ○ **D.** Stored procedure using parameters and Transact-SQL
- ○ **E.** Stored procedure implemented through Web Services

9. You are writing a procedure that will create a permanent table within an existing database. Which of the following will you use in the procedure to store the table?

- ○ **A.** SELECT INTO #TableVar
- ○ **B.** SELECT INTO ##TableVar
- ○ **C.** SELECT INTO tempdb..tablevar
- ○ **D.** SELECT INTO @TableVar
- ○ **E.** SELECT INTO TableVar

10. You need a summary listing of all the user objects within a database. What would you use?

- ○ **A.** sp_Help
- ○ **B.** SELECT * FROM sysobjects
- ○ **C.** SELECT * FROM master..sysobjects
- ○ **D.** SELECT * FROM sys.database_principals
- ○ **E.** SELECT * FROM sys.objects

11. A production server has implemented partitioning, using a function that divides the data into four sections and reserves a fifth partition for future expansion; the fifth partition is currently unused. You need to query the utilization of the four currently used partitions. How would you perform the query?

- ○ **A.** sp_spaceused
- ○ **B.** sp_table_validation
- ○ **C.** sp_server_info
- ○ **D.** $Partition
- ○ **E.** $Identity
- ○ **F.** $RowGUID

12. An application being developed for a production database requires data to be extracted from a comprehensive table and added to another database. The statement must create a new table every time it is executed. Which of the following commands would be used?

   ○ **A.** EXEC ('INSERT INTO ' + @NewTable + ' SELECT * FROM SalesOrders')

   ○ **B.** EXEC ('INSERT ' + @NewTable + ' SELECT * FROM SalesOrders')

   ○ **C.** EXEC ('SELECT * INTO ' + @NewTable + ' FROM SalesOrders')

   ○ **D.** EXEC ('SELECT * INTO #NewTable FROM SalesOrders')

   ○ **E.** EXEC ('SELECT * INTO ##NewTable FROM SalesOrders')

13. You have a text field in an employee table that is used to maintain general information in the form of memos. You would like to make this field searchable. Other tables in the database have the same functionality implemented. What do you need to execute?

   ○ **A.** CREATE FULLTEXT CATALOG

   ○ **B.** CREATE FULLTEXT INDEX

   ○ **C.** CREATE INDEX

   ○ **D.** CREATE PRIMARY XML INDEX

   ○ **E.** CREATE XML INDEX

14. You have an application that accesses data on two servers. When you attempt to execute a query on the first server using both data sets, the query fails when it attempts to access the second server. What do you need to do?

   ○ **A.** Use four-part names in the query.

   ○ **B.** Reference the second database by using an alias.

   ○ **C.** Add the second server as a linked server on the first server.

   ○ **D.** Add the second server as a remote server on the first server.

   ○ **E.** Add the first server as a linked server on the second server.

15. You are working with two servers. You have configured linked server operations. Both servers use SQL Server authentication and different logins. How do you handle connectivity between the two servers?

   ○ **A.** Change security to use Windows authentication.

   ○ **B.** Add additional logins with the same ID and password.

    ○ **C.** Hard-code the user ID and password in the application and use pass-through authentication.

    ○ **D.** Use the sa user ID and password.

    ○ **E.** Configure the linked server to impersonate logins.

16. You are about to perform database analysis against a workload that was taken from the production server. You need to perform a complete analysis of all potential index changes. What is the appropriate setting?

    ○ **A.** Evaluate Utilization of Existing PDS Only

    ○ **B.** Keep All Existing PDS

    ○ **C.** All Recommendations Are Offline

    ○ **D.** Generate Online Recommendations Where Possible

    ○ **E.** Generate Only Online Recommendations

17. You need to configure the settings for an HTTP endpoint on a production SQL Server. It is desired to have the connection performed over SSL (HTTPS). The following definition is being used:

```
CREATE ENDPOINT sql_endpoint
STATE = STARTED
AS HTTP(
    PATH = '/sql',
    AUTHENTICATION = (INTEGRATED),
    PORTS = (CLEAR),
    SITE = 'SERVER'
    )
FOR SOAP (
WSDL = DEFAULT,
    SCHEMA = STANDARD,
    DATABASE = 'master',
    NAMESPACE = 'http://tempUri.org/'
    )
```

What must be changed?

    ○ **A.** AS HTTP should be AS HTTPS.

    ○ **B.** AUTHENTICATION should be BASIC.

    ○ **C.** PORTS setting requires SSL.

    ○ **D.** WSDL should be set to NONE.

    ○ **E.** ENCRYPTION = REQUIRED should be added.

18. You need to find out information about the scheduling of jobs used to perform automated activities. Specifically, you would like to know when was the last time a job was
run. Which procedure would you use?

- ○ **A.** `sp_help_jobschedule`
- ○ **B.** `sp_help_jobs_in_schedule`
- ○ **C.** `sp_help_schedule`
- ○ **D.** `sp_help_job`
- ○ **E.** `sp_help_jobstep`

19. You are using the Database Engine Tuning Advisor and you would like to select options
that give the best recommendations for partitioning performance. What option would
you select?

- ○ **A.** Evaluate Use of Existing PDS Only
- ○ **B.** No Partitioning
- ○ **C.** Aligned Partitioning
- ○ **D.** Full Partitioning
- ○ **E.** Keep Aligned Partitioning

20. Several users are complaining of problems with updating of data through their application. You suspect that locks placed by other users and applications are preventing
updates from occurring. Which of the following will help locate current locks and
blocking? (Select all that apply.)

- ○ **A.** `sys.dm_exec_sessions`
- ○ **B.** `sys.dm_exec_requests`
- ○ **C.** Activity Monitor, Process Info
- ○ **D.** Activity Monitor, Locks by Process
- ○ **E.** System Monitor, SQL Server:Locks

21. Indexes of a table are heavily fragmented. What should you do to decrease the fragmentation of all indexes while keeping the table available to users?

- ○ **A.** Defragment the disk that contains the table.
- ○ **B.** Use `DBCC CLEANTABLE`.
- ○ **C.** Use `ALTER INDEX ALL REORGANIZE`.
- ○ **D.** Use `ALTER INDEX ALL REBUILD`.
- ○ **E.** Use `DBCC CHECKIDENT`.

22. You are working with a database named `Sales` on a server named `SELLER`. You want to mirror `Sales` on a second server named `SELLER2`. Which actions do you perform to prepare `Sales` on `SELLER`? (Select three answers, as each correct answer presents part of the solution.)

    ○ **A.** Set the recovery model to bulk-logged.

    ○ **B.** Set the recovery model to full.

    ○ **C.** Back up `Sales`. Restore the backup on `SELLER2` by using NORECOVERY.

    ○ **D.** Back up `Sales`. Restore the backup on `SELLER2` by using STANDBY.

    ○ **E.** Back up `Sales`. Restore the backup on `SELLER2` by using RECOVERY.

    ○ **F.** Create endpoints on both servers.

    ○ **G.** Set the `Auto Update Statistics` property of `Sales` to `false`.

23. You are moving a database to a new server. The database is used by a data entry application. You need to minimize the amount of time the application is unavailable. What should you do?

    ○ **A.** Set up transactional replication between the servers.

    ○ **B.** Move the data files and provide the new location by using ALTER DATABASE.

    ○ **C.** Back up the database. Restore the database to the new server.

    ○ **D.** Detach the current database. Copy the data files to the new server. Attach the files.

    ○ **E.** Move the database to the new server by using the SMO method in the Copy Database Wizard.

24. You want to use Service Broker to manage data requests. After creation of the broker queue, you need to make other changes and want to ensure that no messages can be received by the service. What should you do?

    ○ **A.** Create the queue with `STATUS OFF`.

    ○ **B.** Create the queue with `ACTIVATION STATUS OFF`.

    ○ **C.** Create the queue with only the `queue_name` argument.

    ○ **D.** Create the queue with `MAX_QUEUE_READERS = 0`.

    ○ **E.** Create the queue with `RETENTION OFF`.

25. One of the daily scheduled jobs aggregates data from multiple sources for reports. The job consists of multiple steps that aggregate data for a specific report. A user reports that the data for some of the reports has not been updated. You need to ensure that every step of the job executes, even when errors occur. What should you do?

- ○ **A.** Configure each step as a separate job.
- ○ **B.** Change the On Failure action to go to the next step.
- ○ **C.** Combine all the steps into a single step that runs once a day.
- ○ **D.** Create a notification that alerts you when an error occurs so that you can correct the error and restart the job.
- ○ **E.** Configure the job to retry the step.

26. You are creating a view to join the Customers and Orders tables. You need to ensure that the view cannot be affected by modifications to underlying table schemas. You want to use the least possible overhead. What should you do?

- ○ **A.** Create a DML trigger to roll back any changes to the tables.
- ○ **B.** Create CHECK constraints on the tables.
- ○ **C.** Create a DDL trigger to roll back any changes to the tables.
- ○ **D.** Create the view, specifying the WITH CHECK option.
- ○ **E.** Create the view, specifying the WITH SCHEMABINDING option.

27. The database schema for an order entry application needs additions. A new column is to be added. You will supply the column with an initial value. You need the column to be modified as necessary. What should you do?

- ○ **A.** Create a DEFAULT constraint.
- ○ **B.** Create an UPDATE trigger.
- ○ **C.** Create a CHECK constraint.
- ○ **D.** Create an INSERT trigger.
- ○ **E.** Create an INSTEAD OF trigger.

28. Your database contains a table that has 500 million rows of data. Some of the data is historical and some is current. You need to partition the data on a single server to increase performance. What should you do?

- ○ **A.** Implement horizontal partitioning.
- ○ **B.** Implement vertical partitioning.
- ○ **C.** Implement a raw partition.
- ○ **D.** Implement distributed partitioning.
- ○ **E.** Implement index partitioning.

29. You are implementing views that are used in ad hoc queries. The views are used to enforce application security policy. Some of these views perform slowly. You create indexes on those views to increase performance but still maintain the security policy. One of the views returns the current date as one of the columns. The view returns the current date by using the GETDATE() function. This view does not allow you to create an index. Which two actions should you perform? (Select two answers, as each correct answer presents part of the solution.)

- ○ **A.** Remove all deterministic function calls from within the view.

- ○ **B.** Remove all date fields from the view.

- ○ **C.** Create the view and specify the WITH CHECK OPTION clause.

- ○ **D.** Remove all nondeterministic function calls from within the view.

- ○ **E.** Schema-bind all functions that are called from within the view.

30. The company website includes a page that customers use to send feedback. Data is stored in the Comments column of a table named Feedback. You need to implement full-text searching so that you can run reports on the comments. Which two actions should you perform? (Select two answers, as each correct answer presents part of the solution.)

- ○ **A.** Create a clustered index on the Comments column.

- ○ **B.** Create a full-text catalog.

- ○ **C.** Create a full-text index on the Comments column.

- ○ **D.** Create a nonclustered index on the Comments column.

- ○ **E.** Execute the USE T-SQL statement against the master.

31. You are creating a database to support a new web-based application that will handle up to 10,000 simultaneous users. This application must quickly display the results of calculation-intensive operations. You need to ensure that the database processes calculations as quickly and efficiently as possible. What should you do?

- ○ **A.** Implement CLR stored procedures in the database.

- ○ **B.** Implement distributed web services.

- ○ **C.** Implement Transact-SQL stored procedures in the database.

- ○ **D.** Have all calculations performed on the client machine.

- ○ **E.** Implement parameterized Transact-SQL queries in the application.

32. You work for a bank that processes 50,000 transactions every day. The application requires a clustered index on the `TransactionID` column. You need to create a table that supports an efficient reporting solution that queries the transactions by date. What are the two ways to achieve this goal? (Select two answers.)

- ○ **A.** Place a nonclustered index on the date column.

- ○ **B.** Create a partitioning scheme that partitions the data by date.

- ○ **C.** Add a unique clustered index on the date column.

- ○ **D.** Map each partition to a filegroup, with each filegroup accessing a different physical drive.

- ○ **E.** Create a `Value()` secondary index.

33. Users report with increasing frequency that they receive deadlock error messages. You need to monitor which objects and SQL Server session IDs are involved when deadlock conditions occur. You want information about each participant in the deadlock. What should you do?

- ○ **A.** Trace the `Lock:Timeout` event by using SQL Server Profiler.

- ○ **B.** Observe the `SQLServer:Locks - Number of Deadlocks/sec` counter by using System Monitor.

- ○ **C.** Observe the `SQLServer:DeadLocks - Number of Deadlocks/sec` counter by using System Monitor.

- ○ **D.** Trace the `Lock:Deadlock` event by using SQL Server Profiler.

- ○ **E.** Trace the `Lock:Deadlock Chain` event by using SQL Server Profiler.

34. You manage a database that contains a table that has many indexes. You notice that data modification performance has degraded over time. You suspect that some of the indexes are unused. You need to identify which indexes were not used by any queries since the last time SQL Server 2005 started. Which dynamic management view should you use?

- ○ **A.** `sys.dm_fts_index_population`

- ○ **B.** `sys.dm_exec_query_stats`

- ○ **C.** `sys.dm_db_index_physical_stats`

- ○ **D.** `sys.dm_db_physical_stats`

- ○ **E.** `sys.dm_db_index_usage_stats`

35. You are modifying a table. You want to add a new Unicode character column that is 35 positions wide. The table currently contains data. All data is not yet known for the content of the column, yet the column will be required. You want to add this new column by using the least amount of effort. What should you do?

   ○ **A.** Define the new column as NULL. Update the column to the same value as the primary key column. Alter the column to be NOT NULL.

   ○ **B.** Define the new column as NULL. Use application logic to enforce the data constraint.

   ○ **C.** Define the new column as NULL with a default value of Undefined.

   ○ **D.** Wait until all data content is known before adding the new column.

   ○ **E.** Define the new column as NOT NULL with a default value of Undefined.

36. A routinely used view that joins the Customers and Sales tables is used to aggregate total sales by customer by month. You need to increase the performance of the view. What should you do?

   ○ **A.** Create two separate views that do not contain any joins.

   ○ **B.** Create a stored procedure to use in place of the view.

   ○ **C.** Create a clustered index on the view.

   ○ **D.** Develop a CLR procedure in place of the views.

   ○ **E.** Update the view to use an outer join.

37. You create an assembly that contains a CLR function. This function reads data from a spreadsheet, performs some calculations, and returns the data to SQL Server. You need to register the assembly by using the CREATE ASSEMBLY statement with the least privileged security permission set. Which permission set should you use?

   ○ **A.** The default

   ○ **B.** EXTERNAL_ACCESS

   ○ **C.** SAFE

   ○ **D.** UNSAFE

   ○ **E.** BLENDER

38. Customer data from your trading partners is imported every night. You need to ensure that the customer record is updated if it already exists. If the record does not exist, the data for the customer needs to be inserted into the Customers table. What should you create?

- ○ **A.** An AFTER trigger
- ○ **B.** A FOR trigger
- ○ **C.** A DDL trigger
- ○ **D.** An INSTEAD OF trigger
- ○ **E.** A CLR trigger

39. You are creating an application that will store original documents as XML documents on a file server. You need to insert the documents into the database. The documents will be retrieved from the database and must be identical to the originals. You need to design a table to store the document data. What should you do?

- ○ **A.** Store the XML in a text column.
- ○ **B.** Store the XML in a varchar(8000) column.
- ○ **C.** Store the XML in an XML column.
- ○ **D.** Shred the XML and store it in a relational structure.
- ○ **E.** Store the XML in an nvarchar(max) column.

40. You are configuring backup jobs. Backup files are written to a tape drive. In the future, backups will go to a new server. Backup files will be written to disk on the new server. To simplify maintenance, you need to configure the backup jobs so that minimal changes will be necessary to back up to the new server. What should you do?

- ○ **A.** Have jobs write to an internal disk. When the new backup server is available, alter the backup jobs.
- ○ **B.** Have jobs write to backup devices. Alter the devices when the new server is available.
- ○ **C.** Have jobs write to the tape drive. Move the tape drive to the new backup server.
- ○ **D.** Have jobs write to an internal disk. Alter the backup jobs to use backup devices after the new server is in place.
- ○ **E.** Have the jobs write to the tape drive. Delete the jobs and re-create them, writing to disk on the new server.

13

Answers to Practice Exam 2

1. B
2. A
3. C
4. E
5. C
6. A, C, D, E
7. D
8. C
9. E
10. A
11. D
12. C
13. B
14. C

15. E
16. D
17. C
18. D
19. D
20. B, D
21. C
22. B, C, F
23. D
24. A
25. B
26. E
27. A

28. A
29. D, E
30. B, C
31. A
32. A, D
33. E
34. E
35. E
36. C
37. B
38. D
39. E
40. B

Question 1

Answer B is correct. The presence of a condition should not affect the addition of an index to the view. You must ensure that the WITH SCHEMABINDING option is performed when creating the view if you are going to be applying indexes. Because this preparatory step had not been completed, it needs to be done. WITH CHECK applies only to data modified through the view and ensures that when a row is modified through a view, the data remains visible through the view after the modification is committed. DROP EXISTING does not apply because there was no previously created index. Clustered or nonclustered applies to the physical properties of the index and is irrelevant in this case.

For more information, see the following sources:

▶ Chapter 2, "Creating Database Objects"

▶ SQL Server 2005 Books Online: "SQL Server Database Engine, Designing and Creating Databases, Views (Database Engine), Designing and Implementing Views, Creating Indexed Views"

Question 2

Answer A is correct. To implement indexes on a view, the first index created must be a unique clustered index. The indexes on the underlying tables are irrelevant. After a unique clustered index is created on the view, other indexes can be created.

For more information, see the following sources:

▶ Chapter 2, "Creating Database Objects"

▶ SQL Server 2005 Books Online: "SQL Server Database Engine, Designing and Creating Databases, Views (Database Engine), Designing and Implementing Views, Creating Indexed Views"

Question 3

Answer C is correct. SQL Server communicates on port 1433 by default. 433 is the TCP/IP NNSP port. 443 is the TCP/IP SSL port. 1443 is the IES (Integrated Engineering Software) port. Pharos uses 4443.

For more information, see the following sources:

▶ Chapter 1, "Installing and Configuring SQL Server 2005"

▶ SQL Server 2005 Books Online: "SQL Server Database Engine, Database Engine How-to Topics, Administration How-to Topics, Database Engine Connectivity How-to Topics, Server Connectivity How-to Topics, How to: Configure a Server to Listen on a Specific TCP Port (SQL Server Configuration Manager)"

▶ "Port Numbers," www.iana.org/assignments/port-numbers

▶ "How to Set Up SQL Server to Listen on Multiple Static TCP Ports," http://support.microsoft.com/default.aspx?scid=kb;en-us;294453

Question 4

Answer E is correct. If all protocols have been configured to not allow for external connections, the only viable connection technique is to use shared memory.

▶ Chapter 1, "Installing and Configuring SQL Server 2005"

▶ SQL Server 2005 Books Online: "SQL Server Database Engine, Administering the Database Engine, Connecting to the SQL Server Database Engine, Client Network Configuration, Choosing a Network Protocol"

▶ "Controlling Net-Libraries and Communications Addresses," http://msdn.microsoft.com/library/default.asp?url=/library/en-us/architec/8_ar_cs_9okz.asp

▶ Within MSDN Library, go to MSDN Home, MSDN Library, Servers and Enterprise Development, SQL Server, SQL Server 2005, Relational Database Components, Communication Components.

Question 5

Answer C is correct. Single-user startup uses the –m switch. The minimal configuration startup (-f) starts an instance of SQL Server with minimal configuration. The option is useful if the setting of a configuration value (for example, overcommitting memory) has prevented the server from starting. The option enables the sp_configure allow updates option. By default, allow updates is disabled.

For more information, see the following sources:

▶ Chapter 1, "Installing and Configuring SQL Server 2005"

- SQL Server 2005 Books Online: "SQL Server Database Engine, Administration How-to Topics, Managing Services How-to Topics, Managing SQL Server from the Command Prompt Using sqlservr.exe, How to: Start an Instance of SQL Server (sqlservr.exe)"

- "Using Startup Options," http://msdn.microsoft.com/library/ default.asp?url=/library/en-us/adminsql/ad_1_start_8m43.asp

- Within MSDN Library, go to MSDN Home, MSDN Library, Servers and Enterprise Development, SQL Server, SQL Server 2000, Starting, Pausing, and Stopping SQL Server, Starting SQL Server, Using Startup Options.

Question 6

Answers A, C, D, and E are correct. SQL Server no longer supports the previously utilized Multiprotocol. You must select one of the other protocols if you are upgrading an instance that uses only Multiprotocol.

For more information, see the following sources:

- Chapter 1, "Installing and Configuring SQL Server 2005"

- SQL Server 2005 Books Online: "SQL Server Database Engine, Administering the Database Engine, Connecting to the SQL Server Database Engine, Client Network Configuration, Choosing a Network Protocol"

- "Controlling Net-Libraries and Communications Addresses," http://msdn.microsoft.com/library/default.asp?url=/library/en-us/ architec/8_ar_cs_9okz.asp

- Within MSDN Library, go to MSDN Home, MSDN Library, Servers and Enterprise Development, SQL Server, SQL Server 2005, Relational Database Components, Communication Components.

Question 7

Answer D is correct. Because the basis for the procedure is data query, T-SQL is preferred over the CLR implementation. The CLR is preferred in situations that involve complex processing, with no data interaction. Parameters are needed to send the options from the client and return the data to the grid.

For more information, see the following sources:

► Chapter 3, "Implementing Database Objects"

► SQL Server 2005 Books Online: "SQL Server Programming Reference, Database Engine .NET Framework Programming, Introduction to Common Language Runtime (CLR) Integration, Overview of CLR Integration"

► "Using CLR Integration in SQL Server 2005," http://msdn. microsoft.com/library/default.asp?url=/library/en-us/dnsql90/html/ sqlclrguidance.asp

► Within MSDN Library, go to MSDN Home, MSDN Library, Servers and Enterprise Development, SQL Server, Using CLR Integration in SQL Server 2005.

Question 8

Answer C is correct. Because the basis for the procedure is complex calculations and not just data-centric activities, using the CLR is preferred over T-SQL. Parameters are needed to send the options from the client and return the data to the grid.

For more information, see the following sources:

► Chapter 3, "Implementing Database Objects"

► SQL Server 2005 Books Online: "SQL Server Programming Reference, Database Engine .NET Framework Programming, Introduction to Common Language Runtime (CLR) Integration, Overview of CLR Integration"

► "Using CLR Integration in SQL Server 2005," http://msdn. microsoft.com/library/default.asp?url=/library/en-us/dnsql90/html/ sqlclrguidance.asp

► Within MSDN Library, go to MSDN Home, MSDN Library, Servers and Enterprise Development, SQL Server, Using CLR Integration in SQL Server 2005.

Question 9

Answer E is correct. The only command that will leave the table behind is one that copies data directly into a table from the current database. The #, ##, and @ identifiers are used solely for variables and create no permanent table. Anything created in `tempdb` is temporary by definition because `tempdb` is erased every time the server starts.

For more information, see the following sources:

- Chapter 2, "Creating Database Objects"

- SQL Server 2005 Books Online: "SQL Server Database Engine, Accessing and Changing Database Data, Changing Data in a Database, Inserting Data into a Table, Adding Rows by Using INSERT and SELECT INTO"

- SQL Server 2005 Books Online: "SQL Server Database Engine, Databases (Database Engine), Understanding Databases, System Databases, tempdb Database"

- SQL Server 2005 Books Online: "SQL Server Database Engine, Designing and Creating Databases, Tables, Understanding Tables, Special Table Types"

Question 10

Answer A is correct. `database_principals` refers to anything that security can be assigned to, such as a user, role, and so on. `sys.objects (sysobjects)` holds information about all objects in the current database and needs a `WHERE` clause to limit the listing to user only (`Type = U`) objects.

For more information, see the following sources:

- Chapter 6, "Database Maintenance"

- SQL Server 2005 Books Online: "SQL Server Database Engine, System Stored Procedures (Transact-SQL), Database Engine Stored Procedures (Transact-SQL), sp_help (Transact-SQL)"

Question 11

Answer D is correct. The $PARTITION function is used for querying by partition number. The ROWGUIDCOL column can be referenced in a SELECT list by using the $ROWGUID keyword. This is similar to the way an IDENTITY column can be referenced by using the $IDENTITY keyword. sp_spaceused displays the number of rows, disk space reserved, and disk space used by a table, indexed view, or Broker queue. sp_table_validation either returns row count or checksum information on a table or an indexed view, or it compares the provided row count or checksum information with the specified table or indexed view. sp_server_info returns a list of attribute names and matching values for SQL Server.

For more information, see the following sources:

- ▶ Chapter 2, "Creating Database Objects," and Chapter 3, "Implementing Database Objects"

- ▶ SQL Server 2005 Books Online: "SQL Server Language Reference, Transact-SQL Reference, $PARTITION (Transact-SQL)"

- ▶ "Partitioned Tables and Indexes in SQL Server 2005," http://msdn.microsoft.com/library/default.asp?url=/library/en-us/dnsql90/html/sql2k5partition.asp

- ▶ Within MSDN Library, go to MSDN Home, MSDN Library, Servers and Enterprise Development, SQL Server, Partitioned Tables and Indexes in SQL Server 2005.

Question 12

Answer C is correct. If you are going to create a process in which a new table is going to be generated on every execution, you need to use SELECT INTO to generate a table and a variable to hold the name of the table. INSERT (INTO) assumes that the table has already been created. # and ## are used for temporary tables.

For more information, see the following sources:

- ▶ Chapter 2, "Creating Database Objects"

- ▶ SQL Server 2005 Books Online: "SQL Server Database Engine, Accessing and Changing Database Data, Changing Data in a Database, Inserting Data into a Table, Adding Rows by Using INSERT and SELECT INTO, Inserting Rows by Using SELECT INTO"

Question 13

Answer B is correct. You must create a full-text index on the columns you would like to utilize. There is already going to be a catalog in place that can be used because similar functionality exists elsewhere in the database. There must also be a unique column identified in the table. No other forms of indexing will help in this scenario.

For more information, see the following sources:

- ▶ Chapter 2, "Creating Database Objects"
- ▶ SQL Server 2005 Books Online: "Full-Text Search"
- ▶ "Breaking Changes to Full-Text Search in SQL Server 2005," http://msdn2.microsoft.com/en-us/library/ms143709(SQL.90).aspx

Question 14

Answer C is correct. You must have a linked server defined at the location at which you are executing the query. A remote server is antiquated technology that should not be used and is not supported for use in SQL Server 2005. An alias does not help the situation; it only provides for another name. Four-part names do not work if no linked server is defined.

For more information, see the following sources:

- ▶ Chapter 1, "Installing and Configuring SQL Server 2005"
- ▶ SQL Server 2005 Books Online: "SQL Server Database Engine, Administering the Database Engine, Managing Servers, Linking Servers"
- ▶ "Configuring Linked Servers," http://msdn.microsoft.com/library/ default.asp?url=/library/en-us/adminsql/ad_1_server_4uuq.asp

Question 15

Answer E is correct. If you are using two servers with different logins, you can easily map them by using the linked-server configuration properties. Logins on one server in this manner can impersonate logins on another server. Hard-coding the user ID and password and/or using the sa user ID and password are both problematic in performing updates and are potential security risks.

For more information, see the following sources:

▶ Chapter 1, "Installing and Configuring SQL Server 2005"

▶ SQL Server 2005 Books Online: "SQL Server Database Engine, Administering the Database Engine, Managing Servers, Linking Servers"

▶ "Configuring Linked Servers," http://msdn.microsoft.com/library/default.asp?url=/library/en-us/adminsql/ad_1_server_4uuq.asp

Question 16

Answer D is correct. Generate online recommendations where possible is the only option that is completely non-limiting in its results; its downfall is that it may provide online implementations where they may be more quickly implemented offline. Using the option All recommendations are offline does not limit any of the indexing recommendations, but it also provides no information about items that could be implemented online. Evaluate utilization of existing PDS only does not evaluate anything other than what already exists, ignoring possible improvements of indexes that could be added. Keep all existing PDS does not evaluate the potential gain in eliminating some of the existing indexes. Generate only online recommendations ignores options that could be eliminated offline.

For more information, see the following sources:

▶ Chapter 8, "Troubleshooting and Optimizing SQL Server"

▶ SQL Server 2005 Books Online: "SQL Server Database Engine, Administering the Database Engine, Monitoring and Tuning for Performance, Tuning the Physical Database Design, Using Database Engine Tuning Advisor, Available Tuning Options"

▶ "SQL Server 2005 Performance," http://msdn.microsoft.com/sql/learning/Perf/

▶ "TechNet Webcast: SQL Server 2005 Database Tuning Advisor (Level 300)," http://msevents.microsoft.com/cui/webcasteventdetails.aspx?eventid=1032275655&eventcategory=5&culture=en-us&countrycode=us

Question 17

Answer C is correct. To define a connection to use SSL, you must set the port to SSL. There is no such option as AS HTTPS; AS HTTP handles standard and SSL definitions. WSDL sets the document generation options and has nothing to do with the protocol used in the communication. BASIC authentication is the poorest of settings and should almost never be used. ENCRYPTION REQUIRED is the default setting when none is specified.

For more information, see the following sources:

- ▶ Chapter 5, "Data Consumption and Throughput"

- ▶ SQL Server 2005 Books Online: "SQL Server Language Reference, Transact-SQL Reference, CREATE ENDPOINT (Transact-SQL)"

- ▶ "Overview of Native XML Web Services for Microsoft SQL Server 2005," http://msdn.microsoft.com/library/default.asp?url=/library/en-us/dnsql90/html/sql2005websvc.asp

- ▶ Within MSDN Library, go to MSDN Home, MSDN Library, Servers and Enterprise Development, SQL Server, Overview of Native XML Web Services for Microsoft SQL Server 2005.

Question 18

Answer D is correct. sp_help_job is the only procedure that provides information on historical executions of tasks. sp_help_job_schedule and sp_help_schedule only give you the time for the next execution, not anything that previously occurred.

For more information, see the following sources:

- ▶ Chapter 6, "Database Maintenance"

- ▶ SQL Server 2005 Books Online: "SQL Server Language Reference, Transact-SQL Reference, System Stored Procedures (Transact-SQL), SQL Server Agent Stored Procedures (Transact-SQL)"

- ▶ "System Stored Procedures," http://msdn.microsoft.com/library/default.asp?url=/library/en-us/tsqlref/ts_sp_00_519s.asp

Question 19

Answer D is correct. Full partitioning allows for the best diagnosis of partitioning possibilities. Selecting No partitioning would not implement at all, and aligned options will use only partitioning that aligns with that currently set.

For more information, see the following sources:

▶ Chapter 8, "Troubleshooting and Optimizing SQL Server"

▶ SQL Server 2005 Books Online: "SQL Server Database Engine, Administering the Database Engine, Monitoring and Tuning for Performance, Tuning the Physical Database Design, Using Database Engine Tuning Advisor"

▶ "SQL Server 2005 Performance," http://msdn.microsoft.com/sql/learning/Perf/

▶ "TechNet Webcast: SQL Server 2005 Database Tuning Advisor (Level 300)," http://msevents.microsoft.com/cui/webcasteventdetails.aspx?eventid=1032275655&eventcategory=5&culture=en-us&countrycode=us

Question 20

Answers B and D are correct. Both Answers B and D provide information about locks and application blocking. Answers A and C provide only process information for those programs currently executing. System Monitor can provide only quantitative information about SQL Server lock requests and deadlock situations.

For more information, see the following sources:

▶ Chapter 7, "Monitoring SQL Server Performance," and Chapter 8, "Troubleshooting and Optimizing SQL Server"

▶ SQL Server 2005 Books Online: "SQL Server Database Engine, Accessing and Changing Database Data, Locking and Row Versioning, Locking in the Database Engine"

▶ "Understanding Locking in SQL Server," http://msdn.microsoft.com/library/default.asp?url=/library/en-us/acdata/ac_8_con_7a_7xde.asp

Question 21

Answer C is correct. To correct fragmentation of indexes, you need to reorganize the indexes. You could rebuild the indexes to correct fragmentation issues, but you would need to take the data offline. Defragmenting the disk does not correct fragmentation within the data and log files. DBCC CLEANTABLE is used to reclaim space dropped from variable-length and text columns. DBCC CHECKIDENT checks the current identity value for a table.

For more information, see the following sources:

- ▶ Chapter 8, "Troubleshooting and Optimizing SQL Server"

- ▶ SQL Server 2005 Books Online: "SQL Server Database Engine, Designing and Creating Databases, Indexes, Optimizing Indexes, Performing Index Operations Online"

- ▶ "ALTER DATABASE," http://msdn.microsoft.com/library/ default.asp?url=/library/en-us/tsqlref/ts_aa-az_4e5h.asp

Question 22

Answers B, C, and F are correct. In setting up for mirroring, you set the full recovery mode instead of bulk-logged or simple. You restore a full backup by using NORECOVERY, allowing for more restores to occur. Mirroring endpoints are connection points used by independent instances of SQL Server.

For more information, see the following sources:

- ▶ Chapter 9, "Implementing High Availability"

- ▶ SQL Server 2005 Books Online: "SQL Server Database Engine, Administering the Database Engine, Configuring High Availability, Database Mirroring, Overview of Database Mirroring"

- ▶ "Managing Database Mirroring (SQL Server Management Studio)," http://msdn2.microsoft.com/en-us/library/ms175134.aspx

- ▶ "Setting Up Database Mirroring," http://msdn2.microsoft.com/en-us/ library/ms190941(SQL.90).aspx

Question 23

Answer D is correct. The fastest way to move a database to another server it to simply take the database offline and transfer the files to the new server. When it is on the new server, you can use the ATTACH method to install the database in the new environment. All-in-all, the process takes only a minimal time over and above the actual file transfer time. Transactional replication does not move the database.

For more information, see the following sources:

- ▶ Chapter 6, "Database Maintenance"

- ▶ SQL Server 2005 Books Online: "SQL Server Database Engine, Databases (Database Engine), Implementing Databases, Modifying a Database, Detaching and Attaching a Database"

▶ "How to: Move a Database Using Detach and Attach (Transact-SQL)," http://msdn2.microsoft.com/en-us/library/ms187858(SQL.90).aspx

Question 24

Answer A is correct. STATUS specifies whether the queue is available or unavailable. RETENTION specifies whether messages sent or received on conversations using this queue are retained. ACTIVATION specifies information about the stored procedure to activate to process messages in the queue. MAX_QUEUE_READERS specifies the maximum number of instances of the activation stored procedure that the queue starts at the same time.

For more information, see the following sources:

▶ Chapter 5, "Data Consumption and Throughput"

▶ SQL Server 2005 Books Online: "SQL Server Service Broker, Service Broker Architecture, Service Architecture, Queues"

▶ "CREATE QUEUE (Transact-SQL)," http://msdn2.microsoft.com/en-us/library/ms190495(SQL.90).aspx

Question 25

Answer B is correct. When a job step fails, you can chose to continue with the remainder of the operations. In the case of the failure, some notification should be made, but the remaining steps could still execute without problems.

For more information, see the following sources:

▶ Chapter 6, "Database Maintenance"

▶ SQL Server 2005 Books Online: "SQL Server Database Engine, Administering the Database Engine, Automating Administrative Tasks (SQL Server Agent), Implementing Jobs, Creating Job Steps"

▶ "How to: Create a Transact-SQL Job Step (SQL Server Management Studio)," http://msdn2.microsoft.com/en-us/library/ms187910 (SQL.90).aspx

Question 26

Answer E is correct. When you implement a view using WITH SCHEMABINDING, SQL Server automatically handles the situation for you. Underlying tables cannot be altered. You would have to drop any object that stated WITH SCHEMABINDING prior to altering the table structure. SCHEMABINDING is utilized for locking in an object schema to prevent changes; this is why it is mandated in setting up indexed views.

For more information, see the following sources:

▶ Chapter 3, "Implementing Database Objects"

▶ SQL Server 2005 Books Online: "SQL Server Database Engine, Designing and Creating Databases, Views (Database Engine), Understanding Views"

▶ "CREATE VIEW," http://msdn.microsoft.com/library/ default.asp?url=/library/en-us/tsqlref/ts_create2_30hj.asp

Question 27

Answer A is correct. A default constraint supplies a column with an initial value that can be changed whenever needed. When you load a row into a table with a DEFAULT definition for a column, you implicitly instruct the engine to insert a default value in the column when a value is not specified for it, but still allow for a value to be entered.

For more information, see the following sources:

▶ Chapter 2, "Creating Database Objects"

▶ SQL Server 2005 Books Online: "SQL Server Database Engine, Designing and Creating Databases, Tables, Designing Tables, Enforcing Data Integrity"

▶ "ALTER TABLE," http://msdn.microsoft.com/library/ default.asp?url=/library/en-us/tsqlref/ts_aa-az_3ied.asp

Question 28

Answer A is correct. The data in partitioned tables and indexes is horizontally divided into units that can be spread across more than one filegroup in a database. Partitioning can make large tables and indexes more manageable and scalable. Vertically dividing a table by columns would not help when the problem is number of rows. Vertical filtering helps to divide tables that have too many columns.

For more information, see the following sources:

- ▶ Chapter 2, "Creating Database Objects," and Chapter 3, "Implementing Database Objects"

- ▶ SQL Server 2005 Books Online: "SQL Server Database Engine, Designing and Creating Databases, Partitioned Tables and Indexes"

- ▶ "Partitioning Data," http://msdn.microsoft.com/library/default.asp?url=/library/en-us/architec/8_ar_cs_5335.asp

- ▶ "Partitioned Tables and Indexes in SQL Server 2005," http://msdn.microsoft.com/library/default.asp?url=/library/en-us/dnsql90/html/sql2k5partition.asp

Question 29

Answers D and E are correct. GETDATE is a nondeterministic function that would not be allowed if you intended to create indexes in the views. The presence of any date fields or deterministic functions would not be problematic.

For more information, see the following sources:

- ▶ Chapter 3, "Implementing Database Objects"

- ▶ SQL Server 2005 Books Online: "SQL Server Database Engine, Designing and Creating Databases, User-defined Functions (Database Engine), Designing User-defined Functions, Deterministic and Nondeterministic Functions"

- ▶ "Creating Indexed Views," http://msdn.microsoft.com/library/default.asp?url=/library/en-us/vdtsql/dvtskcreatingindexedviews.asp

- ▶ "Designing an Indexed View," http://msdn.microsoft.com/library/default.asp?url=/library/en-us/createdb/cm_8_des_06_6ptj.asp

Question 30

Answers B and C are correct. To implement full-text indexes, you need a catalog to store the indexes and an index defined for the text columns in which searches are going to be performed. Other index implementation is irrelevant to the implementation of full-text indexing.

For more information, see the following sources:

- ▶ Chapter 3, "Implementing Database Objects"

- ▶ SQL Server 2005 Books Online: "Full-Text Search"

Question 31

Answer A is correct. If you are dealing with complex calculations that need to interact with the database engine, you will get the best performance by using CLR procedures. If no engine interactions are needed, then client-side process-es may give the advantage of fewer round trips. T-SQL is more advantageous in datacentric operations.

For more information, see the following sources:

▶ Chapter 3, "Implementing Database Objects"

▶ SQL Server 2005 Books Online: "SQL Server Database Engine, Building Database Objects with Common Language Runtime (CLR) Integration, CLR Stored Procedures"

Question 32

Answers A and B are correct. By partitioning and indexing on the data, you seg-regate the data efficiently and more easily present the information for reporting. A value() index is for use with XML data and serves no purpose in this scenario.

For more information, see the following sources:

▶ Chapter 3, "Implementing Database Objects"

▶ SQL Server 2005 Books Online: "SQL Server Database Engine, Designing and Creating Databases, Partitioned Tables and Indexes, Designing Partitioned Tables and Indexes, Special Guidelines for Partitioned Indexes"

Question 33

Answer E is correct. SQL Profiler is the only tool that will provide you with suf-ficient information to trace what is in use when the deadlocks occur. The cor-rect objects to be monitoring are the deadlock chain events.

For more information, see the following sources:

▶ Chapter 7, "Monitoring SQL Server Performance," and Chapter 8, "Troubleshooting and Optimizing SQL Server"

▶ SQL Server 2005 Books Online: "SQL Server Database Engine, Accessing and Changing Database Data, Locking and Row Versioning, Locking in the Database Engine, Deadlocking"

- ▶ "Detecting and Ending Deadlocks," http://msdn2.microsoft.com/en-us/library/ms178104(SQL.90).aspx

Question 34

Answer E is correct. `sys.dm_db_index_usage_stats` returns counts of different types of index operations and the time each type of operation was last performed. `sys.dm_fts_index_population` returns information about the full-text index populations currently in progress. `sys.dm_exec_query_stats` returns aggregate performance statistics for cached query plans. `sys.dm_db_index_physical_stats` returns size and fragmentation information. `sys.dm_db_physical_stats` returns page and row-count information.

For more information, see the following sources:

- ▶ Chapter 8, "Troubleshooting and Optimizing SQL Server"

- ▶ SQL Server 2005 Books Online: "SQL Server Database Engine, System Views (Transact-SQL), Dynamic Management Views and Functions, Index Related Dynamic Management Views and Functions"

Question 35

Answer E is correct. A new column can be created that does not allow NULL content as long as a default value is also supplied.

For more information, see the following sources:

- ▶ Chapter 2, "Creating Database Objects," and Chapter 3, "Implementing Database Objects"

- ▶ SQL Server 2005 Books Online: "SQL Server Database Engine, Designing and Creating Databases, Tables, Designing Tables, Enforcing Data Integrity"

- ▶ "ALTER TABLE," http://msdn.microsoft.com/library/default.asp?url=/library/en-us/tsqlref/ts_aa-az_3ied.asp

Question 36

Answer C is correct. Using a clustered index usually improves performance. Making two separate views is likely to make the situation worse and will definitely make it more difficult to produce the desired results. Using the CLR will rarely improve performance for data-centric activities. A stored procedure is unlikely to perform any better than the view.

For more information, see the following sources:

▶ Chapter 8, "Troubleshooting and Optimizing SQL Server"

▶ "Creating Indexed Views," http://msdn.microsoft.com/library/ default.asp?url=/library/en-us/vdtsql/dvtskcreatingindexedviews.asp

▶ "Designing an Indexed View," http://msdn.microsoft.com/library/ default.asp?url=/library/en-us/createdb/cm_8_des_06_6ptj.asp

Question 37

Answer B is correct. EXTERNAL_ACCESS enables assemblies to access certain external system resources such as files, networks, environmental variables, and the registry. The default setting is SAFE, which is the most restrictive permission set. Code executed by an assembly with SAFE permissions cannot access external system resources such as files, the network, environment variables, or the registry.

For more information, see the following sources:

▶ Chapter 3, "Implementing Database Objects"

▶ SQL Server 2005 Books Online: "Samples and Sample Databases, Samples, SQL Server SQL Server Database Engine Samples, Programmability Samples, CLR Programmability Samples"

▶ "Programmability," http://msdn.microsoft.com/sql/learning/prog/ default.aspx

▶ "Assemblies (Database Engine)," http://msdn2.microsoft.com/ en-us/library/ms186221(SQL.90).aspx

Question 38

Answer D is correct. You can use an INSTEAD OF trigger to perform a different action than what was originally intended. INSTEAD OF triggers are executed in place of the usual triggering action. INSTEAD OF triggers can also be defined on views with one or more base tables, where they can extend the types of updates a view can support.

For more information, see the following sources:

▶ Chapter 2, "Creating Database Objects"

- ▶ SQL Server 2005 Books Online: "SQL Server Database Engine, Designing and Creating Databases, DML Triggers, Understanding DML Triggers, Types of DML Triggers"

- ▶ "Enforcing Business Rules with Triggers," http://msdn.microsoft.com/ library/default.asp?url=/library/en-us/createdb/cm_8_des_08_116g.asp

Question 39

Answer E is correct. If the sole purpose of the storage of XML data is to retrieve the same data later, the best and most effective data type is the nvarchar type. The column should also be sized using max to achieve the most flexibility with the storage. It may be tempting to use the XML type, but doing so is not necessary in this situation.

For more information, see the following sources:

- ▶ Chapter 4, "Supporting the XML Framework"

- ▶ SQL Server 2005 Books Online: "SQL Server Database Engine, Using XML in SQL Server"

- ▶ "XML Best Practices for Microsoft SQL Server 2005," http://msdn.microsoft.com/library/default.asp?url=/library/ en-us/dnsql90/html/sql25xmlbp.asp

- ▶ Within MSDN Library, go to MSDN Home, MSDN Library, Servers and Enterprise Development, SQL Server, XML Best Practices for Microsoft SQL Server 2005.

Question 40

Answer B is correct. Backup devices can easily be changed from one medium to another with little difficulty. The remaining options are all far more involved than simply redefining the devices.

For more information, see the following sources:

- ▶ Chapter 6, "Database Maintenance"

- ▶ SQL Server 2005 Books Online: "SQL Server Database Engine, Administering the Database Engine, Backing Up and Restoring Databases, Managing Backups, Backup Devices"

- "BACKUP," http://msdn.microsoft.com/library/default.asp?url=/library/en-us/tsqlref/ts_ba-bz_35ww.asp

- "sys.backup_devices (Transact-SQL)," http://msdn2.microsoft.com/en-us/library/ms178018(SQL.90).aspx

APPENDIX A

Suggested Readings and Resources

When it comes to SQL Server, there are many resources available to aid the learning process. The help facility SQL Server Books Online is an excellent starting point for digging further into the many topics covered by the exam and related to the product. Many other valuable websites and reference books can also provide further insight.

This appendix lists some of the most useful resources and is organized on a chapter-by-chapter basis for ease of use. You can use the information in this appendix to find additional quality resources that can further your knowledge of SQL Server and database management in general.

Chapter 1: Installing and Configuring SQL Server 2005

Books

Holzner, Steven. *Inside XML*. New Riders Publishing.

Otey, Michael. *Microsoft SQL Server 2005 New Features*. McGraw-Hill/Osborne.

Rizzo, Thomas, et al. *Pro SQL Server 2005*. aPress.

Stanek, William. *Microsoft SQL Server 2005 Administrator's Pocket Consultant*. Microsoft Press.

Watt, Andrew. *Microsoft SQL Server 2005 for Dummies*. Wiley.

On the Web

Microsoft SQL Server: www.microsoft.com/sql/default.mspx

SQL Server Developer Center: http://msdn.microsoft.com/sql

SQL Server Magazine: www.sqlmag.com

MSDN Online Internet Reference/XML Online Developer Center: http://msdn.microsoft.com/xml/default.asp

MSDN Online Internet Reference/Developer Resources for SQL Server: http://msdn.microsoft.com/sql

SQL Server 2005 Books: www.sqlserver2005books.com

TechNet Online Internet Reference: IT Resources for SQL Server: www.microsoft.com/technet/sql/default.asp

SQL Server Books Online Help Facility

"Getting Started with SQL Server Books Online"

"What's New in Microsoft SQL Server 2005"

"Installing SQL Server"

"SQL Server Overview"

"SQL Server Database Engine"

Chapter 2: Creating Database Objects

Books

Turley, Paul, and Dan Wood. *Beginning Transact-SQL with SQL Server 2000 and 2005*. Wrox.

On the Web

Free SQL Server Help: http://sqlservercentral.com

SQL Server Books Online Help Facility

"SQL Server Database Engine -> Designing and Creating Databases"

"What's New in Microsoft SQL Server 2005"

"Full-Text Search"

"SQL Server Language Reference -> Transact-SQL Reference"

Chapter 3: Implementing Database Objects

Books

Ben-gan, Itzik, Dejan Sarka, and Roger Wolter. *Inside Microsoft SQL Server 2005: T-SQL Programming*. Microsoft Press.

Vieira, Robert. *Beginning SQL Server 2005 Programming*. Wrox.

On the Web

Choosing Between the CLR and T-SQL in SQL Server 2005: www.devx.com/dbzone/Article/28412

SQL Server Books Online Help Facility

"SQL Server Language Reference -> Transact-SQL Reference -> System Tables"

"SQL Server Language Reference -> Transact-SQL Reference -> System Views"

"SQL Server Database Engine -> Accessing and Changing Database Data"

"Full-Text Search"

Chapter 4: Supporting the XML Framework

Books

Klein, Scott. *Professional SQL Server 2005 XML*. Wrox.

On the Web

An Interview with Michael Rys on XQuery, SQL Server 2005, and Microsoft XML Technologies: www.stylusstudio.com/michael_rys.html

The Fundamentals of the SQL Server 2005 XML Datatype:
www.developer.com/db/article.php/3531196

SQL Server 2005 Provides True Integration of XML Data:
www.windowsitpro.com/Articles/Index.cfm?ArticleID=45131&DisplayTab=Article

SQL Server Books Online Help Facility

"SQL Server Language Reference -> Transact-SQL Reference -> CREATE ENDPOINT"

"What's New in SQL Server 2005 -> Database Engine Enhancements -> Database Engine XML Enhancements"

"SQL Server Database Engine -> Using XML in SQL Server"

Chapter 5: Data Consumption and Throughput

Books

Hamilton, Bill. *Programming SQL Server 2005*. O'Reilly.

On the Web

SQL Server 2005 Service Broker:
www.securedevelop.net/presentations/HDC2004/HDC2004_SQLServer2005ServiceBroker.pdf#search='SQL%20Server%202005%20service%20broker'

SQL Server Books Online Help Facility

"Tools and Utilities Reference -> Command Prompt Utilities -> bcp Utility"

"SQL Server Database Engine -> Administering the Database Engine -> Importing and Exporting Bulk Data"

"SQL Server Service Broker"

"SQL Server Language Reference -> Transact-SQL Reference -> CREATE ENDPOINT"

Chapter 6: Database Maintenance

Books

Nielson, Paul. *SQL Server 2005 Bible*. Wiley.

On the Web

SQL-Server-Performance.Com Forum/Database Maintenance Plan: www.sql-server-performance.com/forum/topic.asp?TOPIC_ID=9826

SQL Server Reference Guide/Database Maintenance:
www.informit.com/guides/content.asp?g=sqlserver&seqNum=32&rl=1

SQL Server Books Online Help Facility

"SQL Server Database Engine -> Designing and Creating Databases -> Database Snapshots"

"SQL Server Database Engine -> Administering the Database Engine -> Backing up and Restoring Databases"

Chapter 7: Monitoring SQL Server Performance

On the Web

Idera Performance Enhancement: www.sql-server-performance.com

SQL Server Books Online Help Facility

"SQL Server Database Engine -> Administering the Database Engine -> Monitoring and Tuning for Performance"

Chapter 8: Troubleshooting and Optimizing SQL Server

On the Web

Inside SQL Server: www.insidesqlserver.com (The material was based on SQL Server 2000, with the 2005 release to come in the future.)

Solid Quality Learning: www.solidqualitylearning.com

SQL Server Books Online Help Facility

"SQL Server Database Engine -> Administering the Database Engine -> Monitoring and Tuning for Performance"

Chapter 9: Implementing High Availability

On the Web

SQL Server 2005 High-Availability Capabilities/ITPapers: www.itpapers.com/abstract.aspx?docid=154573

SQL Server 2005 Part 3: High Availability and Scalability Enhancements/Failover Clustering: www.databasejournal.com/features/mssql/article.php/3444181

SQL Server Books Online Help Facility

"SQL Server Replication"

"SQL Server Database Engine -> Administering the Database Engine -> Configuring High Availability"

"SQL Server Analysis Services"

APPENDIX B

Accessing Your Free MeasureUp Practice Test

This Exam Cram book features exclusive access to MeasureUp's practice questions, which is an excellent study tool to help you assess your readiness for the 70-431 exam. MeasureUp is a Microsoft Certified Practice Test Provider.

To access your free practice questions, follow these steps:

1. Retrieve your unique registration key on the inside of the back cover of this book.

2. Go to www.measureup.com.

3. Create a free MeasureUp login account or log in to your existing account.

4. On the Learning Locker toolbar, click Register Products.

5. Read and consent to the license agreement by clicking the check box below the License Agreement.

6. Type your registration key number in the key box. Include all dashes and do not substitute any numbers.

7. Click Register.

8. Click the Learning Locker button to display your Personal Test Locker.

9. Click the Practice Test link and follow the instructions to start your test, or click the Learning Locker tab to return to your Learning Locker.

For more details about MeasureUp's product features, see Appendix C, "MeasureUp's Product Features."

APPENDIX C

MeasureUp's Product Features

Since 1997, MeasureUp has helped more than 1 million IT professionals earn certifications from the industry's leading vendors. Created by content developers certified in their areas and with real-world experience, MeasureUp practice tests feature comprehensive questions (some with performance-based simulations, when simulations are relevant to a particular exam), detailed explanations and complete score reporting. MeasureUp is a Microsoft Certified Practice Test Provider, and its practice tests are the closest you can get to the certification exams!

Multiple Testing Modes

MeasureUp practice tests are available in Study, Certification, Custom, Missed Question, and Non-Duplicate modes.

Study Mode

Tests administered in Study mode allow you to request the correct answer(s) and explanation for each question during the test. These tests are not timed. You can modify the testing environment *during* the test by clicking the Options button.

Certification Mode

Tests administered in Certification mode closely simulate the actual testing environment you will encounter when taking a certification exam. These tests do not allow you to request the answer(s) or explanation for each question until after the exam.

Custom Mode

Custom mode allows you to specify your preferred testing environment. You can use this mode to specify the objectives you want to include in your test, the timer length, and other test properties. You can also modify the testing environment *during* the test by clicking the Options button.

Missed Question Mode

Missed Question mode allows you to take a test containing only the questions you missed previously.

Non-Duplicate Mode

Non-Duplicate mode allows you to take a test containing only questions not displayed previously.

Question Types

The practice questions in MeasureUp practice tests simulate the real exam experience. They include the following types:

- ▶ Create a tree
- ▶ Select and place
- ▶ Drop and connect
- ▶ Build list
- ▶ Reorder list
- ▶ Build and reorder list
- ▶ Single hotspot
- ▶ Multiple hotspots
- ▶ Live screen
- ▶ Command line
- ▶ Hot area
- ▶ Fill in the blank

Random Questions and Order of Answers

The Random Questions and Order of Answers feature helps you learn the material without memorizing questions and answers. When this feature is turned on, each time you take a practice test, the questions and answers appear in a different randomized order.

Detailed Explanations of Correct and Incorrect Answers

You'll receive automatic feedback on all correct and incorrect answers on MeasureUp practice tests. The detailed answer explanations are a superb learning tool in their own right.

Attention to Exam Objectives

MeasureUp practice tests are designed to appropriately balance the questions over each technical area covered by a specific exam.

Technical Support

If you encounter problems with the MeasureUp test engine, you can contact MeasureUp at 678-356-5050 or email support@measureup.com. Technical support hours are 8 a.m. to 5 p.m. eastern standard time, Monday through Friday. In addition, you can find FAQs at www.measureup.com.

To purchase additional MeasureUp products, call 678-356-5050 or 800-649-1687 or visit www.measureup.com.

Glossary

ADO (ActiveX Data Objects)
An easy-to-use application programming interface (API) that wraps OLE DB for use in languages, such as Visual Basic, Visual Basic for Applications, Active Server Pages, and Microsoft Internet Explorer Visual Basic Scripting.

aggregate functions   Functions that provide summary data over sets returning a singular value.

alert   A user-defined response to a SQL Server event. Alerts can either execute a defined task or send an email and/or a pager message to a specified operator.

alias   An alternative name for a table or column in expressions that is often used to shorten the name for subsequent reference in code, prevent possible ambiguous references, or provide a more descriptive name in the query output. An alias can also be an alternative name for a server.

ALTER   A command used to change a database object, such as a function or procedure. Using ALTER allows the object to be changed without losing permissions and other database settings.

analysis server   The server component of Analysis Services that is specifically designed to create and maintain multidimensional data structures and provide multidimensional data in response to client queries.

Analysis Services   A service that provides OLAP and data mining functionality for business intelligence solutions.

articles   Data structures made from selected columns from a table or from an entire table that need to be bundled into a publication to be used for replication. A publication is composed of one or more articles. An article represents some or all columns and some or all rows in a single table.

assembly   A managed application module that contains class metadata and managed code as an object in SQL Server. By referencing an assembly, CLR functions, CLR stored procedures, CLR triggers, user-defined aggregates, and user-defined types can be created in SQL Server.

attributes   Characteristics given to an entity, such as PhoneNumber and State; they are usually represented as rows inside an entity. An attribute in data modeling can be thought of as the columns of a table implemented in SQL Server.

backup   A copy of a database, filegroup, file, or transaction log that can be used to restore data, typically after a serious database error or a system failure. Backups can be used alone or as part of a sequence of backups.

batch   A collection of zero, one, or more T-SQL statements sent to SQL Server to be run together. Multiple batches can be combined in a single script or procedure, using the GO keyword to separate the batches.

BCP   A command prompt bulk copy utility that copies SQL Server data to or from an operating system file in a user-specified format.

binding   In SQL application programming interfaces (APIs), associating a result set column or a parameter with a program variable so that data is moved automatically into or out of a program variable when a row is fetched or updated.

blocked process   A process that cannot continue until a lock that another process holds is released.

Books Online   A comprehensive help facility and electronic reference manual.

built-in function   One of a group of predefined functions provided as part of the T-SQL and Multidimensional Expressions (MDX) languages.

cascading actions   Cascading delete or cascading update operations that either delete a row containing a primary key or update a primary key value referenced by foreign key columns in existing rows in other tables. On a cascading delete, all the rows whose foreign key values reference the deleted primary key value are also deleted. On a cascading update, all the foreign key values are updated to match the new primary key value.

CASE   A complex expression that handles multiple-branch conditional logic.

CAST   A function that converts data from one type to another and is based on the American National Standards Institute (ANSI) SQL-92 standard, as opposed to the CONVERT function.

CHECK constraint   A constraint that defines what values are acceptable in a column. You can apply CHECK constraints to multiple columns, and you can apply multiple CHECK constraints to a single column. When a table is dropped, CHECK constraints are also dropped.

client/server   A physically or logically implemented system in which a device or an application called the server requests services or data from another device or application and the server fulfills the request.

CLR (common language runtime) function   A function that is created by referencing a SQL Server assembly. The implementation of the CLR function is defined in an assembly that is created in the .NET Framework CLR.

CLR (common language runtime) stored procedure   A stored procedure that is created by referencing a SQL Server assembly. The implementation of the CLR stored procedure is defined in an assembly that is created in the .NET Framework CLR.

CLR (common language runtime) trigger   A DML trigger or DDL trigger that is created by referencing a CLR assembly. The implementation of the CLR trigger is defined in an assembly that is created in the .NET Framework CLR.

CLR (common language runtime) user-defined type   A user-defined data type that is created by referencing a CLR assembly. The implementation of the CLR user-defined type is defined in an assembly that is created in the .NET Framework CLR.

clustered index   A type of index in which the logical order of key values determines the actual order of the data rows and keeps the data rows sorted. Using a clustered index causes the actual data rows to move into the leaf level of the index.

collation (sequence)   A set of rules that determine how data is compared, ordered, and presented. Character data is sorted using collation information, including locale, sort order, and case-sensitivity.

constraint   A property assigned to a table column that prevents certain types of invalid data values from being placed in the column. For example, a UNIQUE or PRIMARY KEY constraint prevents you from inserting a value that is a duplicate of an existing value; a CHECK constraint prevents you from inserting a value that does not match a search condition; and NOT NULL prevents you from inserting a NULL value.

CREATE   A command used to create a database object, such as a view or stored procedure.

cursor   A construct that holds a rowset from a SELECT statement, which can then be stepped through row-by-row for various operations.

data mart   A subset of the contents of a data warehouse. A data mart tends to contain data focused at the department level or on a specific business area.

data warehouse   A database specifically structured for query and analysis. A data warehouse typically contains data representing the business history of an organization.

database lock   The largest of locking increments, affecting an entire database.

DDL (data definition language) A language, usually part of a database management system, that is used to define all attributes and properties of a database, especially row layouts, column definitions, key columns (and sometimes keying methodology), file locations, and storage strategy.

deadlock   A state in which two users or processes cannot continue processing because they each have a resource that the other needs.

DELETE   A T-SQL statement that can be used to delete data from a table. A fast way to delete all rows is to use TRUNCATE TABLE.

denormalization   The process of adding planned redundancy to an already fully normalized data model.

derived table   A table created by using a SELECT statement in parentheses in a FROM clause.

deterministic   A characteristic of a function that means the function always returns the same output when presented with the same input. Mathematical functions, such as SQRT, are deterministic because they always return the same output, given the same input.

distributed partitioned view   A view that collects data from two or more instances of SQL Server.

distributor   In SQL Server, the server that contains the distribution database, data history, and transactions used in replication; as its name implies, its job is to distribute data to subscribers.

DML (data manipulation language)   The subset of SQL statements used to retrieve and manipulate data.

DROP   A command used to drop a database object, such as a view or stored procedure. Using DROP removes all the permissions for the object, as well as the object itself. For example, the DROP VIEW statement is used to remove a view or indexed view from the database. Dropping a view removes the definition of a view from the database and an entry in the sysobjects while not affecting the underlying tables and views.

encryption A method for keeping sensitive information confidential by changing data into an unreadable form.

execution plan A method in which the query optimizer has chosen to execute a SQL operation.

extended stored procedure A function in a dynamic link library (DLL) that is coded using the SQL Server Extended Stored Procedure application programming interface (API). The function can then be invoked from T-SQL by using the same statements that are used to execute T-SQL stored procedures. Extended stored procedures can be built to perform functionality not possible with T-SQL stored procedures.

extent lock A lock covering eight contiguous data or index pages.

federated database servers A set of linked servers that shares the processing load of data by hosting partitions of a distributed partitioned view.

filegroups In SQL Server, a named collection of one or more files that forms a single unit of allocation. Filegroups are also used for administration of a database.

FILLFACTOR An attribute of an index that defines the amount of free space allotted to each page of the index. FILLFACTOR can be used to allocate space for future expansion. FILLFACTOR is a value from 1 through 100 that specifies the percentage of the index page to be left empty.

filter A set of criteria that controls the set of records returned as a result set. Filters can also define the sequence in which rows are returned.

foreign key A column or multiple columns whose values match the primary key of another table. Foreign keys help in the relational process between two entities by connecting the foreign attribute in the child entity to a primary key in a parent entity.

fragmentation A process that occurs when data modifications are made. It is possible to reduce fragmentation and improve read-ahead performance by dropping and re-creating a clustered index.

FROM The part of the SELECT statement that specifies the tables being accessed. Specifying what tables are being accessed is compulsory for any SELECT data retrieval statement.

Full-Text catalog A special storage space used to house Full-Text indexes. By default, all Full-Text indexes are housed in a single catalog.

Full-Text index A special index that efficiently tracks the words you're looking for in a table. It helps in enabling special searching functions that differ from those used in regular indexes.

GROUP BY The DML operator that creates aggregated sets from a single SELECT statement.

horizontal partitioning
Segmenting a single table into multiple tables based on selected rows. Each of the multiple tables has the same columns but fewer rows.

HTML (Hypertext Markup Language)   A system of marking up, or tagging, a document so that it can be published on the World Wide Web. Documents prepared in HTML include reference graphics and formatting tags. HTML documents are viewed through a web browser (such as Microsoft Internet Explorer).

identity   A column in a table that has been assigned the IDENTITY property, which generates unique incremental numbers.

IN operator   The operator that compares a single value to a set and returns true if the single value occurs within the set.

index   In a relational database, a database object that provides fast access to data in the rows of a table, based on key values. Indexes can also enforce uniqueness on the rows in a table. SQL Server supports clustered and nonclustered indexes. The PRIMARY KEY/UNIQUE constraint automatically causes an index to be built. In full-text searches, a full-text index stores information about significant words and their location within a given column.

indexed view   A view that has an index defined onto it. Indexes on views enable view result sets to be stored in the database's physical storage after an index is created. In contrast, in a non-indexed view, the view is activated at runtime, and the result set is dynamically built.

INSERT   A T-SQL command that is used to add one or more records to a table.

INSERT INTO   A T-SQL statement that can be used to insert rows of data into a table when needed.

INSTEAD OF trigger   A trigger that replaces the action that an INSERT, DELETE, or UPDATE trigger might take.

job   A specified series of operations, called steps, that a SQL Server agent performs sequentially.

join   To combine data in two tables based on matching values found in each of the tables.

key   A column or group of columns that uniquely identifies a row (PRIMARY KEY), defines the relationship between two tables (FOREIGN KEY), or is used to build an index.

latency   The amount of time that elapses when a data change is completed at one server and when that change appears at another within a replication architecture (for example, the time between when a change is made at a publisher and when it appears at the subscriber).

LIKE   A predicate that is used to search through character strings by specifying a search string. A LIKE search is primarily used for searches based on wildcard characters, such as the percent sign (%).

linked server   A database object that represents a particular data source and the attributes, including security and collation attributes, necessary to access the data source.

local partitioned view   A partitioned view in which all member tables reside on the local instance of SQL Server.

lock   A method of ensuring concurrency. Locking enables users to temporarily check out an object, preventing other users from changing the object, for the purpose of ensuring consistency.

log file   A file or set of files containing a record of the modifications made in a database.

log shipping   A process that performs copying, at regular intervals, of the log backup from a read-write database to one or more remote server instances.

master database   The database that controls the operation of each instance of SQL Server. It is installed automatically with each instance of SQL Server and keeps track of user accounts, remote user accounts, and remote servers that each instance can interact with. It also tracks ongoing processes, configurable environment variables, system error messages, tapes and disks available on the system, and active locks.

merge replication   The process of transferring data from the publisher to the subscriber, allowing the publisher and subscriber to update data while connected or disconnected and then merging the updates after they are both connected. Merge replication begins with a snapshot. Thereafter, no data is replicated until the publisher and subscriber do a merge. The merge can be scheduled or done via an ad hoc request. Merge replication's main benefit is that it supports subscribers who are not on the network much of the time. Transactions that are committed, however, may be rolled back as the result of conflict resolution.

metadata   Information about the properties of data, such as the type of data in a column (numeric, text, and so on) or the length of a column. Metadata can also be information about the structure of data or information that specifies the design of objects, such as cubes or dimensions.

Model database   A database that is installed with SQL Server that provides the template for new user databases. SQL Server creates a new database by copying the contents of the Model database and then expanding it to the size requested.

msdb database   A database that the SQL Server agent uses for scheduling alerts and jobs and for recording server operator information.

nonclustered index An index in which the logical order of the index is different from the physical, stored order of the rows on disk. In contrast to clustered indexes, nonclustered indexes are totally separated from the actual data rows, causing an unsorted order of data based on nonclustered keys. Nonclustered indexes differ from clustered indexes at the leaf level. The leaf level of a nonclustered index contains the key value and the row locator. The row locator is either the physical row address (if there is no clustered index) or the clustered index key value (if a clustered index exists).

nondeterministic A characteristic of a function that means the function can return different results when provided with the same input. For example, the RAND function is nondeterministic because it returns a different randomly generated number each time it is called.

normalization Developed by Dr. E. F. Codd in 1970, the process of simplifying data and database design to achieve maximum performance and simplicity. This process involves the removal of useless and redundant data.

ODBC (Open Database Connectivity) A data access application programming interface (API) that supports access to any data source for which an ODBC driver is available. ODBC is aligned with the American National Standards Institute (ANSI) and International Standards Organization (ISO) standards for a database call level interface (CLI).

OLAP (Online Analytical Processing) A technology that uses multidimensional structures to provide rapid access to data for analysis. The source data for OLAP is commonly stored in data warehouses in a relational database.

OLE DB A COM-based application programming interface (API) for accessing data. OLE DB supports accessing data stored in any format (databases, spreadsheets, text files, and so on) for which an OLE DB provider is available.

OLTP (Online Transaction Processing) A data processing system designed to record all the business transactions of an organization as they occur. An OLTP system is characterized by many concurrent users actively adding and modifying data.

operator An individual who can potentially receive messages from SQL Server via email, pager, or Net send.

ORDER BY A substatement found in the SELECT statement that is used to order the rows in a result set in either descending or ascending (DESC and ASC) order.

page lock A lock that covers 8KB of data.

partitioned view A table that has been replaced with multiple, smaller tables. Each smaller table has the same format as the original table, but with a subset of the data. Each partitioned table has rows allocated to it based on some characteristic of the data, such as specific key ranges. The rules that define into which table the rows go must be unambiguous. For example, a table is partitioned into two tables. All rows with primary key values lower than a specified value are allocated to one table, and all rows equal to or greater than the value are allocated to the other. Partitioning can improve application processing speeds and reduce the potential for conflicts in multisite update replication. You can improve the usability of partitioned tables by creating a view. The view, created by a union of SELECT operations on all the partitioned tables, presents the data as if it all resided in a single table.

primary key   A column or set of columns uniquely identifying all the rows in a table. Primary keys do not allow null values. No two rows can have the same primary key value; therefore, a primary key value always uniquely identifies a single row. More than one key can uniquely identify rows in a table; each of these keys is called a candidate key. Only one candidate can be chosen as the primary key of a table; all other candidate keys are known as alternate keys. Although tables are not required to have primary keys, it is good practice to define them. In a normalized table, all the data values

in each row are fully dependent on the primary key. For example, in a normalized employee table that has EmployeeID as the primary key, all the columns should contain data related to a specific employee. This table does not have the column DepartmentName because the name of the department is dependent on a department ID, not on an employee ID.

Profiler   A SQL tool that captures SQL Server events from a server. The events are saved in a trace file that you can later analyze or use to replay a specific series of steps when you want to diagnose a problem.

publication   A container for articles that are capable of being replicated. A publication, which may include one or more articles, is the basic unit of replication. A publication has a single, specific replication type: either snapshot, transactional, or merge. When a subscriber chooses a publication, all the articles contained within the publication are part of the subscription.

publisher   In respect to replication, the server that produces data so that it can be replicated to subscribers.

query optimizer   The SQL Server database engine component responsible for generating efficient execution plans for SQL statements.

RAID (redundant array of independent disks)   A disk system that comprises multiple disk drives (an array) to provide higher performance, reliability, storage capacity, and lower cost. Fault-tolerant arrays are categorized in six RAID levels: 0 through 5. Each level uses a different algorithm to implement fault tolerance.

RDBMS (relational database management system) A system that organizes data into related rows and columns. SQL Server is an RDBMS.

rebuilding indexes A process that helps collect the defragmented pages of information and bring index data back to its original form. Rebuilding indexes increases the overall performance by making it easier for SQL Server to read pages to get data.

recompile To provide effective processing, the queries used by stored procedures and triggers are optimized only when they are compiled. As indexes or other changes that affect statistics are made to the database, compiled stored procedures and triggers may lose efficiency. By recompiling stored procedures and triggers that act on a table, you can reoptimize the queries.

reconfigure A command used to update the currently configured value of a configuration option changed with the `sp_configure` system stored procedure.

recordset The ActiveX Database Objects (ADO) object used to contain a result set. A recordset also exhibits cursor behavior, depending on the recordset properties set by an application. ADO recordsets are mapped to OLE DB rowsets.

recovery model A database property that controls the basic behavior of backup and restore operations for a database. For instance, the recovery model controls how transactions are logged, whether the transaction log requires backing up, and what kinds of restore operations are available.

recursive trigger A trigger that updates, deletes, or inserts data into its own table or another table, which houses a trigger, and then fires another trigger.

relational database A collection of information organized in tables. Each table models a class of objects of interest to the organization. Each column in a table models an attribute of the object. Each row in a table represents one entity in the class of objects modeled by the table. Queries can use data from one table to find related data in other tables.

replication A set of technologies for copying and distributing data and database objects from one database to another and then synchronizing between databases to maintain consistency.

Replication Monitor A tool that provides a systemic view of replication activity, focusing on the movement of data between the publisher and the subscribers. Replication Monitor is a tool for watching real-time activity, troubleshooting problems, and analyzing past replication activity.

roll back　To reverse changes made by transactions that were uncommitted at the point in time to which a database is being recovered.

roll forward　To apply logged changes to data in a roll forward set to bring the data forward in time.

rowset　The OLE DB object used to contain a result set. It also exhibits cursor behavior, depending on the rowset properties set by an application.

schema　In the SQL-92 standard, a collection of database objects that are owned by a single user and form a single namespace. A namespace is a set of objects that cannot have duplicate names. For example, two tables can have the same name only if they are in separate schemas; no two tables in the same schema can have the same name. In T-SQL, much of the functionality associated with schemas is implemented by database user IDs. In database tools, a schema is also the catalog information that describes the objects in a schema or database. In analysis services, a schema is a description of multidimensional objects, such as cubes and dimensions.

SCHEMABINDING　An option for a user-defined function or a view that prevents changes to the objects

referenced by the function or view unless you first drop the view. This makes the views and functions more reliable because they can rely on their database objects always being present.

scope　The lifetime of an object. Specifically, a variable has a scope within a single batch, which means it ceases to exist outside the batch.

script　A collection of batches, usually stored in a text file.

SELECT　The T-SQL statement that is used to return data to an application or another T-SQL statement or to populate a cursor. The SELECT statement returns a tabular result set consisting of data that is typically extracted from one or more tables. The result set contains data from only those rows that match the search conditions specified in the WHERE or HAVING clauses.

SET　The statement used to alter environment settings for a session.

snapshot replication　A type of replication in which data and database objects are distributed by copying published items via the distributor and on to the subscriber exactly as they appear at a specific moment in time. Snapshot replication provides the distribution of both data and structure (tables, indexes, and so on) on a scheduled basis. It can be thought of as a "whole table refresh." No updates to the source table are replicated until the next scheduled snapshot.

SNMP (Simple Network Management Protocol) A protocol that is used for troubleshooting and querying TCP/IP servers.

SQL (Structured Query Language) A language used to insert, retrieve, modify, and delete data in a relational database. SQL also contains statements for defining and administering the objects in a database. SQL is the language supported by most relational databases, and is the subject of standards published by the International Standards Organization (ISO) and the American National Standards Institute (ANSI). SQL Server uses a version of the SQL language called T-SQL.

SQL (Structured Query Language) Profiler A tool used to trace SQL Server activity.

statement permissions An attribute that controls whether a user can execute CREATE or BACKUP statements.

statistics Information about the distribution of the key values in each index and uses these statistics to determine what index(es) to use in query processing.

stored procedure A collection of T-SQL statements with a well-defined set of inputs, called input parameters, and a well-defined set of outputs, which may be output parameters, return values, or cursors. Stored procedures allow the encapsulation of various database operations.

string concatenation Combining of two strings, such as the results of the first name and last name columns. String concatenation can be performed using the plus (+) operator.

subscriber The server that receives replicated data (in the form of publications) from the publisher.

System Monitor The performance monitoring tool available in Windows 2000 and later operating systems. Historically also known as Performance Monitor (PerfMon).

T-SQL (Transact-SQL) The language containing the commands used to administer instances of SQL Server, create and manage all objects in an instance of SQL Server, and insert, retrieve, modify, and delete all data in SQL Server tables. T-SQL is an extension of the language defined in the SQL standards published by the International Standards Organization (ISO) and the American National Standards Institute (ANSI).

table A two-dimensional object consisting of rows and columns that is used to store data in a relational database. Each table stores information about one of the types of objects modeled by the database.

table lock A lock on a table, including all data and indexes.

TCP/IP (Transmission Control Protocol/Internet Protocol) An industry-standard network protocol used by most companies for internetworking computer equipment.

tempdb   The database that provides a storage area for temporary tables, temporary stored procedures, and other temporary working storage needs.

TOP   A keyword that can be used in conjunction with the SELECT statement to select the top *n* rows or a percentage of the result set rows.

trace   The SQL Profiler method for recording server events.

trace flags   Flags that can be enabled to aid in troubleshooting.

transactional replication   A type of replication in which data and database objects are distributed by first applying an initial snapshot at the subscriber and then later capturing transactions made at the publisher and propagating them to individual subscribers. Transactional replication, as with all other replication types, begins with a synchronizing snapshot. After the initial synchronization, transactions, which are committed at the publisher, are automatically replicated to the subscribers.

trigger   A stored procedure that is fired when data is modified from a table using any of the three modification statements DELETE, INSERT, or UPDATE. FOR and AFTER are synonymous and are usually implied when referring to triggers rather than INSTEAD OF triggers. Triggers are often created to enforce referential integrity or consistency among logically related data in different tables.

UNION operator   An operator that can combine two SELECT statements that have identical column numbers and types into one large rowset.

UNIQUE constraint   A constraint that enforces entity integrity on a non-primary key. UNIQUE constraints ensure that no duplicate values are entered and that an index is created to enhance performance.

UNIQUE index   An index in which no two rows are permitted to have the same index value, thus prohibiting duplicate index or key values. The system checks for duplicate key values when the index is created and checks each time data is added with an INSERT or UPDATE statement.

UPDATE   A statement used to modify one or more data values in an existing row or rows. Sometimes, the term update refers to any data modification, including INSERT, UPDATE, and DELETE operations.

UPDATE STATISTICS   A command that updates statistical information for an index. Index statistics need to be up-to-date for the optimizer to decide on the fastest route of access.

updatable subscribers
Subscribers that are capable of updating and modifying data when it is replicated. This option can be used with snapshot replication and transactional replication. A transactional or snapshot publication may allow updatable subscribers. Changes made on the subscriber's replica are propagated to the publisher either in real time via DTC or near real time via a queue.

user A databasewide security context.

user-defined function A collection of T-SQL statements with a well-defined set of input parameters but only one output—which can be a scalar value or a table. User-defined functions allow the encapsulation of various logical and database operations but cannot be used to make changes to a database.

variable A construct that can temporarily hold values for use in a T-SQL batch.

view A relational database object that can be referenced and built by using SELECT statements to join data from one or more base tables. Views are similar to tables in that data can be retrieved and modified and indexes can be built.

WHERE A substatement found in the SELECT statement that uses any of various filter conditions, such as BETWEEN, IN, and LIKE, to limit the number of rows retrieved.

Windows application log The operating system event log used to record application events sent by SQL Server services.

WITH ENCRYPTION A clause that protects the definition of a view. If you specify WITH ENCRYPTION, you encrypt the definition of your view because you may not want users to display it. Encrypting using WITH ENCRYPTION disallows anyone from using sp_heptext to display your view or viewing it via the Enterprise Manager.

WITH SCHEMABINDING An option that specifies that the view be bound to the schema. You need to specify WITH SCHEMABINDING when you want to create views with indexes. Also, when WITH SCHEMABINDING is specified, you have to adhere to the owner.object syntax when referencing tables or views in the creation of a view.

XML (Extensible Markup Language) A hypertext programming language used to describe the contents of a set of data and how the data should be output to a device or displayed in a web page. XML is used to move data between systems.

Index

A

Activity Monitor

  filtering imformation in, 163

  process information columns, 162-163

Advanced Tuning Options section (DTA), 195

AFTER triggers, cascading actions, 53

Agent (SQL Server), 153, 198

alerts, setting via SQL Server Agent, 198

Aligned Partition option (DTA), 194

ALTER DATABASE statements, 33

  partitioned tables, 56

  SET RECOVERY option, 138-139

ALTER ENDPOINT statements, 112

ALTER FULLTEXT INDEX command, 81

ALTER INDEX REBUILD statements, 91

ALTER TABLE statements

  CHECK CONSTRAINT clause, 91

  DEFAULT option, 46

  NOCHECK CONSTRAINT clause, 91

Analysis Services

  MSAS, 219

  SSAS, 218-219

ANSI NULLS, indexed views, 36

ANSI PADDING, indexed views, 36

ANSI WARNINGS, indexed views, 36

answer keys (practice exams), 237-257, 273-291

Application column (Activity Monitor), 162

assemblies, 41

asymmetric design (partitioning tables), 54

asynchronous processing, 124

authentication

   dialogues, 128

   SQL Server, 113

authorization, dialogues, 128

AUTO mode, FOR XML statements, 103

B

BACKUP command, 136, 139-141

BACKUP statements

   CHECKSUM option, 144

   CONTINUE AFTER ERROR
   option, 145

   COPY ONLY option, 146

   FORMAT option, 144

   INIT option, 143

   NO CHECKSUM option, 145

   NO LOG option, 145

   NO TRUNCATE option, 142

   NOFORMAT option, 144

   NOINIT option, 144

   NORECOVERY option, 142, 145

   NOREWIND option, 144

   NOSKIP option, 143-144

   NOUNLOAD option, 144

   REWIND option, 144

   SKIP option, 143-144

   STANDBY option, 146

   STOP ON ERROR option, 145

   TRUNCATE ONLY option, 145

   UNLOAD option, 144

BACKUP VERIFYONLY option, 135

backups (databases), 136, 139

   appending, 144

   as system databases, 146

   differential, 140

   extra backups, 146

   full, 140

   initializing headers, 144

   integrity of, 141

   master databases, 146

   media sets, creating, 144

   model databases, 146

   msdb databases, 146

   overwriting, 141, 143

   read-only secondary servers, 146

   recovery models, 137

      ALTER DATABASE statements,
      SET RECOVERY option,
      138-139

      sp dboption stored procedure,
      136-138

      T-SQL, 138-139

   reliability of, 141

   removing inactive log entries, 145

   restoring data from, 146-149

   rewinding tape, 144

   tail-log, 142

   transaction logs, 137, 141-142

   truncating logs, 145

   unloading tape, 144

   validating data, 144

   warm backup secondary
   databases, 145

baselines, SQL Server performance, 161

BASIC authentication (SQL Server), 113

BCP (Bulk Copy Program), 119-121

bcp command, 118-121

BETWEEN keyword, 78

bigint data type, 43

binary data type, 43

bit data type, 43

Blocked By column (Activity Monitor), 163

**BlockedAndBlocking filter (Activity
Monitor), 163**

**BlockedOrBlocking filter (Activity
Monitor), 163**

Blocking column (Activity Monitor), 163

Blocks, troubleshooting, 186

Broker event class (SQL Profiler), 174

BULK COPY option, bcp command, 121

BULK INSERT statements, 118, 121

bulk-logged recovery models, 136-137

C

Cartesian join statements. *See* CROSS JOIN statements

cascading actions, 52-53

central publisher and multiple subscribers strategies (replication), 212

central subscriber replication, 210

char data type, 43

CHECK CONSTRAINT clause, 91

CHECK constraints, 61-62

CHECK CONSTRAINTS hint, 120

CHECKSUM option, BACKUP statements, 144-145

CISA exam self-assessment, 7

educational background, 9

exam readiness, 11-12

hands-on experience, 10

ideal Certified Information Systems Auditor candidate, 8

CLR

stored procedures, 88

system views, 87-88

CLR event class (SQL Profiler), 174

CLR UDT, 45

clustered indexes, 47-49, 188

clusters, failover clustering, 209

COLUMN CHECK constraints, 61-62

columns, 34, 42

access patterns (partitioning tables), 55

combining, 72

computed, 46, 92

headers, renaming, 72

identity, 46

NOT NULL property, 45

NULL property, 45

timestamp data type, 47

Command column (Activity Monitor), 162

COMMIT statements, 93

computed columns, 46, 92

CONCAT NULL YIELDS NULL, indexed views, 36

conditional data filtering, 78-80

connected techniques. *See* live updates

constraint checking, 91

constraints, 42

CONTAINS command, 81

CONTAINSTABLE command, 81

contention (locks), reducing, 185

CONTINUE_AFTER_ERROR option, 135, 145

conversations. *See* dialogues

COPY ONLY option, BACKUP statements, 146

covering indexes, 188

CPU column (Activity Monitor), 162

CREATE CONTRACT statements, 126

CREATE DATABASE statements, 33

CREATE ENDPOINT statements, 112

CREATE FUNCTION statements, 62

CREATE INDEX command, 48-50

CREATE PARTITION FUNCTION statements, 56-57

CREATE PARTITION SCHEME statements, 56-58

CREATE REMOTE SERVICE BINDING statements, dialogues, 128

CREATE TABLE statements, 46

credentials, 26, 64

CROSS JOIN statements, 77-78

cursor data type, 43

Cursors event class (SQL Profiler), 174

D

data consumption

importing/exporting data

BCP, 119-121

BULK INSERT statements, 121

disconnected techniques, 118

live updates, 118

OPENROWSET statements, 122

SSIS, 122-124

readings/resources, 296

Service Broker, 124

assembling components into services, 127

components of, 125

creating queues, 126-127

defining message type, 125

dialogues, 127-128

providing contract details, 126

data filtering, conditional filtering, 78-80

data heaps, 48

data marts, 219

data partitioning

indexes, 193

joins, 193

performance, improvements to, 193

tables, 193

advantages of, 55

ALTER DATABASE statements, 56

asymmetric design, 54

CREATE PARTITION FUNCTION statements, 56-57

CREATE PARTITION SCHEME statements, 56-58

data storage, 56-57

indexes, 56

$PARTITION queries, 59-60

row/column access patterns, 55

strategies for, 55

symmetric design, 55

table size, 55

views, 39-40, 192

data querying

conditional data filtering, 78-80

full-text indexes, 80-81

SELECT statements, 70-71

GROUP BY clause, 74

HAVING clause, 74

ORDER BY clause, 74

TABLESAMPLE clause, 75

TOP clause, 73

WHERE clause, 74

tables

combining columns, 72

filtering data, 74

grouping data, 74

joining, 76-78

listing contents of, 71-72

renaming columns, 72

returning top rows, 73

sampling stored data, 75-76

selecting null value rows, 76

trimming white space, 73

data storage, partitioned tables, 56-57

data types

list of, 42-43

timestamp, 47

UDT, 44-45

xml, 45

XML schema collections, 45

data updates

computed columns, 92

data from previous SQL Server releases, 93

filtered updates, 92

multiple records, 92

object schemas, 93

positioned updates, 92

single records, 92

transaction processing, 92

data warehouses, 219

Database column (Activity Monitor), 162

Database Diagram tool, 34

Database event class (SQL Profiler), 174
Database Properties dialog, 136
databases
  administrators, replication, 211
  ALTER DATABASE statements, 33
  assemblies, 41
  backups
    appending, 144
    as system databases, 146
    differential, 140
    extra backups, 146
    full, 140
    initializing headers, 144
    integrity of, 141
    master databases, 146
    media sets, creating, 144
    model databases, 146
    msdb databases, 146
    overwriting, 141-143
    read-only secondary servers, 146
    recovery models, 136-139
    reliability of, 141
    removing inactive log entries, 145
    restoring data from, 146-149
    rewinding tape, 144
    tail-log, 142
    transaction logs, 141-142
    truncating logs, 145
    unloading tape, 144
    validating data, 144
    warm backup secondary databases,
      145
  components of, 34
  CREATE DATABASE statements,
    33
  Database Diagram tool, 34
  database diagrams, 40
  DTA, 193-194
  indexing strategies, 188
    analyzing existing indexes, 191
    determining what not to index,
      190

    determining what to index, 189
    fill factor, 191
    indexed views, 191
    maintaining indexes, 191
  maintenance
    readings/resources, 297
    SQL Server, 134-155
  master databases, 32, 146
  mirroring, 207-209
  model databases, 32, 146
  msdb databases, backups, 146
  objects
    associated objects, viewing, 34
    creating, 294
    implementing, 295
  proxies, 41
  roles, 64
  snapshots, 135, 150-153
  statistics, 40
  synonyms, 40
  sys.databases catalog view, 33
  system databases, backups as, 146
  tables, 34
  triggers. *See* DDL triggers
  views, 34
    aggregate data, 36
    benefits of, 35
    indexed, 36-39
    partitioned, 39-40
    standard, 35
  warm copies, 205
datetime data type, 43
DBCC (Database Console Command)
  maintenance operations, 197
  miscellaneous operations, 197
  options of, 195-196
  server maintenance, 195
  SQL Server performance, 167-168
  validation operations, 196-197
DBCC INDEXDEFRAG command, 50

DBMS (database management system), SQL Server installations, 21

DDL triggers, 54

deadlocks, 185-186

decimal data type, 43

DEFAULT option, 46

defragmenting indexes, 191

delegations, 24-25

DELETE statements, 93-94

deleting

table data

DELETE statements, 93-94

DENY statements, 95

escalating deletion privileges, 95

GRANT statements, 95

REVOKE statements, 95

TRUNCATE TABLE method, 94

tables, cascading actions, 52

DENY statements, data deletion privileges, 95

Deprecation event class (SQL Profiler), 174

dialogues

security, 128

Service Broker, creating in, 127-128

differential backups, 140

DIGEST authentication (SQL Server), 113

DISABLE INDEX statements, 91

DISABLE TRIGGER statements, 91

DISABLED state (endpoints), 113

disconnected techniques, 118

disk systems, SQL Server installations, 20

distributed partitioned view, 39

distributors, role in replication, 210, 213

DML triggers, 53-54

Do Not Keep Any Existing PDS option (PDS), 194

document returns (XML), 102

drives, SQL Server installations, 20

DROP DATABASE statements, deleting database snapshots, 152

DROP EXISTING option, 50

DTA (Database Engine Tuning Advisor), 177, 193

Advanced Tuning Options section, 195

Partitioning Strategy to Employ section, 194

PDS, 194

dynamic management functions and views, 86-87, 166

E - F

educational background, self-assessment, 9

ENABLE TRIGGER statements, 91

error handling, TRY/CATCH constructs, 93

Errors and Warnings event class (SQL Profiler), 174

Evaluate Utilization of Existing PDS Only option (PDS), 194

exams

practice

answer keys, 237-257, 273-291

questions, 224-235, 260-271

readiness, 11-12

exclusive locks, 184

EXECUTE AS statements, deletion privileges, 95

Execution Context column (Activity Monitor), 163

execution plans, 183

exist() method, 107-109

experience, self-assessment, 10

EXPLICIT mode, FOR XML statements, 105

exporting/importing data, standard view, 35

extended stored procedures, 60

failover clustering, 209

fast recovery (databases), 135

federations, 192

FILELISTONLY option, RESTORE statements, 150

fill factor, 191

FILLFACTOR setting, indexes, 50

filtered updates, 92

filtering data, 74, 78-80

FIRE TRIGGERS hint, 120

float data type, 43

FOR XML statements, 106

AUTO mode, 103

EXPLICIT mode, 105

PATH mode, 102, 105

RAW mode, 104-105

FOREIGN KEY constraints, 52

FORMAT option, BACKUP statements, 144

FREETEXT command, 81

FREETEXTTABLE command, 81

FROM clause, system views, 89

From Device (Restore Database dialog), 148

full backups, 140

full recovery models, 136-138

Full Text event class (SQL Profiler), 174

full-text catalogs, 63-64, 80

full-text indexes, 63-64, 80-81

G - H

General page (Restore Database dialog), 147

Generate Online Recommendations Where Possible option (DTA), 195

Generate Only Online Recommendations option (DTA), 195

GRANT statements, data deletion privileges, 95

GROUP BY clause, 74

grouping data, 74

hands-on experience, self-assessment, 10

hardware

performance tuning, 182

requirements, SQL Server installations, 15

HAVING clause, 74

HEADERONLY option, RESTORE statements, 150

heaps (data), 48

high-availability

data mirroring, 207-209

failover clustering, 209

implementing, readings/resources, 298

log shipping, 205-206

MSAS, 219

replication

central publisher and multiple subscribers strategies, 212

database administrators, 211

distributors role in, 210, 213

latency, 215

merge, 211, 217

multiple publishers and multiple subscribers strategies, 213

multiple publishers and single subscriber strategies, 213

publishers role in, 210-213

push/pull subscriptions, 212

single publisher and a remote distributor strategies, 213

site autonomy, 215

snapshot, 211, 216

subscribers role in, 210-213

transactional, 211, 217

transactional consistency, 215

SSAS, 218-219

warm backups, 204

Host column (Activity Monitor), 163

I

ideal Certified Information Systems
Auditor candidate, 8

identity columns, 46

IGNORE DUP KEY, indexed views, 36

image data type, 43

IMPERSONATE permissions, deletion
privileges, 95

impersonations, 24-25

importing/exporting data
BCP, 119-121
BULK INSERT statements, 121
disconnected techniques, 118
live updates, 118
OPENROWSET statements, 122
SSIS, 122-124
standard view, 35

IN keyword, 79

indexed views
ANSI NULLS, 36
ANSI PADDING, 36
ANSI WARNINGS, 36
CONCAT NULL YIELDS NULL,
36
IGNORE DUP KEY, 36
implementation settings, 36-37
Query Optimizer, 36
QUOTED IDENTIFIER, 36
SCHEMABINDING clause, 37-39
SET command, 37
tables, binding, 37-38

indexes, 42
ALTER INDEX REBUILD
statements, 91
clustered, 47-49, 188
covering, 188
CREATE INDEX command, 48-50
database tuning strategies, 188
analyzing existing indexes, 191
determining what not to index,
190

determining what to index, 189
fill factor, 191
indexed views, 191
maintaining indexes, 191
DBCC INDEXDEFRAG command,
50
defragmentation, 191
DISABLE INDEX statements, 91
FILLFACTOR setting, 50
full-text, 63-64, 80-81
nonclustered, 47-49, 188
pad index setting, 192
PADINDEX setting, 50
partitioned tables, 56
partitioning, 193
storage structure of, 47
unique values, importance of, 49
XML, 111-112

INIT option, BACKUP statements, 143

INNER JOIN statements, 76-77

INSERT ... SELECT * FROM OPEN-
ROWSET(BULK) statements, 118

INSERT SELECT statements, system
views, 90

INSERT statements, system views, 87-89

int data type, 43

INTEGRATED authentication (SQL Server),
113

inter-application messaging. See Service
Broker

INTO clause, system views, 89-90

ISNULL function, 76

J - K - L

Job Schedule Properties dialog, 155

job scheduling, database maintenance,
153-155

joining tables, 76-78

joins, partitioning, 193

KERBEROS authentication (SQL Server), 113

keys, 42

  foreign key relationships, 52

  many-to-many relationships, 52

  one-to-many relationships, 51

  one-to-one relationships, 51

  primary key relationships, 51

LABELONLY option, RESTORE statements, 150

Last Batch column (Activity Monitor), 163

latency, replication, 215

Leave the Database Ready for Use by Rolling Back the Uncommitted Transactions option (Restore Database dialog), 148

LEFT JOIN statements, 78

LIKE keyword, 79

linked server configurations (SQL Server), 22-25

Linked Server Properties dialog, 25

live updates, 118

local partioned views, 39

locks

  contention, reducing, 185

  deadlocks, 185

  events, trapping, 187

  exclusive, 184

  levels of, 185

  shared, 184

  sp lock stored procedures, 186

  SQLServer:Locks object, 187

  sys.dm exec requests dynamic managment view, 186

  sys.dm exec sessions dynamic management view, 186

  sys.dm tran locks dynamic management view, 186

  system monitor lock counters, 187

  troubleshooting, 186

Locks event class (SQL Profiler), 174-176

Log File Viewer, 164

  SQL Server logs, 165-166

  Windows NT logs, 165

log shipping, 205-206

Login Time column (Activity Monitor), 163

logins, 64

  credentials, 26

  SQL Server

    impersonations, 24-25

    security, 26-27

LTRIM (left trim) function, 73

M

maintenance

  databases

    readings/resources, 297

    SQL Server, 134-155

  servers, DBCC, 195-197

managed code, 88

Management Studio, 160, 164-166

many-to-many relationships, 52

master databases, 32

  backups, 146

  common system views list, 82-84

Memory Usage column (Activity Monitor), 163

merge replication, 211, 217

messaging (inter-application). See Service Broker

metadata, viewing in SQL Server

  DBCC, 167-168

  dynamic management functions and views, 166

  SNMP, 169

  trace flags, 168

Migration Assistant, 19

mirrored backup sets, 135

mirroring (data), 207-209

model databases, 32, 146

modify() method, 107, 110

money data type, 43

MSAS (Microsoft Analysis Services), 219

msdb databases, backups, 146

multiple publishers and multiple sub-scribers strategies (replication), 213

multiple publishers and single subscriber strategies (replication), 213

N

Native XML Web Services, 112-113

nchar data type, 43

Network Address column (Activity Monitor), 163

Network Library column (Activity Monitor), 163

NO CHECKSUM option, BACKUP state-ments, 145

NO LOG option, BACKUP statements, 145

NO TRUNCATE option, BACKUP state-ments, 142

NOCHECK CONSTRAINT clause, 91

nodes() method, 107, 110-111

NOFORMAT option, BACKUP statements, 144

NOINIT option, BACKUP statements, 144

nonclustered indexes, 47-49, 188

NORECOVERY option, BACKUP statements, 142

NOREWIND option, BACKUP statements, 144

NOSKIP option, BACKUP statements, 143-144

NOT NULL property, columns, 45

NOUNLOAD option, BACKUP statements, 144

ntext data type, 43

NTLM authentication (SQL Server), 113

NULL property, columns, 45

NULL values, selecting rows by, 76

numeric data type, 43

nvarchar data type, 43

O - P

object schemas, 93

Objects event class (SQL Profiler), 174

OLEDB event class (SQL Profiler), 174

one-to-many relationships, 51

one-to-one relationships, 51

Open Transactions column (Activity Monitor), 162

OPENROWSET statements, importing data with, 122

operating systems

performance tuning, 182

SQL Server installation require-ments, 15

optimizing SQL Server, readings/resources, 298

Options page

Database Properties dialog, setting recovery model type, 136

Restore Database dialog

Leave the Database Ready for Use by Rolling Back the Uncommitted Transactions option, 148

Prompt Before Restoring Each Backup option, 149

Restrict Access to the Restored Database option, 149

ORDER BY clause, 74

ORDER hint, 121

orphan children (foreign key relation-ships), 52

OUTER JOIN statements, 77

PADINDEX setting, 50, 192

partial database restores, 135

$PARTITION queries, 59-60

partitioning data

  indexes, 193

  joins, 193

  performance, improvements to, 193

  tables, 193

    advantages of, 55

    ALTER DATABASE statements, 56

    asymmetric design, 54

    CREATE PARTITION FUNC-TION statements, 56-57

    CREATE PARTITION SCHEME statements, 56-58

    data storage, 56-57

    indexes, 56

    $PARTITION queries, 59-60

    row/column access patterns, 55

    strategies for, 55

    symmetric design, 55

    table size, 55

  views, 39-40, 192

Partitioning Strategy to Employ section (DTA), 194

PATH mode, FOR XML statements, 102, 105

PDS (physical design structures), DTA, 194

PerfMon (Performance Monitor). *See* System Monitor

performance

  databases, DTA, 193-194

  hardware, tuning, 182

  operating systems, tuning, 182

  partitioning, effects on, 193

  SQL Server

    Activity Monitor, 162-163

    baselines, 161

    DBCC, 167-168

    DTA, 177

    dynamic management functions and views, 166

    Log File Viewer, 164-166

    readings/resources, 298

    SNMP, 169

    SQL Profiler, 172-177

    System Monitor, 169-171

    trace flags, 168

Performance event class (SQL Profiler), 174

permissions, 26, 64

Physical IO column (Activity Monitor), 163

Playback feature (SQL Profiler), 176

point-in-time data restorations, 148

positioned updates, 92

practice exams

  answer keys, 237-257, 273-291

  questions, 224-235, 260-271

PRIMARY KEY constraints, 51

primary XML indexes, 112

Process ID column (Activity Monitor), 162

Profiler (SQL), 172

  data captures, 173

  data storage, 173

  event class categories list, 174-175

  lock events, trapping, 187

  Playback feature, 176

  Results window, 176

  templates, 173

  traces, 173

    defining, 174-175

    locking diagnosis example, 175-176

    replaying, 177

    workload sampling, 177

Progress Report event class (SQL Profiler), 175

Prompt Before Restoring Each Backup option (Restore Database dialog), 149

proxies, 41

publishers, role in replication, 210

  central publisher and multiple sub-scribers strategies, 212

multiple publishers and multiple subscribers strategies, 213

multiple publishers and single subscriber strategies, 213

single publisher and a remote distributor strategies, 213

push/pull subscriptions, replication, 212

Q

Query Optimizer (SQL Server)

execution plans, 183

indexed views, 36

statistics, 183

query() method, 107-108

querying data

conditional data filtering, 78-80

full-text indexes, 80-81

SELECT statements, 70-71

GROUP BY clause, 74

HAVING clause, 74

ORDER BY clause, 74

TABLESAMPLE clause, 75

TOP clause, 73

WHERE clause, 74

tables

combining columns, 72

filtering data, 74

grouping data, 74

joining, 76-78

listing contents of, 71-72

partitioned tables, 59-60

renaming columns, 72

returning top rows, 73

sampling stored data, 75-76

selecting null value rows, 76

system tables, preferred
methods, 41

trimming white space, 73

**questions (practice exams), 224-235,
260-271**

queues

dialogues, 127-128

Service Broker, creating in, 126-127

QUOTED IDENTIFIER, indexed views, 36

R

**RAID (redundant array of
independent/inexpensive disks)**

configurations, 183

SQL Server installations, 20

RAM, SQL Server installations, 19

**RAW mode, FOR XML statements,
104-105**

read-only secondary servers, 146

readiness for CISA exam, 11-12

real data type, 43

RECEIVE statements, dialogues, 128

recovery models

ALTER DATABASE statements,
SET RECOVERY option, 138-139

sp dboption stored procedure,
136-138

T-SQL, 138-139

replication

central subscriber, 210

database administrators, 211

distributors role in, 210, 213

latency, 215

merge, 211, 217

publishers role in, 210-213

push/pull subscriptions, 212

site autonomy, 215

snapshot, 211, 216

subscribers role in, 210-213

transactional, 211, 215-217

RESTORE command, 139

Restore Database dialog

From Device option, 148

General page, 147

Options page, 148-149

RESTORE statements, 147

FILELISTONLY option, 150

HEADERONLY option, 150

LABELONLY option, 150

VERIFYONLY option, 150

WITH RECOVERY option, 149

WITH REPLACE option, 142

WITH STANDBY option, 149

WITH STOPAT option, 142

RESTORE VERIFYONLY option, 135

Restrict Access to the Restored Database option (Restore Database dialog), 149

Results window (SQL Profiler), 176

REVOKE statements, data deletion privileges, 95

REWIND option, BACKUP statements, 144

RIGHT JOIN statements, 78

ROLLBACK statements, 92

rows, 34

access patterns (partitioning tables), 55

deleting data, TRUNCATE TABLE method, 94

null value rows, selecting, 76

top rows, returning, 73

RTRIM (right trim) function, 73

S

sampling stored data, 75-76

scalar-valued functions, 63

Scans event class (SQL Profiler), 175

SCC (System Configuration Checker), SQL Server installations, 19

SCHEMABINDING clause, 37-39

secondary databases, 145

secondary servers, read-only, 146

secondary XML indexes, 112

security

credentials, 64

database roles, 64

dialogues, 128

linked server configurations (SQL Server), 23-24

logins, 26-27, 64

permissions, 64

server roles, 64

Security Audit event class (SQL Profiler), 175

SELECT INTO option, bcp command, 121

SELECT INTO statements, system views, 89-90

select into/bulkcopy database option, 138

SELECT statements, 70-71

GROUP BY clause, 74

HAVING clause, 74

ORDER BY clause, 74

TABLESAMPLE clause, 75

TOP clause, 73

WHERE clause, 74

self-assessment, 7

Certified Information Systems Auditor candidate, 8

educational background, 9

exam readiness, 11-12

hands-on experience, 10

SEND statements, dialogues, 127

Server event class (SQL Profiler), 175

servers

federations, 192

maintenance, DBCC, 195-197

roles, 64

Service Broker, 124

components of, 125

contracts, providing details, 126

dialogues, 127-128

message type, defining, 125

queues, creating, 126-127

services, assembling components into, 127

Sessions event class (SQL Profiler), 175

SET command, indexed views, 37

SET RECOVERY option, 138-139

shared locks, 184

simple recovery models, 136-137

single publisher and a remote distributor strategies (replication), 213

site autonomy, replication, 215

SKIP option, BACKUP statements, 143-144

smalldatetime data type, 43

smallint data type, 43

smallmoney data type, 43

snapshots
  databases, 135, 150-153
  replication, 211, 216

SNMP (Simple Network Management Protocol), SQL Server performance, 169

software requirements for SQL Server installation, 17-18

sp dboption stored procedure, setting recovery models, 136-138

sp lock stored procedures, 186

sp_dboption stored procedure. See ALTER DATABASE statements

SQL Profiler, 172
  data captures, 173
  data storage, 173
  event class categories list, 174-175
  templates, 173
  traces, 173-175

SQL Server
  database maintenance, 134
    automating, 153
    BACKUP VERIFYONLY option, 135
    CONTINUE_AFTER_ERROR option, 135
    database backups, 136-149
    database snapshots, 135, 150-153
    fast recovery, 135
    job scheduling, 153-155
    mirrored backup sets, 135

    partial database restores, 135
    RESTORE VERIFYONLY option, 135

high availability, implementing, 298

impersonations, 24-25

installing, 14
  DBMS, 21
  hardware requirements, 15
  installation process, 18
  Migration Assistant, 19
  operating system requirements, 15
  postinstallation procedures, 22-27
  preparations for, 19-22
  RAID, 20
  SCC, 19
  support software requirements, 17-18

linked server configurations, 22-25

login security, 26-27

metadata, viewing, 166-169

optimizing, readings/resources, 298

performance
  Activity Monitor, 162-163
  baselines, 161
  DBCC, 167-168
  DTA, 177
  dynamic management functions and views, 166
  Log File Viewer, 164-166
  readings/resources, 298
  SNMP, 169
  SQL Profiler, 172-177
  System Monitor, 169-171
  trace flags, 168

readings/resources, 293-294

troubleshooting, readings/resources, 298

user authentication, 113

SQL Server Agent, 153, 198

SQL Server logs, Log File Viewer, 165-166

SQL Server Profiler, trapping lock events, 187

SQL Server Query Optimizer, 183

sql variant data type, 43

SQLServer:Locks object, 187

sqlsrvr.exe command, 208

SSAS (SQL Server Analysis Services), 218-219

SSIS (SQL Server Integration Services)
  importing data with, 122-124
  uses of, 123

standard view, importing/exporting data, 35

STANDBY option, BACKUP statements, 146

STARTED state (endpoints), 113

statistics, 40-42, 183

Status column (Activity Monitor), 162

STOP ON ERROR option, BACKUP statements, 145

STOPPED state (endpoints), 113

stored procedures, 60, 85
  CLR, 88
  sp_dboption. *See* ALTER DATABASE statement
  system views, 88

Stored Procedures event class (SQL Profiler), 175

storing data, partitioned tables, 56-57

string concatenation, 72

subscribers, role in replication, 210
  central publisher and multiple subscribers strategies, 212
  multiple publishers and multiple subscribers strategies, 213
  multiple publishers and single subscriber strategies, 213

subscriptions (push/pull), 212

support software requirements, SQL Server installations, 17-18

symmetric design (partitioning tables), 55

synchronous processing, 124

synonyms, 40

sys.databases catalog view, 33

sys.dm exec requests dynamic management view, 186

sys.dm exec sessions dynamic management view, 186

sys.dm tran locks dynamic management view, 186

syscomments system tables, 41

sysobjects system tables, 41

system databases, backups as, 146

System Monitor
  counters list, 170-171
  prefixes list, 169

System Process column (Activity Monitor), 162

system tables, 41

system views, 81
  ALTER INDEX REBUILD statements, 91
  ALTER TABLE NOCHECK CONSTRAINT statements, 91
  CLR, 87-88
  common views list, 82-84
  DISABLE INDEX statements, 91
  DISABLE TRIGGER statements, 91
  dynamic management views, 86-87
  ENABLE TRIGGER statements, 91
  FROM clause, 89
  INSERT SELECT statements, 90
  INSERT statements, 87-89
  inserting
    complete recordsets, 89-90
    data, disabling functionality, 90-91
    individual records, 88-89
  SELECT INTO statements, 89-90
  stored procedures, 85, 88
  temporary tables, 90
  UDT, 87
  VALUES keyword, 89

system-stored procedures, 60

T

TABLE CHECK constraints, 62

table-valued, 63

tables. *See also* **views**

ALTER TABLE statements, DEFAULT option, 46

columns, 34, 42

   computed, 46

   identity, 46

   NOT NULL property, 45

   NULL property, 45

   timestamp data type, 47

constraints, 42

CREATE TABLE statements, DEFAULT option, 46

customizing

   combining columns, 72

   renaming columns, 72

   returning top rows, 73

   trimming white space, 73

data types

   list of, 42-43

   timestamp, 47

   UDT, 44

   UDT. CLR, 45

   xml, 45

   XML schema collections, 45

deleting data

   DELETE statement, 93-94

   DENY statements, 95

   escalating deletion privileges, 95

   GRANT statements, 95

   REVOKE statements, 95

   TRUNCATE TABLE method, 94

determining purpose of, 41

filtering data, 74

grouping data, 74

indexed views, 37-39

indexes, 42

   clustered, 47-49

   CREATE INDEX command, 48-50

   DBCC INDEXDEFRAG command, 50

   FILLFACTOR setting, 50

   nonclustered, 47-49

   PADINDEX setting, 50

   storage structure of, 47

   unique values, importance of, 49

joining, 76

   CROSS JOIN statements, 78

   INNER JOIN statements, 77

   LEFT JOIN statements, 78

   OUTER JOIN statements, 77

   RIGHT JOIN statements, 78

keys, 42

   foreign key relationships, 52

   many-to-many relationships, 52

   one-to-many relationships, 51

   one-to-one relationships, 51

   primary key relationships, 51

listing contents of, 71-72

object assignments, 41

partitioning, 193

   advantages of, 55

   ALTER DATABASE statements, 56

   asymmetric design, 54

   CREATE PARTITION FUNCTION statements, 56-57

   CREATE PARTITION SCHEME statements, 56-58

   data storage, 56-57

   indexes, 56

   $PARTITION queries, 59-60

   row/column access patterns, 55

   strategies for, 55

   symmetric design, 55

   table size, 55

rows, 34, 76

statistics, 42

stored data, sampling, 75-76

system tables, 41

temporary tables (system views), 90

triggers, 42

    DDL, 54

    DML, 53-54

    updates, 92

TABLESAMPLE clause, 75

TABLOCK hint, 121

tail-log backups, 142

templates, SQL Profiler, 173

temporary tables (system views), 90

tests

    practice

        answer keys, 237-257, 273-291

        questions, 224-235, 260-271

    readiness, 11-12

text data type, 44

throughputs

    importing/exporting data

        BCP, 119-121

        BULK INSERT statements, 121

        disconnected techniques, 118

        live updates, 118

        OPENROWSET statements, 122

        SSIS, 122-124

    readings/resources, 296

    Service Broker, 124

        assembling components into services, 127

        components of, 125

        creating queues, 126-127

        defining message type, 125

        dialogues, 127-128

        providing contract details, 126

timestamp data type, 44, 47

tinyint data type, 44

TOP clause, 73

trace flags

    data mirroring, 208

    SQL Server performance, 168

traces, SQL Profiler, 173

    defining in, 174-175

    locking diagnosis example, 175-176

    replaying in, 177

transaction log backups, 137, 141-142

transaction processing, 92

transactional consistency, 215

transactional replication, 211, 215-217

Transactions event class (SQL Profiler), 175

triggers, 42

    AFTER, cascading actions, 53

    DDL, 54

    DISABLE TRIGGER statements, 91

    DML, 53-54

    ENABLE TRIGGER statements, 91

TRIM function, 73

troubleshooting

    alerts, setting via SQL Server Agent, 198

    blocks, 186

    deadlocks, 186

    locks, 186

    SQL Server, readings/resources, 298

TRUNCATE ONLY option, BACKUP statements, 145

TRUNCATE TABLE method, 94

TRY/CATCH constructs, 93

TSQL event class (SQL Profiler), 175

U - V

UDF, 62-63

UDT (user-defined data types), 44

    CLR UDT, 45

    system views, 87

uniqueidentifier data type, 44

UNLOAD option, BACKUP statements, 144

untyped XML, 106

UPDATE statements, 91-92

updating data
   computed columns, 92
   data from previous SQL Server
      releases, 93
   filtered updates, 92
   multiple records, 92
   object schemas, 93
   positioned updates, 92
   single records, 92
   tables, cascading actions, 52
   transaction processing, 92
user authentication, SQL Server, 113
User column (Activity Monitor), 162
**User Configurable event class (SQL
Profiler), 175**

V

value() method, 107-109
VALUES keyword, system views, 89
varbinary data type, 44
varbinary(max) declarations, 101
varchar data type, 44
varchar(max) declarations, 101
**VERIFYONLY option, RESTORE state-
ments, 150**
views. *See also* **tables**
   aggregated data, 36
   benefits of, 35
   indexed
      ANSI NULLS, 36
      ANSI PADDING, 36
      ANSI WARNINGS, 36
      binding tables, 37-38
      CONCAT NULL YIELDS
         NULL, 36
      IGNORE DUP KEY, 36

   implementation settings, 36-37
      Query Optimizer, 36
      QUOTED IDENTIFIER, 36
      SCHEMABINDING clause,
         37-39
      SET command, 37
   partitioned, 39-40
   partitioning, 192
   standard, 35
   system views, 81
      ALTER INDEX REBUILD
         statements, 91
      ALTER TABLE NOCHECK
         CONSTRAINT statements, 91
      CLR, 87-88
      common views list, 82-84
      DISABLE INDEX statements, 91
      DISABLE TRIGGER state-
         ments, 91
      dynamic management views,
         86-87
      ENABLE TRIGGER
         statements, 91
      FROM clause, 89
      INSERT SELECT statements,
         90
      INSERT statements, 87-89
      inserting complete recordsets,
         89-90
      inserting data, disabling function-
         ality, 90-91
      inserting individual records, 88-89
      SELECT INTO statements,
         89-90
      stored procedures, 85, 88
      temporary views, 90
      UDT, 87
      VALUES keyword, 89

W

Wait Resources column (Activity Monitor), 162

Wait Time column (Activity Monitor), 162

Wait Type column (Activity Monitor), 162

warm backups, 145, 204

warm copies, 205

WHERE clause, 74

wildcard searches, 64, 79

Windows NT logs, Log File Viewer, 165

Windows System Monitor. *See* System Monitor

WITH RECOVERY option, RESTORE command, 149

WITH REPLACE option, RESTORE statements, 142

WITH STANDBY option, RESTORE command, 149

WITH STOPAT option, RESTORE statements, 142

WITH TIES option, 73

workload sampling, SQL Profiler, 177

WSDL (Web Service Description Language), 112-113

X - Y - Z

XML (Extensible Markup Language), 100
    document returns, 102
    elements of, 103
    FOR XML statements, 106
        AUTO mode, 103
        EXPLICIT mode, 105
        PATH mode, 102, 105
        RAW mode, 104-105

frameworks, readings/resources, 296
    indexes, 111-112
    Native XML Web Services, 112-113
    outputting data, 103-105
    schema collections, 45
    untyped XML, 106
    varbinary(max) declarations, 101
    varchar(max) declarations, 101
    xml data type, 101, 106
        exist() method, 107-109
        modify() method, 107, 110
        nodes() method, 107, 110-111
        query() method, 107-108
        value() method, 107-109
    XML DML, 101
    XQuery, 101

XSINIL, 105